produce

LYNNE MULLINS

Photographers

Craig Abraham

James Alcock

Joe Armao

Narelle Autio

Steve Baccon

Natalie Boog

Mario Borg

Matthew Bouwmeester

Sonia Byrnes

Joe Castro

Patrick Cummins

Simone De Peak

Marco Del Grande

Jill Dupleix

Nicole Emmanuel

George Fetting

Jerry Galea

Kate Geraghty

Jacky Ghossein

Rebecca Hallas

Paul Harris

Sahlan Hayes

Tina Haynes

Jessica Hromas

Eddie Jim

Quentin Jones

Gary Medlicott

Fiona Morris

Shannon Morris

Lynne Mullins

Richard Mullins

Marina Oliphant

Michel O'Sullivan

Edwina Pickles

Robert Rough

Ben Rushton

Peter Schofield

Jennifer Soo

Penny Stephens

Cathryn Tremain

Tim Winborne

Other book titles available from *The Age* and *The Sydney Morning Herald* stores:

Whip it Up, a collection of quick and tasty recipes by Lynne Mullins

Blokes, tasty no-fuss recipes

Summer, *Autumn*, *Winter* and *Spring* cookbooks

Epicure Chocolate

The Kitchen Gardener, a practical guide to growing vegetables

The Food and Wine Atlas of Australia

The Beer Bible Updated Edition, by Willie Simpson

52 Wine Lessons, a year of good drinking

Why It's Good For You, helping you make healthy food and lifestyle choices

Kitchen Basics, a beginner's guide to setting up a kitchen and home cooking

The Age Good Food Guide

The SMH Good Food Guide

The Foodies' Guides to Melbourne

The Foodies' Guide to Sydney

The New Retirement, how to afford the good life

Super Made Simple

Writing Good English series (for students and business professionals)

The Ultimate Guide to Buying and Renting Houses and Apartments, by Jimmy Thomson

Good Weekends Away, featuring 100 of the best short-break holidays

You're Leaving Tomorrow, conscripts and correspondents caught up in the Vietnam War

Long Shadows, 100 years of Australian cricket

Gallipoli: Untold Stories

Reflections, celebrating 150 years of The Age

The Big Picture, 175 years of articles and images from The Sydney Morning Herald

Plus a range of Word Puzzle, Sudoku and Crossword titles

To find out more about these titles and other great offers please contact either
The Age Store on 1300 656 052 or www.theage.com.au/store or
The SMH Store on 1300 656 059 or www.smh.com.au/store

Publisher John Fairfax Publications Pty Ltd.

Cover design and internal page layouts by Peter Schofield
Cover picture Natalie Boog. Photographed at Fratelli Fresh, 7 Danks Street, Waterloo with permission from the owners Barry and Jamie McDonald.
Design Fiona James
Chief sub-editor Patrick Witton
Managing Editor Fairfax Books Michael Johnston
Senior Product Manager Fairfax Books Linda MacLennan
Publishing Manager Fairfax Books Stephen Berry
Group General Manager Fairfax Enterprises Kevin Stokes

For copyright or marketing enquiries, contact Linda MacLennan on (02) 9282 3054
Printed in China by the Australian Book Connection
ISBN 978-1-921190-67-4

produce

LYNNE MULLINS

FAIRFAX BOOKS

OVEN TEMPERATURES

	Celsius	Fahrenheit	Gas mark
very slow	120	250	1
slow	150	300	2
moderately slow	160	325	3
moderate	180-190	350-375	4
moderately hot	200-210	400-425	5
hot	220-230	450-475	6
very hot	240-250	500-525	7

OTHER MEASURES

1 cup (level) 250ml

1 tsp (level) 5ml

eggs used in these recipes are large (60g)

DRY MEASURES

metric	imperial
15g	½oz
30g	1oz
60g	2oz
90g	3oz
125g	4oz
155g	5oz
185g	6oz
220g	7oz
250g	8oz
280g	9oz
315g	10oz
345g	11oz
375g	12oz
410g	13oz
440g	14oz
470g	15oz
500g	16oz (1lb)
750g	24oz
1kg	32oz (2lb)

LIQUID MEASURES

metric	imperial
30ml	1 fluid oz
60ml	2 fluid oz
100ml	3 fluid oz
125ml	4 fluid oz
150ml	5 fluid oz (½ pint)
190ml	6 fluid oz
250ml	8 fluid oz
300ml	10 fluid oz
500ml	16 fluid oz
600ml	20 fluid oz (1 pint)
1000ml	1¾ pints

Top: Angouleme Market, France
Right: Campo di Fiori Market, Rome

Contents

Introduction

Produce, fresh fruit and vegetables, has been a heartfelt passion of mine ever since I became seriously interested in cooking and writing.

I love to travel, I love to visit new places and the best new places are the fresh produce markets. For a cook this can be paradise. It is where you learn not only about the seasonal fruit and vegetables but also about the people, their cooking traditions and their culture. It all evolves at the local market reflecting the climate and the seasons.

Buying in season means better value and superior flavour and occasional gluts provide the opportunity to bottle tomatoes, preserve pickles and boil jams. Farmers' markets are becoming increasingly popular, springing up in many country areas as well as the cities. Much of this produce is organically grown and it's where you'll find the new varieties of apples, potatoes and peaches which are often a revelation in texture and flavour. These stalls are moulded by the seasons and are much more inspirational than supermarkets or greengrocers where imported products are sometimes displayed but suffer from prolonged periods of storage.

Huge bunches of pungent basil in summer, crisp white asparagus in spring, exotic mushrooms in autumn, crunchy fennel in winter are all special ingredients to be enjoyed at their peak. The wide-ranging climatic conditions in Australia make it possible not only to enjoy freshly picked fruit and vegetables but the seasons are often extended enabling us to enjoy fragrant Queensland strawberries during winter and luscious Victorian varieties during summer.

Mercado De Triana, Seville

Some plant breeders are seeking out newer varieties of fruit and vegetables that transport well, have lower acid content or increased yields but the heirloom varieties are also enjoying a resurgence because they taste superior. Hydroponics have created the theory that tomatoes should be perfectly shaped and bright red though many lack flavour. Lettuce and other perky salad greens grown hydroponically are easy to identify as the roots are usually sold attached.

Seasonality is the key to great cooking. Choose fresh rather than frozen, local rather than imported and use the produce thoughtfully and simply. Most fruits and vegetables are quick and easy to prepare with panache and minimum effort so use these recipes as a guide and they will bring a world of tantalising possibilities to your table.

Lynne Mullins

*For convenience some produce such as tomatoes, avocadoes and rhubarb are listed in the section under which they are most commonly used.

Acknowledgements

I would like to thank the team at Fairfax Books, in particular, Linda MacLennan, Michael Johnston, Patrick Witton and Peter Schofield. Also the photographers who contributed delicious images and Trish Heagerty for her creativity.

Thanks to my wonderful recipe tasters, Kate, Carter and Steve for their candid comments.

And to Richard for his continued warm-hearted support.

Marrakech, Morocco

Fruit

Top: Place d'Aligre Market, Paris
Above left: Poznan Market, Poland
Left: Cahors Market, France
Right: Place d'Aligre Market, Paris

Apples

You can buy apples in the markets year-round, but crisp new-season varieties take pride of place on the shelves when the cooler weather arrives and thoughts turn to tarts, pies, cakes and other dishes starring the indispensable fruit. There is nothing more warming than the aroma of a hot apple pie fresh from the oven.

Each season brings new arrivals: pink lady, extremely popular and perfect in pies, sauces and salads; bonza; golden delicious; gala; red fuji sundowner; braeburn and lady williams to name just a few.

Of course, one of the most popular varieties remains the tart, crisp granny smith, which has a greasy skin when fresh. But don't let that put you off because it is one of the most common cooking apples in the world, great for stewing, baking, sauces and pureeing. It was originally grown in 1860 as a chance seedling by Maria Ann Smith in what is now Sydney's Eastwood.

Apples taste best plucked ripe from the tree, but fruit picked fully ripe does not keep well. So at the markets and in the shops choose firm, smooth, shiny-skinned apples that feel heavy for their size, with stalks intact.

Store them in a ventilated plastic bag in the crisper of the fridge – all varieties lose crispness rapidly at room temperature.

Most apples are now stored in temperature-controlled units so in theory they emerge as fresh as they went in. However, they gradually lose their flavour and crisp texture in storage.

If preparing apples ahead of time, brush the cut surface with lemon juice to prevent browning.

Buttered apples with pecans and calvados

3 large granny smith apples, unpeeled

4 tbsp butter

4 tbsp honey

2 tbsp calvados or other liqueur

2 tbsp orange juice

2 tsp orange zest

90g (³/₄ cup) pecan nuts, toasted and
    coarsely chopped

frozen vanilla yoghurt or ice-cream, to serve

Halve, core and thinly slice apples. Melt 2 tablespoons butter in a large frying pan over medium heat and add half the apples and cook for 3-5 minutes on each side or until golden. Remove apples and cook remaining slices, then remove from pan.

Add remaining butter to pan with honey, calvados, orange juice, grated orange zest and pecan nuts. Bring to the boil, stirring continuously, then remove from heat.

Divide apples among 4 serving bowls, drizzle with sauce and serve with frozen vanilla yoghurt or ice-cream.

Serves 4

Quick apple tarts

2 sheets bought puff pastry

2 large granny smith apples, unpeeled

juice of ¹/₂ lemon

2 tbsp butter

4 tsp sugar

thick cream, to serve

Preheat oven to 200C.

Using a saucer as a guide, cut 4 circles of pastry from 2 sheets of puff pastry. With a small, sharp knife make concentric circles 1cm in from the edge of each round, taking care not to cut right through pastry. Crimp or pinch the border to form pleats. This will allow the border of the tarts to rise to form an edge. Place pastry rounds on lightly greased oven trays.

Cut apples into quarters and core. Thinly slice and place in a bowl. Sprinkle with lemon juice and toss gently to combine. Arrange apple slices on pastry circles, overlapping slightly so they cover pastry completely except for the borders. Dot each with ¹/₂ tablespoon butter and sprinkle each with 1 teaspoon of sugar and bake for 15-20 minutes or until pastry is cooked and golden.

Serve with thick cream.

Serves 4

Fragrant apple custard tea cake

Custard

1 cup milk

55g caster sugar

3 large egg yolks

30g plain flour

2 tsp vanilla extract

200g soft butter

110g caster sugar

2 eggs

225g self-raising flour, sifted

2 small apples, peeled, cored and thinly sliced
   (about 140g each)

1 tbsp butter, melted

2 tsp caster sugar, extra

1 tsp fragrant, sweet spices or nutmeg

For the custard, place milk in a small saucepan and bring to a simmer over medium heat. Remove.

Whisk egg yolks and sugar in a small bowl until thick then add flour and whisk until smooth. Pour hot milk onto egg yolk mixture and stir until smooth. Return mixture to saucepan and stir over low heat until mixture comes to the boil. Stir constantly for 1-2 minutes until thick then remove from heat, stir in vanilla and allow to cool, then chill, covered, in the fridge.

Preheat oven to 180C.

Combine butter and sugar in a bowl and beat with an electric mixer until pale and fluffy. Add eggs, one at a time, beating well after each. Fold in flour. Spread half the mixture into a 22cm greased and baking-paper-lined cake tin, add custard and smooth with a spatula. Add spoonfuls of remaining cake mix and spread carefully with a spatula to cover custard.

Arrange apples on top of cake mixture and brush with melted butter. Combine sweet spice mix (or nutmeg) with extra caster sugar and sprinkle over apples.

Bake for 60-70 minutes or until cooked when tested with a skewer. Cool in pan before turning out.

Serves 6-8

Apple and currant chutney

4 granny smiths, peeled, cored and chopped

75g ($\frac{1}{2}$ cup) currants

100g ($\frac{1}{2}$ cup) firmly packed brown sugar

$\frac{1}{3}$ cup white-wine vinegar

1 tbsp flat-leaf parsley, chopped

pinch of ground nutmeg

pinch of dried chilli

$\frac{1}{2}$ tsp salt

Combine all the ingredients with a cup of water and stir frequently in a heavy-based saucepan over low heat for 45 minutes or until mixture is thick. Cool.

Makes about 2$\frac{1}{2}$ cups

Apricots

Apricots belong to the rose family and are closely related to almonds, peaches, plums and cherries. They make a luscious dessert, superb jam or can be simply eaten as a snack or chopped and scattered over muesli.

Fresh or cooked, they enhance other summer fruits and marry particularly well with chicken, duck, lamb and pork. Apricots are an excellent source of vitamins A and C, potassium and dietary fibre. The thin skin doesn't need peeling.

Succulent dried apricots, by far the most plentiful sun-dried tree fruit, will keep for long periods in an airtight container in the fridge. Many are treated with sulphur dioxide before being dried, which helps retain the rich, golden colour; untreated fruit has a darker appearance and a caramelised, almost fig-like flavour.

Select firm fruit with a hint of delicate perfume and rich, golden-orange skin. Avoid any that are greenish-yellow. Unless you plan to eat them immediately, choose slightly firm fruit and let them ripen in the bowl. Remove the stone before cooking, as it is very bitter. Generally, the stronger the colour, the sweeter the apricot.

Salamanca Market, Hobart

Apricot and coconut crumble

10 large apricots, seeded and cut into quarters

1 tsp lemon zest

2 tbsp fresh lemon juice

150g (²/₃ cup) caster sugar

large pinch of ground star anise

Topping

75g (¹/₂ cup) self-raising flour

50g unsalted cold butter, chopped

65g (¹/₃ cup, firmly packed) brown sugar

20g (¹/₄ cup) desiccated coconut

20g (¹/₄ cup) flaked almonds, chopped

For the topping, place flour in a medium-sized bowl and rub in the butter until mixture resembles coarse breadcrumbs. Add brown sugar, coconut and almonds and stir well.

Combine apricots, lemon zest and juice, sugar and 2 tablespoons of water in a large bowl.

Heat a non-stick frying pan over medium heat until hot and add apricot mixture and stir for 2-3 minutes until apricots have softened slightly. Add ground star anise, stir and cool.

Transfer apricot mixture to a lightly greased 6-cup-capacity ovenproof dish and sprinkle with topping. Bake at 180C for 25-30 minutes or until topping is golden and apricots are cooked.

Serve hot or warm with good quality vanilla ice-cream or vanilla custard.

Serves 4

Apricot and nectarine sundaes with honey cream and pistachios

6 large apricots (about 90g each) halved, seeded and sliced

3 white nectarines, halved seeded and thinly sliced

2 tbsp kirsch

750ml vanilla bean ice-cream

1 cup (150g) pistachios, coarsely chopped

Honey cream

2 tbsp honey

300ml pouring cream, whipped

For the honey cream, place honey and cream in a bowl and stir until well combined.

Place apricots and nectarines in a large bowl, sprinkle with kirsch then toss gently to combine and stand for 5 minutes.

To serve, take 8 1¹/₂-cup capacity glasses and place a scoop of vanilla bean ice-cream in the bottom of each, top with some of the fruit, then a spoonful of honey cream. Repeat layering with remaining ice-cream, fruit and honey cream.

Sprinkle apricot sundaes with pistachios and serve immediately.

Serves 8

Baked ham with dried apricots

1 leg of ham

cloves

$^1/_4$ cup dry sherry

3 tbsp Dijon mustard

1 tbsp Chinese five-spice powder

2 cups brown sugar

1$^1/_2$ cups pineapple juice

500g dried apricots

Preheat oven to 150C.

Cut skin from ham and peel back carefully, leaving a layer of fat. Score fat with a sharp knife, moving diagonally across the fat and press in the cloves. Pour sherry over ham.

Rub mustard over fat and then sprinkle with five-spice powder. Press brown sugar onto ham to coat fat and place ham in a large baking tray. Bake for 30 minutes. Baste with pineapple juice, add apricots and bake for a further 10 minutes. Continue basting every 10 minutes for a further 50 minutes.

Remove and rest for at least 1 hour before carving.

Serve with drained apricots, baby potatoes with parsley, roast sweet potato and a large green salad.

Serves 8-10

Warm sugared apricots and nectarines with chocolate cinnamon wafers

6 large, ripe nectarines, halved and stoned

4 ripe apricots, halved and stoned

55g ($^1/_4$ cup) caster sugar

30g ground hazelnuts

300g ricotta

2 tbsp icing sugar

Chocolate cinnamon wafers

1 tsp ground cinnamon

100g shortbread biscuits

75g dark chocolate, melted

For the chocolate wafers, process cinnamon and biscuits in a food processor until fine. Combine crumb mixture and melted chocolate and mix well. Place biscuit mixture between 2 sheets of baking paper and, using a rolling pin, roll very thinly into a rectangle about 20cm x 24cm. Remove top sheet and, using a sharp knife, mark 8 rectangles (about 5cm x 8cm). Replace paper and freeze until firm (10-15 minutes) or needed.

For the fruit, place nectarines and apricots, cut-side up, on a foil-lined baking tray and sprinkle with combined sugar and hazelnuts. Cook under a hot grill for about 5 minutes or until fruit is warmed through.

Combine ricotta and icing sugar in a small bowl and mix well.

To serve, place a dollop of ricotta on the side of the warm fruit, and pass the chocolate wafers.

Serves 4

Bananas

Low in fat, bananas are the perfect high-energy snack food. The carbohydrate in this fruit has a low glycemic index, meaning it is absorbed slowly to give you sustained energy. The creamy flesh tastes delectable and very ripe fruit is great to cook with.

Bananas are native to the humid tropical climates of South-East Asia and the flowers, leaves and trunk are also used in cuisines of the Pacific Islands.

Cavendish is the most widely grown variety in Australia, with smaller types such as lady finger and goldfinger becoming increasingly plentiful. Petite senoritas, just 5-6cm with light-orange flesh, are ideal as a snack. Red daccas, plump and red with delicate pinkish flesh, are very tasty cooked on the barbecue.

Plantains, also known as cooking bananas, are very large fruit with thick green skin and starchy flesh that is too astringent to eat raw. Popular in African and Asian cooking, this non-sweet variety is often used as an alternative to rice and potatoes, and is very tasty cooked with coconut milk, curry leaves, lemongrass and chillies.

Bananas are normally harvested green and ripened under contolled temperature. It is easy to assess what stage the fruit is at: when the skin has a waxy sheen and is light green at the ends the flesh is firm and barely sweet; bright-yellow skin still with some sheen and a brown mark or two means softer, sweeter flesh; and, as the skin dulls and becomes more brown-speckled, the flesh ripens to a luscious texture.

Choose fruit still in bunches and free from blemishes and bruises. They are best stored at room temperature, where they will ripen gently, however, bananas can be stored in the fridge if becoming overripe (the skins will turn brown but it won't harm the fruit). Speed up the ripening process by putting the banana in a closed bag with an apple or an orange.

Good Living Growers Market, Sydney

Caramel bananas on brioche

(pictured page 21)

¹/₂ cup pouring cream

1 cup maple syrup

1 cup toasted pecan nuts, halved

4 bananas

4 tbsp butter

4 slices brioche

low-fat yoghurt or vanilla ice-cream, to serve

Combine cream, maple syrup and pecans in a medium-sized saucepan, bring to the boil and simmer, stirring occasionally, for 3-5 minutes or until slightly reduced and thickened.

Slice bananas diagonally and cook in 2 tablespoons of butter in a large frying pan for 1-2 minutes each side, until light-golden.

Spread remaining butter on brioche and toast under a preheated hot grill until golden.

Top brioche with banana, spoon over warm sauce and serve with yoghurt or ice-cream.

Serves 4

Banana toffee cake

1 cup water

1 cup (220g) caster sugar

1-2 bananas (depending on size), sliced 1cm thick

³/₄ cup (150g) brown sugar

1 tsp vanilla extract

2 eggs, lightly beaten

160ml vegetable oil

¹/₃ cup (50g) self-raising flour

²/₃ cup (100g) plain flour

1 tsp bicarb soda

1¹/₂ tsp ground cinnamon

1 cup mashed banana (about 2 medium)

vanilla ice-cream, to serve

Preheat oven to 180C.

Combine water and caster sugar in a saucepan and stir over medium heat until sugar dissolves. Bring to the boil and cook for about 10 minutes or until mixture turns a caramel colour. Pour caramel into a 22cm greased and baking-paper-lined cake tin and arrange banana slices on toffee to cover.

Combine brown sugar, vanilla, eggs and oil in a medium-sized bowl and stir. Sift combined flours, bicarb soda and cinnamon into brown sugar mixture and stir well. Stir in mashed banana.

Pour mixture over bananas in cake tin and bake for about 40-45 minutes or until a cake is cooked.

Serve warm or at room temperature with vanilla ice-cream.

Serves 8

Chocolate and pistachio pavlova with bananas and raspberries

5 egg whites

pinch of salt

330g caster sugar

1$\frac{1}{2}$ tsp white-wine vinegar

1$\frac{1}{2}$ tsp vanilla extract

2 tbsp cocoa powder

1 tsp cornflour

300ml pouring cream, whipped

100g pistachios, toasted and chopped

2 large bananas, sliced

1 x 150g punnet raspberries

Preheat oven to 150C.

Line a baking tray with foil, mark a 23cm circle onto the foil and lightly grease the circle.

Beat egg whites and salt until soft peaks form, then gradually add sugar, beating well after each addition. Continue beating until all the sugar is dissolved and the mixture is thick and glossy, then whisk in vinegar, vanilla, cocoa and cornflour.

Spread two-thirds of the mixture evenly over the circle. Spoon remaining meringue around the edge of pavlova, forming a rim.

Reduce oven temperature to 100C and bake for 60 minutes. Turn oven off and leave pavlova in oven to cool.

To serve, spread whipped cream over pavlova, top with bananas and raspberries (or other berries if these are not available) and sprinkle with pistachios.

Serves 8

Banana, dried apricot and sultana bread

2 cups self-raising flour

1 tsp ground cinnamon

110g caster sugar

50g ($\frac{1}{3}$ cup) dried apricots, chopped

55g ($\frac{1}{3}$ cup) sultanas

1 cup milk

2 eggs

1 cup mashed, very ripe bananas (about 2 large)

Preheat oven to 180C.

Sift flour and cinnamon together in a large bowl. Add sugar, apricots and sultanas and stir to combine.

Combine milk, eggs and banana in a bowl and stir well. Fold into flour mixture and continue to stir. Spoon mixture into a 13cm x 23cm greased and baking-paper-lined loaf tin and bake for 45-50 minutes or until a cake tester comes out clean.

Rest for 5 minutes then turn onto a rack to cool.

Serve with unsalted butter. Toasts well.

Berries

Strawberries are one of the most widely grown berries. Many varieties are low in acid, so enhance their flavour with slightly acidic foods such as oranges, red-wine or balsamic vinegar. Complement their sweet perfume with other aromatic ingredients such as vanilla, rose petals, chocolate, sugar and mint leaves.

New varieties arrive at markets each year as growers search for the perfect berry; most are harvested a little under-ripe so they don't bruise en route. All strawberries should be picked with their green crowns intact. Before buying, turn the punnet upside down and reject any that are soft, squashed or oozing juice. Store briefly in the fridge.

Alpine strawberries or fraises du bois, sold in specialist shops, have a pungent aroma and intense flavour and are superb eaten unadorned. Tangy, sweet blueberries (known as bilberries in America) are reported to be one of the richest sources of disease-fighting antioxidants. They are naturally sweet, low in calories and freeze successfully. Choose plump berries that are a light powdery blue with a waxy gloss. Blueberries are harvested ripe, but spoil quickly at room temperature so best to keep them unwashed and dry in an airtight container in the fridge. Serve at room temperature for maximum flavour.

Raspberries, the king of berries, are not a true berry but a collection of drupelets. The hollow fruit, grown on prickly bushes, is held together by a network of fine, interlacing hairs. Yellow raspberries have an exquisite flavour and an almost velvety texture, but are not as readily available as the red varieties.

Blackberries remain sour for a short time after they turn black so are best eaten slightly soft. They contain high levels of pectin, which makes them ideal for jams and jellies. As well as raspberries, blackberries have been used to create hybrids such as youngberries, boysenberries and loganberries, which can be used as a substitute in most recipes. Choose plump, dry fruit – store in the crisper of the fridge, but bring to room temperature before serving.

Panna cotta with warm strawberries

750ml pouring cream

220g (1 cup) caster sugar

$^1/_3$ cup milk

1 tbsp powdered gelatine

1 tsp vanilla extract

2 tbsp amaretto liqueur

Strawberries

1 tbsp unsalted butter

2 punnets (500g) strawberries, hulled and halved

$^1/_2$ cup (100g) brown sugar

juice of 1 large orange

Combine cream, sugar and milk in a medium-sized saucepan and cook over low heat until almost boiling, stirring until sugar dissolves. Remove from heat.

Place 2 tablespoons of hot water in a small cup, sprinkle gelatine over then stand in a saucepan of simmering water and stir until gelatine dissolves. Pour dissolved gelatine into cream mixture and stir well to combine.

Cool slightly and add vanilla extract and amaretto and stir well to combine.

Pour cream mixture into 6 x 200ml moulds that have been rinsed in cold water. Cover and refrigerate until set.

For warm strawberries, melt butter in a large frying pan over medium heat, add strawberries and sprinkle over brown sugar. Toss gently and add orange juice. Stir over medium heat until strawberries are just soft.

To serve, unmould panna cotta by dipping moulds in hot water for a few seconds. Serve with warm strawberries and a little of the juices poured over.

Accompany with biscotti if desired.

Serves 6

Positano, Italy

Best-ever sponge cake with raspberry jam and fresh raspberries

4 large eggs, separated

$^3/_4$ cup (165g) caster sugar

1 cup (150g) plain flour

$^1/_2$ tsp cream of tartar

$^1/_4$ tsp bicarb soda

pinch of salt

1 tsp butter

3 tbsp hot water

raspberry jam

whipped cream

icing sugar, for dusting

450g (3 punnets) ripe raspberries

Preheat oven to 180C.

Beat egg whites in an electric mixer until thick. Gradually add sugar, about a tablespoon at a time, beating until sugar is dissolved in between additions. Fold in egg yolks. Sift combined flour, cream of tartar, bicarb soda and salt 3 times onto paper, then sift again into egg mixture and lightly fold in. Pour combined butter and hot water down the side of the bowl and gently fold through.

Pour mixture evenly into 2 x 20cm well-greased round cake tins and smooth top to edges with a metal spoon. Bake for about 20 minutes, until cooked. Turn onto wire racks covered with baking paper to cool.

Place one sponge on serving plate, spread with raspberry jam and whipped cream. Top with remaining cake, dust with sifted icing sugar and serve with fresh raspberries.

Serves 6-8

Warm buttered blackberries with lime creme brulee

2 vanilla beans, split

3 cups pouring cream

7 egg yolks

$^1/_2$ cup (110g) caster sugar

3 tsp lime zest

$^3/_4$ cup (165g) caster sugar, extra

1 tbsp butter

450g blackberries

100g brown sugar

juice of 1 orange

For the lime brulees, place beans in a saucepan with pouring cream and bring to the boil over low heat. Remove. Whisk egg yolks with 110g sugar until thick. Remove vanilla beans and stir cream into egg-yolk mixture. Transfer mixture to a clean, heavy-based saucepan and cook, stirring constantly, over low heat until mixture thickens enough to coat the back of a wooden spoon. Do not boil. Remove from heat and strain. Stir in lime zest and divide custard evenly among six 1-cup ramekins. Cover with plastic wrap and refrigerate for 3 hours or overnight.

Sprinkle surface of creme brulees with extra caster sugar to form a layer 2-3mm thick. Place under a preheated hot grill and cook until sugar caramelises. Chill for 15 minutes before serving. Alternatively, use a small blow-torch to caramelise sugar.

Melt butter in a frying pan over medium heat, add blackberries and sprinkle over brown sugar. Toss gently and add orange juice. Stir over medium heat for 2-3 minutes, until blackberries are just soft.

Serve creme brulees with a small pot of warm blackberries (and juices) on the side.

Serves 6

Fresh blueberries with sabayon sauce

2 punnet blueberries

4 egg yolks

$^1/_2$ cup (110g) caster sugar

$^1/_2$ cup marsala

$^1/_4$ cup water

Beat egg yolks with sugar in the top half of a double boiler or in a bowl over a saucepan of simmering water. Add marsala and water and cook, stirring constantly, until thick and foamy.

Remove from heat and divide fresh berries evenly between 4 serving dishes. Pour sabayon sauce over berries.

Serves 4

Warm blueberries and strawberries with Grand Marnier, orange and black pepper

25g butter

100g brown sugar

160ml fresh orange juice

2 tsp orange zest

2 punnets blueberries

1 punnet strawberries, hulled and halved

10 turns of the pepper mill

2 tbsp Grand Marnier

Melt butter in a large frying pan over low heat and add brown sugar and orange juice. Stir for 2 minutes and then add orange zest. Add blueberries and strawberries and stir to coat. Add pepper and cook for about 3 minutes or until berries are glossy and juices are reduced and slightly thickened.

Remove from heat and stir in Grand Marnier. Spoon warm berries into serving dishes and pour sauce over. Serve with thick cream or ice-cream.

Serves 4

Blueberry and almond muffins

300g (2 cups) self-raising flour

110g ($^1/_2$ cup) caster sugar

1 cup milk

$^1/_3$ cup vegetable oil

2 eggs

$^1/_2$ cup fresh or frozen blueberries

40g ($^1/_2$ cup) flaked almonds

Preheat oven to 200C.

Combine flour and sugar in a large bowl. Combine milk, oil and eggs in a separate bowl and whisk lightly, then stir in berries.

Make a well in the centre of flour mixture, pour in liquid and mix lightly. Spoon batter into 6 greased muffin tins ($^1/_2$ cup capacity) until two-thirds full then scatter tops with almonds. Bake for 20-25 minutes or until golden and cooked.

Turn onto a wire rack to cool. Serve with unsalted butter.

Makes 6

Sugared mixed berries with chocolate mousse

375g quality dark cooking chocolate, broken into pieces

3 eggs

1 tbsp caster sugar

300ml cream

1 tbsp brandy or cognac

3 punnets (750g) mixed berries

3-4 tbsp icing (confectioner's) sugar

Melt chocolate in a bowl over a saucepan of simmering water or in the microwave and then cool slightly. Stir eggs into chocolate until smooth.

Whip cream with sugar until firm and then fold into chocolate mixture. Stir in brandy or cognac and spoon chocolate mousse into small dishes. Cover and refrigerate until ready to serve.

Place strawberries in a bowl and sprinkle with icing sugar. Set aside until ready to serve.

Serve strawberries beside pots of mousse.

Serves 6

Summer berry pudding

1 loaf white bread (lightly buttered, optional)

2 cups mixed berries (blackberries, raspberries, blueberries)

2 large eggs

300ml pouring cream

165g (³/₄ cup) caster sugar

icing sugar, to serve

Lightly grease a medium-sized ovenproof dish.

Remove crusts from bread and cut in triangle halves. Sprinkle 1 cup of the mixed berries over the base of the dish. Top with slices of bread overlapping slightly. Sprinkle ¹/₂ cup of the remaining berries over bread. Top with a layer of bread. Sprinkle over remaining berries.

Put eggs, cream and caster sugar in a medium-sized bowl and whisk to combine. Pour egg mixture over pudding and bake at 180C for 30-45 minutes or until golden and cooked.

Sprinkle with icing sugar before serving.

Serves 4

Raspberry and ricotta tartlets

Pastry

225g (1¹/₂ cups) plain flour

2 tbsp icing sugar

150g cold unsalted butter, chopped

1 egg yolk

Filling

500g ricotta cheese

5-6 tbsp icing sugar

1¹/₂ tsp vanilla extract

2-3 punnets raspberries

extra icing sugar, for dusting

Process flour, icing sugar and butter in a food processor until mixture resembles coarse breadcrumbs. Add egg yolk and 2 tablespoons of iced water and process until mixture just comes together. Form dough into a disc, wrap in plastic and refrigerate for 1 hour.

Divide pastry into 8 pieces; roll out 1 piece on a lightly floured surface until 5mm thick and line an 8cm greased tart tin with removable base, trimming pastry. Repeat process with remaining pastry. Prick base lightly with a fork and freeze for about 20 minutes.

Place tart tins on an oven tray and bake at 190C for 12-15 minutes or until pastry is light golden and dry, then cool.

For the filling, combine ricotta and icing sugar (to taste) with vanilla and stir until smooth.

Spread ricotta mixture into tart cases and top with fresh raspberries. Dust with extra icing sugar.

Makes 8

Strawberry fruit salad with lemongrass syrup

300g grated palm sugar

2 sticks lemongrass, bruised

2 tsp lime juice

1 punnet (250g) strawberries, hulled and halved

3 kiwifruit, peeled and cut into chunks

¹/₂ rockmelon, peeled and cut into chunks

1 cup light coconut cream

Combine palm (or brown) sugar with lemongrass and 300ml water in a saucepan and stir over medium heat until sugar dissolves. Bring to the boil and simmer for 5 minutes. Cool syrup to room temperature, then strain. Add lime juice and mix well.

Combine strawberries, kiwifruit and rockmelon in a large bowl. Add lemongrass syrup and toss gently to combine. Serve drizzled with coconut cream.

Serves 4

Goat's curd cheesecake with warm cinnamon raspberries

Spend a few minutes in the kitchen during summer and you'll be well rewarded with this divine cheesecake and warm raspberries. The cheesecake will keep in an airtight container in the refrigerator for up to 2 days.

165g ($^3/_4$ cup) caster sugar, plus extra for dusting

400g goat's curd, at room temperature

100g ricotta cheese

1 tsp vanilla extract

1 tsp lemon rind, grated

2 tsp lemon juice

6 large eggs, separated

30g plain flour

Warm cinnamon raspberries

50g unsalted butter

75g ($^1/_3$ cup) caster sugar

$^3/_4$ tsp ground cinnamon

4 x 150g punnets raspberries

Preheat oven to 180C.

Grease a 22cm springform pan and dust with a little caster sugar, shake out excess and line base with baking paper.

Using an electric mixer, beat sugar, goat's curd, ricotta, vanilla, lemon rind and juice until combined, then add egg yolks and beat until smooth. Reduce speed to low, add flour and beat until just combined. Set aside.

Using an electric mixer, whisk egg whites until stiff peaks form. Fold one-third into cheese mixture to loosen, then fold in remaining egg whites. Pour mixture into pan and bake for 30-35 minutes or until a cake tester comes out clean. Rest in pan for 15 minutes, then transfer to a wire rack to cool.

For warm raspberries, melt butter in a large frying pan over low heat and stir in sugar and cinnamon. Add raspberries and stir very gently for 1-2 minutes or until raspberries are warm and release some of their juices.

Transfer cheesecake to a large plate and dust generously with icing sugar. Cut into wedges and serve with warm raspberries on the side.

Serves 8

Roasted summer fruit salad

1 punnet (250g) strawberries, hulled

2 large nectarines, halved and stoned

2 medium freestone peaches, halved and stoned

2 large blood plums, halved and stoned

$^1/_2$ cup marsala

3 tbsp water

2 tbsp brown sugar

1 vanilla bean, very thinly sliced lengthways

2 tbsp mint, chopped

Preheat oven to 200C.

Place fruit, cut side up, in an ovenproof dish Combine marsala and water, stir and pour over fruit. Sprinkle with sugar and vanilla bean and bake for about 15-20 minutes or until fruit is soft.

Remove and cool to room temperature.

Serve drizzled with pan juices and scattered with mint.

Serves 4

Cherries

The cherry season is short, so make the most of them and serve a big bowl of crushed ice topped with a pile of the shiny red fruit and a few sprigs of mint. It makes a wonderful edible centerpiece, particularly on the Christmas table.

There are two main types of cherries, sweet and sour, and more than 100 species. Sweet cherries are not commonly sold by varietal name, except perhaps for the glossy crimson rons, bing and supremes. White cherries, in reality a creamy gold with a rosy-pink blush, are slightly acidic and not as big or as sweet as the large red varieties.

Sweet cherries have almost no fat and are a good source of vitamin C and potassium (but they are low in pectin so if you are making jam you will need to add powdered pectin or apple juice for good consistency). Sour cherries, grown mainly in colder areas, appear sporadically in specialist fruit shops. They have higher levels of pectin so are better for cooking and team well with duck. Morellos, the most common variety, are delicious in savoury dishes and with turkey.

Select plump, firm, shiny examples but look especially for green stems – cherries stay fresher longer if the stems are attached. The fruit doesn't ripen any further after harvesting, so is best eaten within three to four days of purchase. Store in a plastic bag in the crisper of the fridge and wash just before eating.

Cherry and almond crumble with vanilla bean creme anglaise

Creme anglaise

2 cups milk

1 vanilla bean, split

6 egg yolks

65g caster sugar

1kg cherries, stems and pips removed

110g (1/2 cup) caster sugar

1 1/2 tbsp kirsch

110g (3/4 cup) self-raising flour

100g butter, chopped

3/4 cup (75g) flaked almonds

100g brown sugar

For the vanilla bean creme anglaise, heat milk with vanilla bean in a saucepan until almost boiling. Remove from heat and set aside for 5 minutes for flavours to infuse. Beat egg yolks with caster sugar in a bowl until thick and pale, then gradually whisk in milk. Return to saucepan and cook over low heat, stirring constantly, until mixture thickens enough to coat the back of a wooden spoon. Do not boil. Cool to room temperature and remove vanilla bean.

Preheat oven to 200C.

For the crumble, combine a quarter of the cherries in a food processor with caster sugar and kirsch and process to a puree. Grease a 1.5-litre ovenproof dish and scatter with remaining cherries. Pour over cherry puree.

For the topping, place self-raising flour in a bowl and rub in chopped butter. Add flaked almonds and brown sugar and mix well. Spread crumble mixture over the cherries and bake for 30-40 minutes, until cherries are cooked and crumble is golden.

Serve warm or cold with vanilla bean creme anglaise.

Serves 4

Cherry Ripe slice

500g dark cooking chocolate, chopped

500g desiccated coconut

100g copha, melted

395g tin condensed milk

100g glace cherries, chopped

few drops of red food colouring

Melt half the chocolate and spread evenly over the base of a foil-lined 30cm x 20cm cake tin. Rest, covered, in the fridge until set.

Place coconut, copha, condensed milk and cherries in a large bowl and stir well to combine. Add a few drops of food colouring and mix until evenly coloured. Spoon coconut mixture over top of chocolate and use the back of a spoon to press evenly. Refrigerate until set.

Melt remaining chocolate and spread over coconut mixture and return to fridge until set.

Cut into bars with a hot knife.

Store in an airtight container in the fridge.

Cherry and chocolate cakes with cherries and vanilla ice-cream

These cakes are great for entertaining, as they can be made well ahead. Unfilled cakes will keep in an airtight container for up to 4 days. Add ice-cream just before serving. The kids will love them, too.

60g soft unsalted butter

75g ($^1/_3$ cup) caster sugar

2 eggs

110g ($^3/_4$ cup) self-raising flour

2 tbsp cocoa

1 tsp baking powder

2 tbsp milk

100g cherries, pitted and chopped

1 cup vanilla ice-cream

icing sugar, for dusting

Preheat oven to 180C.

Using an electric mixer, beat butter and caster sugar until light and fluffy. Add eggs, one at a time, beating well after each. Sift together flour, cocoa and baking powder, then fold into butter mixture alternately with milk and mix until smooth.

Fold in half the cherries, then divide mixture among 6 paper case-lined muffin tins and bake for about 25 minutes or until a cake skewer comes out clean. Cool in tin for 5 minutes before transferring to a wire rack to cool.

Cut tops from cakes and scoop out a little cake from the centre, then spoon 2 tablespoons of ice-cream and remaining cherries into cakes. Dust with icing sugar and serve immediately.

Serves 6

Cherries in balsamic syrup with vanilla ice-cream

1 cup caster sugar

$^3/_4$ cup water

1 tablespoon balsamic vinegar

400g pitted cherries

vanilla ice-cream, to serve

Combine sugar and $^1/_2$ cup of water in a small saucepan over low heat. Stir until sugar is dissolved then bring to the boil and simmer without stirring until mixture is a pale-caramel colour. Remove from heat and add remaining water and balsamic vinegar. (Be careful, as mixture will spit.) Return to low heat and stir until smooth.

Place cherries in a heatproof bowl and pour syrup over. Allow to cool and serve with a scoop of vanilla ice-cream.

Serves 4

Chestnuts

With their rich, earthy appeal chestnuts are among the most exciting flavours of autumn. They are versatile, too, starring in savoury dishes as well as desserts. Their nutty, mealy taste makes them delicious in silky smooth soups, poached whole in vanilla syrup or folded through cooked apple puree.

Chestnuts have a thin skin (pellicle) and are encased in a glossy brown shell. Once cooked, the creamy flesh has a delicate flavour with a texture similar to a roast potato.

To prepare them, cut a cross in the base of each with a small, sharp knife before cooking, as they can explode when heated. Boil the nuts in water for 15-20 minutes and peel while they are still hot and the tough inner skin will be much easier to remove. Roast prepared nuts in a hot oven (200C) for about 20 minutes or until soft, then peel.

Select the largest nuts because they will take less time to prepare. The best ones have shiny, undamaged shells and feel heavy for their size. The firmer the nuts, the fresher they will be. Avoid any that rattle in the shell, as it indicates they are drying out.

Because of their high moisture content, chestnuts are best stored in the refrigerator in a sealed container to prevent them from shrivelling, and should be consumed within a couple of weeks.

Most nuts are high in fat, but chestnuts rate as a healthy choice containing about 2.7 per cent fat, most of which is unsaturated. They are a good source of fibre and contain vitamins C, B1, B6 and E, as well as potassium, folate and magnesium.

Roasted mushrooms with fresh chestnuts and herbs

8 large chestnuts (about 25g each)

1$\frac{1}{2}$ cups chicken stock

4 large flat mushrooms

1 clove garlic, finely chopped

$\frac{1}{2}$ tsp dried chilli flakes

1 tbsp oregano, chopped

1 tbsp flat-leaf parsley, chopped

1 tsp thyme leaves

2 tbsp breadcrumbs

1 tbsp butter

Preheat oven to 200C.

Score the skin of each chestnut with a sharp knife to prevent them from bursting when cooked. Simmer in chicken stock for 10 minutes.

Remove from stock a few at a time and peel both the skin and the inner layer while still warm. Reserve stock. Coarsely chop chestnuts.

Remove the stalks from the mushrooms and chop stalks finely. In a bowl, combine the chopped stalks, garlic, chilli flakes, oregano, parsley, thyme and breadcrumbs and season to taste with sea salt. Add chestnuts and stir to combine.

Place the mushrooms, stalk side up, in a shallow, lightly greased ovenproof dish and spoon chestnut mixture over mushrooms. Dot with butter and drizzle with remaining chicken stock.

Roast for 30 minutes or until mushrooms are cooked.

Serves 4 as an entree

Chestnut and carrot soup with fresh herbs

300g chestnuts, base scored with a sharp knife

1 tbsp butter

1 tbsp extra virgin olive oil

300g carrots, peeled and chopped

1 onion, peeled and chopped

2 sticks celery, sliced

1 bay leaf

2 sprigs thyme

2 sprigs flat-leaf parsley

4 cups chicken stock

salt and cracked black pepper

$\frac{1}{2}$ cup light pouring cream (optional)

2 tbsp flat-leaf parsley, chopped

Microwave chestnuts on high for 2-3 minutes until shells open and flesh is soft (or bake at 200C for about 15 minutes). Peel while still warm and chop.

Melt butter in a large saucepan with olive oil over medium heat and add carrots, onion, celery, bay leaf, thyme and flat-leaf parsley and cook, stirring often, for 4-5 minutes. Add chestnuts, chicken stock and salt and pepper and simmer, covered, for about 20 minutes, until chestnuts are tender. Remove herbs and reserve 2 tablespoons of vegetable and chestnut mixture.

Mix remaining vegetables and stock in a food processor or blender until smooth then return to saucepan. Add cream (optional) and stir continually to heat through. Check seasoning. Do not boil. Ladle soup into 4 warm bowls, top with reserved chestnuts and vegetables and sprinkle with flat-leaf parsley.

Serves 4

Coconuts

The creaminess of coconut milk rounds out a fiery chilli sauce, while coconut flesh makes delectable macaroons, cakes, ice-creams and puddings and coconut cream adds a richness to curries and a luscious finish to many dishes.

Eaten young (about 6 months), the flesh is soft, creamy and fruity. Mature coconut meat commonly used in Asian dishes adds a mellow flavour to curries, soups and salads.

When buying a coconut, ensure the shell is dry with no mould or dampness. It should feel heavy for its size and the three "eyes" on top of the coconut should be uniformly dark. Shake it to make sure there is liquid inside – if not, the flesh will be rancid.

The easiest way to prepare the nut is to push a screwdriver through two of the holes and drain the liquid, which can be used in cooking and also makes a refreshing drink.

To make the flesh easier to remove, bake the coconut at 180C for about 20 minutes, then cool and hit it with a hammer to crack open. Peel away the brown skin using a small, sharp knife or vegetable peeler.

The flesh can be frozen and sealed in a plastic bag for up to a month.

Prawn, lemongrass and coconut soup

375ml (1½ cups) fish or vegetable stock

2 cups light coconut milk

1 tbsp caster sugar

1 stick lemongrass, chopped

2 cloves garlic, chopped

½ tsp dried chilli flakes

½ tsp ground turmeric

2 coriander roots

16 large green (raw) prawns, shelled and deveined

¾ cup light coconut cream

2 tbsp fish sauce

1½ tbsp lime juice

4 tbsp coriander leaves

Combine stock and coconut milk in a large saucepan, add sugar and a good pinch of salt and bring to the boil. Place lemongrass, garlic, chilli flakes, turmeric and coriander roots in a small food processor and whiz until finely ground (or pound in a mortar and pestle). Add lemongrass mixture to hot stock and simmer for 5 minutes. Add prawns and simmer until they just change colour. Add coconut cream, fish sauce and lime juice and stir.

Ladle soup into warm bowls and top with coriander leaves.

Serves 4

Little lamingtons

125g soft butter, chopped

165g (¾ cup) caster sugar

½ tsp vanilla extract

2 eggs

225g (1½ cups) plain flour, sifted

3 tsp baking powder, sifted

¼ cup milk

250g flaked coconut, for coating

Icing

500g (3¼ cups) icing sugar, sifted

50g Dutch cocoa

40g soft butter

½ tsp vanilla extract

20ml cognac

Using an electric mixer, beat butter, sugar and vanilla until light and creamy. Add eggs, one at a time, beating well after each addition. Stir in combined flour and baking powder alternately with milk, in two batches, until smooth. Spoon mixture into a greased 23cm-square cake tin lined with baking paper and bake at 190C for 25-30 minutes or until cooked when tested with a cake skewer. Stand in tin for 10 minutes before turning out on a wire rack to cool. Wrap in plastic wrap and store for 1 day.

For the icing, combine all the ingredients with 100ml of boiling water and mix until smooth.

Cut cake into 4cm squares and dip each one briefly into icing, then into coconut.

Place lamingtons on a rack for 1-2 hours, until dry.

Makes about 25

Custard apples

Custard apples taste like a tropical fruit salad and have a creamy, velvety texture that makes them a luscious sweet snack or dessert. Grown in sub-tropical areas, the two main varieties have shiny black seeds and mellow flesh.

Pinks mammoth weigh up to 3kg and have yellowish-green skin and a lumpy exterior. African prides, medium in size and weighing 500-800g, have thin, smoother, skin with firm flesh and more seeds. Both turn from mid-green to a light-jade colour when ripe and team well with nutmeg, cinnamon, oranges, honey and vanilla.

The shelf life of custard apples is short, so buy small quantities of firm, mature fruit. Avoid black, overripe, squashy examples. They are ready to eat when soft to the touch, as with an avocado. Quicken the ripening process by placing them in a brown paper bag with an apple or banana.

Open a ripe custard apple by placing your thumbs in the indent where the stem joins the fruit and gently pull the fruit apart into quarters or segments, discarding the smooth, black seeds. The flesh discolors quickly so eat it straight away or rub the surface with a little lemon or lime juice.

Custard apple smoothie

1 cup full-cream milk

1 cup custard apple flesh (seeds removed)

2 tbsp honey

$^1/_4$ tsp ground nutmeg

Combine milk and custard apple flesh in a food processor or blender until smooth. Add honey and whiz until combined. Pour mixture into a tall glass and sprinkle with nutmeg.

Serves 1

Custard apple cheesecake

Pastry

225g (1$^1/_2$ cups) plain flour

125g butter, chopped

1 tbsp icing sugar

1 egg yolk

Filling

Pulp from 1 large custard apple, seeds removed

150ml cream

110g ($^1/_2$ cup) caster sugar

300g ricotta cheese

$^1/_2$ tsp vanilla extract

3 tsp powdered gelatine

$^1/_2$ cup flaked almonds, toasted

Preheat oven to 180C.

For the pastry, combine flour, butter, icing sugar and a pinch of salt in a food processor until mixture resembles coarse breadcrumbs. Add 1-2 tablespoons chilled water, egg yolk and process until mixture just comes together. Shape pastry into a disc, cover with plastic wrap and refrigerate for 30 minutes.

Roll out pastry on a lightly floured surface and line a round, 23cm tart tin with removable base. Prick base of pastry lightly with a fork, cover with plastic wrap and refrigerate for 30 minutes.

Line pastry with baking paper, fill with dried beans or rice and bake blind for 15 minutes. Remove paper and weights and bake for a further 10-15 minutes, until pastry is golden and dry. Cool.

For the filling, combine custard apple, cream, sugar, ricotta and vanilla in a medium-sized bowl and mix well. Dissolve gelatine in 2 tablespoons of hot water then stir in to cream mixture. Pour mixture into pastry case and refrigerate until firm. Serve topped with toasted flaked almonds.

Serves 6

Dates

The date palm is perhaps the oldest cultivated plant in the world, thought to have originated in Mesopotamia about 3500BC. Dates have been an essential food for thousands of years in the Middle East, where they appear in savoury and sweet recipes.

There are many varieties of date, but the big, meaty medjool are the ideal healthy snack and the most prized of the soft dates. Beige-coloured deglet noors have a smooth skin and chewy texture and are often sold dried or semi-dried. Barhi are small Australian dates.

Select plump, dark-brown, shiny fruit and avoid very hard dates. The high sugar content in soft, buttery medjools makes them suitable for freezing, but they can also be stored at room temperature for several weeks. Semi-dried dates are often sold pressed into blocks and can be difficult to separate. These are best used in biscuits, pies and tarts – once the packet is open, store them in an airtight container.

When chopping fresh dates, use a pair of scissors dipped in hot water, as they can be very sticky. Dates will also be easier to chop if they have been stored in the fridge for a couple of hours.

Dust dates with a little plain flour before you put them into your cake or sticky date pudding so they won't all sink to the bottom.

Moroccan chicken with fresh dates and preserved lemon

4 chicken marylands, halved

4 tbsp extra virgin olive oil

2 cloves garlic, finely chopped

$^1/_2$ tsp paprika

$^1/_2$ tsp ground cumin

$^1/_4$ tsp ground turmeric

1 tsp ginger, grated

salt and cracked black pepper

$^1/_2$ lemon, finely sliced

2 onions, finely chopped

2 small carrots, peeled and thinly sliced

$^3/_4$ cup frozen peas

120g ($^3/_4$ cup) green olives

8 large fresh dates, halved and pitted

$^1/_4$ preserved lemon, finely chopped

2 tbsp coriander, chopped

Preheat oven to 200C.

Place chicken pieces in a large bowl and drizzle with 3 tablespoons of oil.

Combine garlic, paprika, cumin, turmeric and fresh ginger in a small bowl and then sprinkle over chicken. Season with salt and pepper and turn chicken to coat. Add lemon slices, cover with plastic wrap and refrigerate for 1 hour.

Heat a large ovenproof dish with remaining olive oil and once hot add onions and stir over medium heat for 2-3 minutes. Add 1 cup of water and stir well. Place chicken on top of onions, turn to coat and bake covered for 20 minutes. Add carrots and bake for 10 minutes. Add peas, olives and dates and bake for a further 10 minutes, until chicken is tender.

Serve chicken with juices and vegetables spooned over and top with preserved lemon and coriander.

Serve with couscous or mash.

Serves 4

Little Christmas puddings with brandy sauce

Puddings

160g fresh dates, pitted and chopped

1 cup water

50g glace cherries, chopped

1 tsp bicarb soda

60g soft, unsalted butter

2 eggs, lightly beaten

165g caster sugar

185g self-raising flour, sifted

$^1/_2$ tsp vanilla extract

Brandy Sauce

6 egg yolks

$^1/_2$ cup orange juice

110g ($^1/_2$ cup) caster sugar

$^1/_2$ cup brandy

125g ($^1/_2$ cup) melted butter

Preheat oven to 190C.

For the puddings, cook dates in water over low heat for about 10 minutes until they reach jam consistency. Transfer to a bowl and beat in remaining ingredients and mix well. Grease eight 200ml ovenproof dishes and dust with flour. Pour pudding mixture evenly between them. Bake for 18-20 minutes or until cooked when tested with a skewer. Remove from the moulds and serve with brandy sauce or custard or cream.

For the brandy sauce, combine yolks, orange juice and sugar in a bowl and whisk over a pan of simmering water until thick. Remove from heat and whisk in brandy. Stir in melted butter. Serve warm.

Serves 8

Figs

Hailed as the fruit of the gods, figs have been cultivated for thousands of years. They originated in Asia Minor and are mentioned in numerous ancient texts. They have been an important part of the Mediterranean diet for millennia and are prized for their energy value and as a source of iron, potassium and calcium.

There are many varieties. Black genoas are early market arrivals, then come brown turkeys, with a green tinge on the skin. White adriatics, with amber-to-green skin and reddish flesh, arrive later. Mission figs, with their deep-purple-black skin and sweet, lush flavour are widely grown in California.

The fruit must be picked by hand – even then some varieties remain perfect for a few days only. They need to be harvested when soft and mature and require expensive packaging, hence the high price tag.

Dried figs will keep in an airtight container in a cool, dark place for several weeks but will gradually darken and harden. As with most dried fruits, they make excellent snacks.

Fresh figs should smell sweet: sour odours mean they are overripe. They should feel heavy for their size and the skin should not be split. Green, immature figs are firm and have a bland flavour.

Eat figs as soon as possible; they can be stored in the crisper of the fridge for a couple of days. Trim the stem before using, as it contains a white milky substance that is unpleasant to eat.

Pancetta-wrapped figs with goat's curd and pecan dressing

200g pecan nuts

$^1/_2$ bunch coriander, coarsely chopped

$^1/_2$ small red onion, finely sliced

$^1/_2$ small red chilli, finely chopped

50ml extra virgin olive oil

1 tbsp lemon juice

salt and cracked black pepper

12 fresh ripe figs

12 thin slices spicy pancetta

400g fresh goat's curd

2 tbsp olive oil, extra

Preheat oven to 200C.

Toast pecans on an oven tray for 4-5 minutes. Remove and, when cool, coarsely chop.

For the dressing, combine pecans, coriander leaves, red onion and red chilli with 50ml extra virgin olive oil, lemon juice, salt and pepper in a small bowl and stir well.

Score the tops of 12 ripe, fresh figs into quarters without completely cutting through and wrap each in a slice of pancetta. Place on an oven tray and bake for 5-6 minutes, until pancetta is crisp and figs are warm.

To serve, spoon dressing evenly into the centre of 4 serving plates. Place 3 dollops of goat's curd on top of dressing then a fig on top of each dollop of curd. Sprinkle with salt and pepper and drizzle each plate with 2 teaspoons extra virgin olive oil.

Serves 4

Figs poached in red wine and vanilla with thick cream

165g (³/₄ cup) caster sugar

³/₄ cup water

750ml red wine

2 vanilla beans, split

8 figs

1 cup thick cream

Combine sugar and water in a large saucepan and stir over low heat until sugar is dissolved. Add wine and vanilla beans and stir. Bring to the boil over medium heat and add figs. Simmer, covered, over low heat for 4-8 minutes (depending on ripeness) or until figs are just tender. Remove figs.

Reduce wine mixture over high heat, uncovered, until it has a syrup consistency. Cool and remove beans.

Place 2 figs on serving plates, drizzle with syrup and serve thick cream on the side.

Serves 4

Black figs with pepperoni, rocket and fresh goat's curd

(pictured page 45)

6 black figs, quartered

24 thin slices pepperoni salami

24 small rocket leaves, stems removed

24 toothpicks

200g fresh goat's curd, to serve

You can assemble fig, pepperoni and rocket on the morning of the party and refrigerate, covered.

Place 1 piece of fig and 1 slice of pepperoni on one or two rocket leaves (depending on size). Roll leaf and secure with a toothpick. Repeat with remaining figs, pepperoni and rocket leaves. Cover and chill.

Serve fig canapes with a dollop of goat's curd.

Makes 24

Roasted figs with honey, almonds and creme fraiche

8 large, ripe figs

2 tbsp honey

2 tbsp blanched almonds, chopped

2 tbsp creme fraiche

Preheat oven to 220C.

Cut figs in quarters, leaving the bases intact, and place in a lightly buttered ovenproof dish. Drizzle each with 1 teaspoon of honey and sprinkle with 1 teaspoon of chopped almonds. Spoon a teaspoon of creme fraiche into the centre of each fig and roast in a hot oven for about 10 minutes or until figs are soft.

Serve figs with warm juices spooned over.

Serves 4

Angouleme Market, France

Grapefruit

The clean, sharp tang of grapefruit is delightful in both savoury and sweet recipes. A cross between a sweet orange and a pomelo, they are so named because they grow in bunches on the tree.

Grapefruit were originally white fleshed with many seeds and much smaller than the newer varieties. Ruby (pink) grapefruit are often called the glamour members of the citrus family and are very juicy and lower in acid than their yellow cousins. They have very smooth rind and few seeds, but a shorter season than yellow grapefruit, which are available all year. Red grapefruit are sweet with no sour overtones and have skin that varies from pale-yellow with a slight blush to an intense red-orange.

Choose firm fruit, avoiding any with brown spots. They should feel heavy for their size, indicating good juice content.

Grapefruit are tree ripened, so are ready to eat when you buy them. They can be stored in the fruit bowl for about a week or in the crisper of the fridge for up to a month – but bring them to room temperature before serving for maximum flavour.

Ruby grapefruit, avocado, prawn and pickled walnut salad

2 large ruby grapefruit

2 tsp chardonnay vinegar

4 tbsp extra virgin olive oil

salt and cracked black pepper

2 ripe avocadoes, peeled and sliced

20 large, cooked king prawns, shelled and
    deveined, tails intact

100g wild rocket leaves

2 green onions, finely sliced

3 pickled walnuts, coarsely chopped

Peel grapefruit and then cut in between each membrane to release segments. Place segments in a large bowl. Squeeze juice from remaining grapefruit cores and reserve.

To make a dressing, measure 2 tablespoons of juice and pour into a small bowl. Add vinegar and olive oil. Season with salt and pepper and whisk well.

Add avocadoes and prawns to the grapefruit segments. Toss rocket leaves with 1 tablespoon of the dressing and divide rocket evenly between 4 serving plates.

Add green onions to grapefruit and prawn mixture and add remaining dressing. Toss gently to combine and pile grapefruit salad on top of rocket leaves. Sprinkle with pickled walnuts.

Serves 4

Salmon, grapefruit and fennel salad

500g cooked salmon, skin and bones removed
    and flesh flaked

1 grapefruit, peeled and segmented

1 bulb fennel, halved, cored and sliced

1 avocado, peeled and sliced

$^1/_2$ bunch watercress, trimmed

50g salmon roe

Dressing

$^1/_3$ cup grapeseed oil

2 tbsp fresh orange juice

1 tsp lemon juice

salt and cracked black pepper

pinch of sugar

Combine salmon, grapefruit, fennel, avocado and watercress in a large bowl and toss gently.

For the dressing, whisk all the ingredients together until combined. Pour dressing over salad and toss gently.

Serve topped with salmon roe.

Serves 4 as a starter or light lunch

Red grapefruit and chocolate tart

The citrus flavour combines beautifully with the chocolate in this unusual tart. Make it the day before serving, and use a bought pastry shell if you're short of time.

Pastry

225g plain flour

125g unsalted butter, chopped

55g caster sugar

1 tbsp ground almonds

1 egg yolk

$^1/_4$ cup iced water

100g dark chocolate

175g unsalted butter, chopped

$2^1/_2$ tbsp cream

$^1/_2$ cup orange juice

4 egg yolks

$^1/_2$ cup caster sugar

2 tsp gelatine powder (dissolved in 2 tbsp
    hot water)

2 red grapefruit, peeled, segmented and drained
    on absorbent paper

Preheat oven to 180C.

For the pastry, process flour, butter, sugar and ground almonds in a food processor until mixture resembles coarse breadcrumbs. Add egg yolk and iced water and process until mixture just comes together. Gently knead on a lightly floured surface until smooth. Wrap in plastic wrap and refrigerate for 30 minutes.

Roll pastry out on a lightly floured surface. Line a round 23cm flan tin (with removable base) with the pastry. Cover and refrigerate for 1 hour.

Line tart shell with baking paper, fill with dried beans or rice and bake blind for 10 minutes. Remove paper and beans and bake for a further 10 minutes or until pastry is dry and lightly coloured.

For the filling, melt chocolate, 50g butter and cream in the top of a double saucepan or in a heatproof bowl over a saucepan of simmering water, stirring occasionally, until melted and smooth. Pour over base of cooled pastry case and refrigerate for 30 minutes or until set.

Combine orange juice, remaining butter, egg yolks and sugar in the top of a double saucepan or heatproof bowl over a pan of simmering water and stir until mixture thickens enough to coat the back of a wooden spoon. Do not boil. Remove and cool for 5 minutes.

Stir gelatine into orange juice mixture. Pour mixture over chocolate and place grapefruit segments on top. Cover and refrigerate for 4-6 hours or overnight, until set.

Serve with thick cream.

Serves 6

Grapes

This ancient fruit is also used to make the increasingly popular verjuice, which according to *Larousse Gastronomique*, was made from the juice of large unripened grapes in the Middle Ages and used commonly in sauces and as a condiment. Grapeseed oil is quite bland – use it in recipes calling for mild seasoning.

Grapes are classified as green, black, white or red and there are thousands of varieties grown throughout the world. Grapes are an excellent source of vitamin C and dietary fibre and also contain vitamin B6 and potassium.

Select bunches of grapes that are plump and firm and avoid any with the slightest withering around the stalks. The stem should be green and pliable, not brown and brittle. The fruit does not ripen any further once plucked from the vine and a gentle shake will indicate whether they are fresh: the grapes will fall from the stem if the bunch is old.

Store grapes in a plastic bag or airtight container in the fridge. Don't wash until ready to use as wet grapes deteriorate quickly.

Orange, New South Wales

Grape and poppyseed muffins with orange honey butter

300g (2 cups) self-raising flour

110g (1/2 cup) caster sugar

pinch of salt

1/2 tsp ground nutmeg

1 1/2 tbsp poppyseeds

1 cup milk

1/3 cup vegetable oil

2 eggs

1/2 cup small black seedless grapes

Orange honey butter

125g soft unsalted butter

3 tsp orange rind, finely grated

2 tbsp honey

Preheat oven to 200C.

Combine flour, sugar, salt, nutmeg and poppyseeds in a large bowl. In a separate bowl, combine milk, oil and eggs and whisk lightly, then stir in grapes.

Make a well in the centre of flour mixture, pour in liquid and mix lightly. Spoon batter into 6 greased muffin tins (1/2 cup capacity) until two-thirds full then bake for 20-25 minutes or until golden and cooked.

Turn onto a wire rack to cool and serve with orange honey butter.

For the orange honey butter, beat all the ingredients together until well combined.

Makes 6

Baked ricotta slices with grapes, chilli, herbs and olives

600g ricotta cheese, well-drained

salt and cracked black pepper

200g large, seedless green grapes, halved

100g large kalamata olives, pitted and chopped

2 tbsp flat-leaf parsley, coarsely chopped

leaves from 3 sprigs thyme

1/2 tsp dried oregano

1 tsp dried chilli flakes

2 tbsp extra virgin olive oil

crusty bread, to serve

Preheat oven to 200C.

Spread the ricotta in the base of a lightly greased medium-sized ovenproof dish. Season with salt and pepper. Top with grapes and scatter over chopped kalamatas and herbs. Sprinkle with chilli flakes and drizzle with olive oil.

Bake for about 20-25 minutes or until ricotta is firm with browned edges.

Serve warm with crusty bread.

Serves 4

Grapes in red wine with hazelnut shortbread and thick cream

110g caster sugar

250ml red wine

2 x 1cm-wide strips orange peel

1 cinnamon stick

50g unsalted butter, chopped

600g black seedless grapes

thick cream, to serve

shortbreads

250g soft unsalted butter, chopped

55g caster sugar

225g plain flour, sifted

35g rice flour, sifted

100g ground hazelnuts

Preheat oven to 160C.

For the shortbread, beat butter and sugar until thick and creamy, fold in sifted flours, then stir in hazelnuts. Spread mixture into a lightly greased, baking-paper-lined 3cm x 18cm x 25cm cake tin and, using a sharp knife, mark into fingers. Bake for 25-30 minutes or until lightly browned. Cut into fingers while still warm.

Combine sugar and red wine in a large saucepan and stir over medium heat until sugar dissolves, then stir in orange peel, cinnamon and butter. Simmer over medium heat for 5-8 minutes or until reduced and slightly thickened. Stir in grapes and simmer a further 3 minutes. Remove from heat and discard orange peel and cinnamon.

To serve, spoon grapes into serving dishes, pour some of the syrup over, add a dollop of thick cream and serve with shortbread fingers.

Makes about 25 hazelnut shortbread fingers

Grape and almond friands

100g ground almonds

240g (1¹/₂ cups) icing sugar

75g plain flour, sifted

5 large egg whites

grated rind of 1 lemon

185g unsalted butter, melted

¹/₂ tsp ground cinnamon

100g very small seedless grapes (about 50)

Combine almonds, icing sugar and flour in a bowl and mix well. Add egg whites and lemon rind and mix until just combined. Add butter and cinnamon and stir until smooth.

Pour mixture evenly among 10 lightly greased and floured friand moulds (100ml capacity) and top each with 5 grapes. Bake at 200C for 25-30 minutes or until cooked when tested with a skewer.

Perfect served with green tea.

Makes 10

Guava

There are many varieties of this subtropical round or pear-shaped fruit with yellow, pink, red or white flesh. The delicate rind on guavas can be pale-green to yellow when the fruit is mature or pink to red. Native to the American tropics, the whole fruit is edible, but many people prefer to remove the seeds and rind, which can be slightly bitter tasting.

Guavas are rich in vitamins A, B and C and high in calcium. They have a musky, penetrating odour so store at room temperature until ripe (when they will be slightly soft with a creamy texture) then in an airtight container in the fridge. Guavas bruise easily so handle with care.

Kick start your day with fresh guava juice or serve with ice-cream or sorbet. Enjoy them in a fruit salad or do as they do in Thailand and eat them under-ripe, dipped in a mixture of salt and chilli powder or fish sauce.

Brown bread ice-cream with caramel sauce and guavas

8 slices wholemeal bread, crusts removed

100g brown sugar

4 egg yolks

110g ($^1/_2$ cup) caster sugar

$^1/_2$ tsp vanilla extract

300ml cream, whipped

Caramel Sauce

330g (1$^1/_2$ cups) caster sugar

250ml (1 cup) cream

100g mascarpone

8 guavas, peeled and halved

For the ice-cream, sprinkle bread slices with brown sugar and grill until caramelised. Cool and cut into 1cm pieces. Beat yolks, sugar and vanilla in a bowl until thick and pale. Fold whipped cream into egg mixture, add bread pieces and stir to combine. Place mixture in a freezer-proof container, cover and freeze until firm around the edges. Remove from freezer and break up crystals with a fork. Return to the freezer until almost firm. Remove and break up crystals again. Freeze until firm. Alternatively ice-cream can be churned in an ice-cream maker.

For the caramel sauce, combine sugar and $^1/_4$ cup water in a heavy-based saucepan and stir over low heat, without boiling, until sugar is dissolved. Increase heat and boil, without stirring, until golden. Remove from heat and slowly whisk in cream until well-combined, then whisk in mascarpone. Drizzle over ice-cream and serve with guavas.

Serves 8

Nutmeg rice custards with guavas

660g (3 cups) caster sugar

2 tbsp Grand Marnier

3 cups milk

200g (1 cup) arborio rice

pinch of salt

60g unsalted butter, chopped

1 cup caster sugar

1 tsp grated nutmeg

finely grated rind of $^1/_2$ an orange

5 eggs

6 ripe guavas, peeled and halved

Preheat oven to 200C.

Combine 2 cups caster sugar and $^1/_2$ cup water in a heavy-based saucepan and stir over low heat until sugar dissolves. Increase heat and boil, without stirring, until pale-golden.

Remove from heat and divide half the caramel evenly among six lightly greased 150ml ovenproof moulds. Slightly cool remaining caramel, carefully stir in 2 tablespoons hot water, return to heat and stir until smooth. Remove from heat and stir in the Grand Marnier.

Heat 3 cups milk in a large saucepan, bring to the boil and add rice and a pinch of salt and cook over low heat, stirring occasionally, for about 15 minutes or until rice is tender. Remove from heat, stir in butter and remaining caster sugar, nutmeg and orange rind and stir until sugar dissolves. Add eggs one at a time, stirring well after each.

Pour rice mixture into prepared moulds, place in a baking dish, then pour in enough boiling water to reach halfway up the sides of the moulds. Bake for about 25 minutes or until cooked when tested with a skewer.

Rest for 5 minutes then run a knife around the edge of custards and turn onto serving plates. Serve drizzled with warm sauce and accompany with guavas.

Serves 6

Kiwifruit

This fruit is native to China (where there are hundreds of varieties) and is in fact a Chinese gooseberry, but more recently enterprising New Zealand growers have named it kiwifruit. It is packed with vitamin C (far more than oranges).

The brown, furry skinned, egg-shaped type has brilliant emerald-green flesh while the newer golden-fleshed kiwifruit has smooth brown skin and a cap at one end. The fruit grows on a lush, vigorous vine and is picked while very firm then allowed to ripen to full softness after harvesting.

Kiwifruit contain an enzyme (actinidin) that dissolves protein and can be used as a meat tenderiser. It is not suitable, however, for uncooked dairy recipes because it will turn the dish bitter.

New kiwiberries are small fruit weighing 5-20 grams that have smooth, hairless, edible skins with varying shapes from round to elongated. This healthy snack is also rich in vitamins A and C, but is more perishable and needs to be refrigerated.

Purchase hard kiwifruit and ripen at room temperature. They will store well in the crisper of the fridge for several weeks. When ripe, kiwifruit should yield to gentle pressure, but should not be wrinkled or very soft.

To speed ripening, place in a brown paper bag with an apple or banana, which produces ethylene gas that hastens the process.

Golden syrup puddings with kiwifruit

100g soft butter, chopped

110g (^{1}/$_2$ cup) caster sugar

^{1}/$_2$ tsp vanilla extract

2 eggs

1 small apple, peeled and grated

100g self-raising flour, sifted

25g plain flour, sifted

2^1/$_2$ tbsp buttermilk

3 tbsp golden syrup

3 tbsp golden syrup, extra

4 kiwifruit, peeled and sliced

Preheat oven to 200C.

Butter 4 x 200ml individual ovenproof moulds.

Beat butter, sugar and vanilla until light and creamy. Add eggs, one at a time, beating well after each addition. Add apple, combined flours and buttermilk and mix until smooth.

Pour golden syrup into the base of the moulds. Spoon mixture carefully on top, cover each with foil and place in a bain-marie (baking dish with hot water that comes halfway up the sides of the moulds). Bake for 35-40 minutes or until cooked.

Heat extra syrup, turn puddings out onto serving plates and pour extra syrup over.

Serve with kiwifruit and vanilla bean ice-cream

Serves 4

Marinated lamb cutlets with kiwifruit salsa

2 green kiwifruit, peeled

2 cloves garlic, chopped

12 lamb cutlets

Salsa

1 cob of corn

3 green kiwifruit, peeled and finely chopped

1 tomato, seeded and chopped

1 avocado, chopped

1 tbsp extra virgin olive oil

1 tbsp lemon juice

^{1}/$_4$ cup coriander leaves, coarsely chopped

Combine kiwifruit and garlic in a food processor and process until just smooth, but seeds not broken. Place cutlets in a large bowl and spoon marinade onto both sides. Rest, covered, in the refrigerator for 15-30 minutes.

For the salsa, grill or barbecue corn until cooked. Remove kernels from cob. Combine salsa ingredients in a medium-sized bowl and toss gently to combine.

Remove excess marinade from lamb cutlets and barbecue or grill for 2-3 minutes on each side or until done to your liking.

Serve with salsa on the side.

Serves 4

Lemons

Packed with tart juice, vitamin C and pungent aromatic oils, lemons are indispensable in the kitchen. Piquant puddings, golden marmalade and thick curd can all be made with the tangy fruit. Or drizzle it on barbecued fish.

Firm, thick-skinned eureka lemons are excellent for cooking and juicing and have a squeaky-clean citrus flavour. Hybrid meyer lemons are easily identified at the markets by their smooth, thin, orange-yellow skin and round shape. Sweetly fragrant with lots of low-acid juice, they are also high in natural sugars and have a milder taste. Lisbons, the third-most common variety, are sharply astringent like eurekas, but have a smoother rind and pointed tip. A close relative, lemonade fruit, is refreshing squeezed into chilled water for a zesty drink, but not so suitable for cooking because of its low acidity.

The outer part of lemon peel contains the essential oil that makes lemon zest so fantastic in cooking and the pith, the white layer around the flesh, contains pectin necessary for the setting of marmalades and jams.

Lemon juice is a fabulous all-rounder. It can be used to preserve the colour in other fruits, as a tenderiser, to flavour dressings, sauces and icings and, of course, for squeezing on seafood.

Select firm lemons with bright, unblemished skin. They should feel heavy for their size. Lemons do not ripen further after picking so are best stored in the refrigerator.

Lemon Delicious

zest of 1 lemon

1/3 cup lemon juice

4 tbsp butter

220g (1 cup) caster sugar

3 eggs, separated

75g (1/2 cup) self-raising flour

1 1/2 cups milk

Preheat oven to 180C.

Combine lemon zest, butter and sugar in a food processor until smooth. Add egg yolks and process briefly. Add flour and milk alternately, whizzing briefly to make a smooth batter. Transfer to a bowl and add lemon juice and stir until combined.

Whisk egg whites until firm then fold into butter mixture. Pour mixture into a greased 1-litre ovenproof dish and stand in a baking dish. Pour hot water to halfway up the sides of the ovenproof dish and bake for 55-60 minutes.

Serve warm with cream or ice-cream.

Serves 6

Tangy little lemon cheesecakes

If you are short on time make these cute little desserts with bought shortcrust pastry.

They're also delicious made with limes instead of lemons.

Pastry

225g (1 1/2 cups) plain flour

180g butter, chopped

1 tbsp icing sugar

2 tbsp iced water

1 egg yolk

Filling

500g cream cheese (room temperature)

110g (1/2 cup) caster sugar

1 tsp vanilla extract

2 tbsp lemon juice

1 tbsp lemon zest

2 eggs, lightly beaten

icing sugar, to serve

vanilla bean ice-cream, to serve

For the pastry, combine flour, butter and icing sugar in the bowl of a food processor until the mixture resembles breadcrumbs. Add water and egg yolk and process briefly until mixture just comes together. Remove and shape into a disc, wrap in plastic wrap and rest in the fridge for 30 minutes.

Roll pastry out on a lightly floured bench and cut 6 circles about 11-12cm in diameter. Gently press each circle into a pastry tin (10cm diameter) and trim excess pastry with a sharp knife. Place on a tray and rest in the fridge for 30 minutes.

Line tart shells with baking paper and fill with rice or dried beans. Bake at 190C for 15 minutes. Remove paper and weights and bake for a further 5 minutes. Cool slightly.

For the filling, combine cheese, sugar, vanilla, lemon juice and zest in a medium-sized bowl and mix until smooth. Add eggs and, when combined, spoon mixture into pastry shells and bake at 170C for 20-25 minutes or until just firm to touch.

Sprinkle cheesecakes with icing sugar before serving and accompany with vanilla bean ice-cream.

Makes 6

Seared tuna steaks with lemon, watercress and herb salad

(pictured page 61)

3 large lemons, peeled

1 tbsp caster sugar

1 long red chilli, deseeded and very finely sliced

1/2 cup torn mint leaves

salt and cracked black pepper

4 x tuna steaks (about 180g each)

4 tbsp extra virgin olive oil

4 cups watercress sprigs

chunky chips, to serve (optional)

Cut away white pith from lemons and cut between each membrane to remove segments. Cut each segment in half and place in a bowl with caster sugar, chilli, mint leaves, salt and pepper.

Brush tuna steaks with 2 tablespoons extra virgin olive oil and sear in a non-stick frying pan for 1-2 minutes each side or until cooked as desired.

Toss water cress sprigs with remaining olive oil and divide between 4 serving plates. Place tuna steaks on watercress and top with lemon salad.

Serve with chunky chips.

Serves 4

Lemon chicken

75g plain flour

1/2 tsp paprika

salt and cracked black pepper

4 chicken 1/2 breasts (with bone and skin on)

1/2 cup vegetable oil

finely grated rind and juice of 2 lemons

1 clove garlic, finely chopped

2 tbsp soy sauce

Preheat oven to 200C.

Place flour, paprika, salt and pepper in a large plastic bag. Add chicken pieces and shake to coat with flour mixture. Remove chicken and shake off excess flour.

In a medium-sized bowl, mix vegetable oil with rind and juice of lemons, garlic and soy sauce and stir well. Place chicken, skin side down, in a shallow ovenproof dish. Pour lemon mixture evenly over chicken. Bake, covered, for 30 minutes. Remove cover, turn chicken pieces over and bake a further 20 minutes or until golden and cooked.

Serve with couscous or mash and a green salad.

Serves 4

Pan-fried cutlets with caper and lemon sauce

150g (1 cup) rice flour

salt and cracked black pepper

12 lamb cutlets

2 tbsp extra virgin olive oil

3 tbsp lemon juice

1 clove garlic, finely chopped

zest of 1/2 lemon

1 tbsp salted capers, rinsed

steamed asparagus and mash to serve (optional)

Season rice flour with salt and pepper and dust 12 lamb cutlets in flour mixture, shaking off excess. Pan-fry cutlets in olive oil for 3-4 minutes each side over medium heat or until cooked as desired, adding more oil if necessary. Remove and keep warm.

In the same pan, add lemon juice, garlic, lemon zest, capers and 180ml water and stir over medium heat for 2-3 minutes or until slightly reduced. Check seasoning. Spoon sauce over warm cutlets and serve with steamed asparagus and mash.

Serves 4

Lemon tart with vanilla ice-cream

1¹/₂ cups plain flour

125g butter, chopped

pinch of salt

1 tbsp icing sugar

1-2 tbsp iced water

¹/₂ tsp vanilla extract

1 egg yolk

icing sugar, for dusting

vanilla ice-cream, to serve

Filling

2 tsp lemon rind, finely grated

³/₄ cup lemon juice

³/₄ cup caster sugar

¹/₂ cup cream

1 tsp vanilla extract

5 eggs

For the pastry, combine flour, butter, icing sugar and a pinch of salt in a food processor until mixture resembles breadcrumbs. Add 1-2 tablespoons iced water, vanilla and egg yolk, and process until mixture just comes together. Shape pastry into a flat disc, cover with plastic wrap and refrigerate for 30 minutes.

Roll out pastry on a lightly floured surface. Prick base of pastry lightly with a fork, cover with plastic wrap and refrigerate for 30 minutes. Place pastry in a lightly greased, round, 28cm tart tin with a removable base. Line pastry with baking paper, fill with dried beans or rice and bake blind for 10 minutes at 200C. Remove paper and beans, reduce heat to 180C and bake for another 10 minutes or until pastry is crisp and golden. Cool.

For the filling, whisk lemon rind, lemon juice, sugar, cream and vanilla in a bowl until well combined. Add eggs, one at a time, beating well after each. Pour lemon mixture into tart shell and bake at 180C for 20-25minutes or until filling is just set.

Serve dusted with icing sugar and accompanied by vanilla ice-cream.

Serves 8

Preserved lemons

250g coarse salt

10 thick-skinned lemons, cut into quarters

extra lemon juice

Sprinkle a tablespoon of salt into the base of a 1-litre sterilised jar. Tip lemons into a large dish with remaining salt and mix well. Pack lemons into the jar and add any remaining salt mixture. Cover fruit with extra lemon juice.

Seal top tightly and store in a cool, dry place for at least 1 month. Rinse before using.

Bay leaves, cinnamon sticks and cloves can be added for extra flavour.

If a wedge of lemon is not covered with juice it may develop white mould, which is harmless. Use only the rind but not the pulp.

Lemon and pea risotto with asparagus

Creamy, comforting risotto is the perfect Sunday night dish or a great start to a dinner party. The trick lies in the stirring, which releases the starch in the rice and gives the dish its fabulous texture. Use an Italian rice such as arborio, carnaroli or vialone nano and let it rest for a few minutes after cooking, for extra creaminess.

5 tbsp butter

1 onion, chopped

2 cups arborio rice

$1/2$ cup dry white wine

6-7 cups hot chicken stock

1 bunch asparagus, cut into 2cm pieces

$1/2$ cup fresh green peas

40g grated parmesan

finely grated rind of 1 lemon

Melt 3 tablespoons of butter in a large saucepan over medium heat. Cook onion, stirring for 3-4 minutes, until pale-yellow. Add rice and stir to coat rice with butter. Add white wine and stir until wine is evaporated. Add chicken stock, 1-2 ladles at a time, stirring until each addition is absorbed before adding the next. When rice is half cooked add asparagus and peas and continue cooking until rice is al dente. Stir in remaining butter, parmesan and lemon rind and serve immediately with extra parmesan, if desired.

Serves 4

Street market, Amalfi, Italy

Limes/Kaffir

Tangy, refreshing limes are a close relative of lemons and can be substituted for them in many recipes, but their flavour is more assertive. Small, round, Mexican or key limes grow in very hot climates while the Tahitian or Persian lime has more yellow flesh and a wider climatic range.

The thick, warty rind on kaffir limes makes them easily identifiable in the markets. They grow on a thorny tree, are the size of a normal lime with a knob at the top end and have their own special fragrance, but very little juice. Also known in Thailand as makrut lime, the juice is rarely used in cooking, but the lumpy rind is extremely aromatic and can be used to flavour salads, curries and soups. The zest marries well with coconut milk and adds a floral character to green curries, but avoid the unpleasant white pith or the curry may taste bitter.

The pungent kaffir leaves are the primary appeal of this unique citrus, however. They have an alluring aroma and are easy to spot in the shops, as they have the appearance of two glossy leaves joined end to end and are often called guitar-shaped leaves. Because they are tough and leathery, the centre vein needs to be removed before the two pieces of leaf can be thinly sliced or julienned.

Fingerlimes have smooth skin that can be red, yellow, green or purple and are found in the subtropical rainforests of Queensland and northern NSW. They are finger-sized and once split open reveal translucent rows of seeds that are perfect in salads or other dishes requiring the sharpness of lime.

Choose brightly coloured, firm limes that are heavy for their size, indicating good juice content. They are ripe when green skinned; avoid any with soft spots or brown patches.

Store in the crisper of the fridge. Fresh kaffir lime leaves freeze satisfactorily when stored in a sealed plastic bag, but eventually turn brown and lose their shine.

Grilled summer fruits with low-fat lime ricotta

2 large nectarines, halved and stoned

4 apricots, halved and stoned

4 plums, halved and stoned

55g (¹/₄ cup) caster sugar

30g ground hazelnuts

Low-fat lime ricotta

300g low-fat ricotta

2 tbsp icing sugar

2 tsp lime juice

zest of 2 limes

For the lime ricotta, combine all the ingredients in a small bowl and mix well.

Place nectarines, apricots and plums, cut-side up, on a foil-lined baking tray and sprinkle with combined sugar and hazelnut. Cook under a hot grill for 5 minutes or until fruit is warmed through.

Serve immediately with ricotta.

Serves 4

Kaffir lime and coconut tart

If kaffir limes are not available, substitute with zest of 2 limes and juice of ¹/₂ a lime.

110g caster sugar

2 egg yolks

150g (3 cups) shaved coconut

2 kaffir lime leaves, very finely sliced

1 egg white

Filling

Grated rind and juice of 2 kaffir limes

Grated rind and juice of 2 lemons

165g (³/₄ cup) caster sugar

6 egg yolks

¹/₂ tsp vanilla extract

150g unsalted butter, chopped

Whisk sugar and egg yolks until pale and thick, then add coconut and lime leaves and stir until well combined. Beat egg white until stiff peaks form and fold gently into yolk mixture.

With damp fingers, press mixture evenly over base and sides of a lightly greased 23cm round tart tin with removable base. Bake at 150C for about 25 minutes or until golden. Cool.

For the filling, whisk grated lime and lemon rinds and juice with caster sugar, egg yolks and vanilla in a heatproof bowl over simmering water until well combined. Whisk in butter, a little at a time, whisking well after each addition. Stir until mixture thickens enough to coat the back of a wooden spoon; do not boil. Remove and cool.

Spoon filling into coconut crust, cover and refrigerate overnight.

Serve with thick cream.

Serves 6-8

Chicken on lemongrass skewers with lime and soy marinade

4 chicken breast fillets, cut into 4cm pieces

8 sticks lemongrass

Marinade

$^1/_3$ cup vegetable oil

1 clove garlic, finely chopped

2 green onions, very finely sliced

2 tbsp coriander, chopped

1 tsp turmeric

1 tsp ground cumin

2 tbsp soy sauce

1 tsp palm sugar

zest of 1 lime

1 tbsp lime juice

For the marinade, combine all the ingredients in a large bowl and mix well.

Add chicken pieces to marinade, cover and refrigerate for at least 1 hour.

Trim lemongrass stalks to about 20cm and cut root end on the diagonal.

Use a sharp skewer to pierce each piece of chicken, then thread 2 or 3 pieces on each stick of lemongrass. Barbecue, char-grill or grill skewers, turning occasionally, for 8-10 minutes.

Serve with steamed rice and a cucumber and chilli salad topped with chopped peanuts.

Serves 4

Lime and watermelon salsa

Try the following salsa accompanied by green prawns that have been marinated in equal quantities of lime juice and extra virgin olive oil, salt and cracked black pepper, then barbecued for the ultimate low-fat lunch.

1 Lebanese cucumber, halved lengthways, seeded and cut into 1cm pieces

1kg watermelon, rind removed and flesh cut into 1cm pieces

4 green onions, thinly sliced

1 lime, peeled and segmented, removing any pith

1 tbsp mint, finely chopped

1 tbsp fresh coriander, finely chopped

1 small fresh red chilli, finely chopped (or to taste)

Combine all the ingredients, season to taste and toss gently. Cover and refrigerate for 20-30 minutes. Serve with grilled or barbecued king prawns.

Serves 4

Lime and pistachio tea cake with cream cheese frosting

220g soft unsalted butter

180g caster sugar

3 eggs

200g self-raising flour

90g plain flour

finely grated rind of 1 lime

$^1/_4$ cup lime juice

$^1/_3$ cup (50g) shelled pistachios, coarsely chopped

Frosting

200g cream cheese

110g caster sugar

$^1/_2$ tsp vanilla extract

1-2 tbsp lime juice

$^1/_3$ (50g) shelled pistachios, coarsely chopped

Preheat oven to 170C.

Beat butter and sugar in an electric mixer until light and fluffy. Add eggs, one at a time, beating well after each addition. Stir in combined sifted flours, lime rind and lime juice and stir until combined. Fold in pistachios and spoon mixture into a greased and baking-paper-lined 13cm x 23cm loaf pan and bake for 60-65 minutes or until cooked when tested with a cake skewer. Cool then turn out onto serving plate.

For the frosting, combine cream cheese, sugar and vanilla extract in a food processor until smooth. Add lime juice to taste and process until well combined. Spread frosting over cake and sprinkle with pistachio nuts.

Serves 8

Thai prawn and coconut soup with kaffir lime leaves (Tom Kha Goong)

4 cups coconut milk

2 thin slices galangal, peeled

1 tbsp lemongrass, thinly sliced

$^1/_4$ cup galangal (or ginger), peeled and sliced

5 kaffir lime leaves

2 stalks lemongrass, cut into 5cm pieces

2 red eschalots, peeled and very thinly sliced

20 green (raw) king prawns, shelled and deveined

3 tbsp lime juice

3 tbsp fish sauce

small bird's-eye chillies, chopped (to taste)

coriander leaves and kaffir leaves, for garnish

Place coconut milk in large saucepan and bring to the boil over medium heat. Process slices of galangal and 1 tablespoon of lemongrass in a food processor until finely ground (or pound in a mortar and pestle). Add to coconut milk and stir well. Add lime leaves, lemongrass pieces, and eschalots and simmer for 5 minutes. Add prawns and cook just until they change colour. Remove from heat and add lime juice, fish sauce and chillies and stir well.

Serve warm or at room temperature garnished with coriander leaves.

Serves 4

Thai fish cakes with cucumber dipping sauce

500g boned firm white fish fillets

3 tbsp red curry paste

1 egg

2 tbsp fish sauce

100g green beans, very finely sliced

$^1/_2$ tsp caster sugar

2 tbsp Thai basil, chopped

4 very finely shredded kaffir lime leaves

vegetable oil, for frying

Cucumber dipping sauce

200ml rice-wine vinegar

75g caster sugar

1 lebanese cucumber, unpeeled, finely chopped

1 tbsp coriander, chopped

2 small red chillies, very finely chopped

1 red eschalot, very finely chopped

1 tbsp toasted peanuts, chopped

Place fish fillets in a food processor and process for about 20 seconds until smooth. Remove to a bowl and add red curry paste and egg and stir to combine. Add fish sauce, green beans, caster sugar, Thai basil and kaffir lime leaves and mix well. Using wet hands, form mixture into flattish cakes (about 2 tablespoons each) and refrigerate until ready to cook.

Heat vegetable oil in a wok or large frying pan over medium heat and shallow-fry cakes, a few at a time for about 2-3 minutes each side or until browned and cooked. Drain on paper towel and serve immediately with cucumber dipping sauce.

For the sauce, combine rice-wine vinegar with caster sugar in a small saucepan and stir over low heat until sugar is dissolved. Remove from heat and cool. Add cucumber, chopped coriander, red chillies, eschalot and peanuts.

Makes about 16 cakes

Mojito mangoes with lime sorbet and coconut

2 limes, cut into small pieces (skin on)

³/₄ cup caster sugar

1 cup mint leaves

1¹/₂ cups white rum

3-4 ripe mangoes (depending on size), peeled and sliced

toasted shaved coconut, to serve

Lime sorbet

440g (2 cups) caster sugar

1³/₄ cup water

1 cup strained lime juice (about 6-8 limes)

250ml (1 cup) still mineral water

1 kaffir lime leaf, very finely chopped (optional)

2 egg whites, lightly whisked

For the sorbet, combine sugar and water in a saucepan and stir over low heat until sugar dissolves. Bring to the boil then remove from heat and cool. Strain mixture, then combine 1³/₄ cups of the syrup with lime juice and mineral water, stir in chopped kaffir lime leaf, if using, and freeze in an ice-cream maker according to manufacturer's instructions. Add egg whites about two-thirds of the way through the churning.

Combine limes, sugar and mint in a mortar or glass or ceramic bowl and crush and grind with a pestle until juices start to run. Add rum and stir very well, until most of the sugar dissolves. Pour mixture over mangoes, cover and refrigerate for 45-60 minutes.

Remove mango slices from bowl using tongs and place in serving glasses or dishes; discard lime pieces and juice. Serve with scoops of lime sorbet topped with toasted coconut.

Serves 6

Loquats

When picked fully ripe, loquats are sweet and beautifully juicy. They take their name from the Cantonese word *lu-kwyit* and are members of the same family as apples and pears.

This sweet, mildly acidic fruit has been cultivated for more than a thousand years in China and southern Japan, and is very popular candied or made into jelly. They are particularly tasty in salads where the lemon juice or vinegar in the dressing creates a sweet/sour tang.

Loquats are best eaten as soon as possible after purchasing. The skin should be smooth and firm with a slight shine; most varieties have a fine down on the surface.

Store at room temperature until they are well coloured and have the texture of a firm plum – then they can be stored in the crisper of the fridge for a couple of days.

The sweet-perfumed fruit is high in potassium and vitamin A and contains significant amounts of calcium and phosphorus.

Loquat, almond and cinnamon crumble

10-15 loquats (depending on size), peeled, seeded and sliced
80ml brandy
caster sugar, to taste
thickened cream, to serve

Topping
60g soft butter
$^1/_2$ cup (100g) firmly packed brown sugar
1 egg yolk
$^1/_2$ cup (60g) ground almonds
$^1/_2$ cup (60g) walnuts, chopped
$^1/_4$ tsp ground cinnamon

Preheat oven to 170C.

Combine loquats, brandy and sugar to taste and divide among four 1-cup ovenproof dishes.

For the topping, beat butter and brown sugar until light and fluffy, add egg yolk and beat until well combined. Add almonds, walnuts and cinnamon and mix well. Spoon mixture over loquats to cover, place dishes on an oven tray and bake for 30 minutes or until topping is golden and loquats are tender. Serve warm with thick cream.

Serves 4

Roasted loin of pork with glazed loquats

12-16 loquats (depending on size)
120ml Madeira
1.3kg loin of pork, boned
1 tbsp Dijon mustard
1 tbsp brown sugar
salt and cracked black pepper

Preheat oven to 200C.

Peel loquats, place in a bowl and pour Madeira over.

Trim fat from pork, roll up and tie with string at 3cm intervals. Rub mustard into pork and sprinkle with brown sugar and a little salt and pepper. Place on a wire rack in a roasting pan and roast for 30 minutes.

Add loquat mixture to pan and roast a further 30 minutes or until pork is cooked as desired. Rest in a warm place for 10 minutes.

Serve pork sliced with loquats, skimmed pan juices and mash. Follow with a green salad.

Serves 4

Lychees, longans and rambutans

Lychees were introduced to Australia by Chinese gold miners in the late 1800s. The translucent flesh beneath the reddish brittle skin is high in vitamin C and B group vitamins as well as phosphorus. The prickly skinned fruit has been cultivated in China for thousands of years and is also known as litchi.

Smooth-skinned longans are a close cousin of the lychee, and similar in taste. They are smaller and have firm brown, brittle skin. Rambutans are often called hairy lychees (which refers to its soft red and yellow spines). Most varieties are red when ripe and have similar translucent pearly flesh, although they are a little more acidic.

Lychees, longans and rambutans are best eaten raw, but can be added to curries and stir-fries at the end of cooking. Their lush texture doesn't survive long, slow cooking and much of the clean flavour and exquisite perfume of lychees is lost when tinned.

Lychees and longans will last longer if a little of the stem is attached. Select bright-red, fragrant lychees; the skin loses its glorious red shade several days after harvesting, so colour indicates freshness. Choose longans that are not cracked, without any moist spots, and buy them with the twiggy branches attached. Rambutans should have fresh, plastic-looking spines that are not brown and withered.

Keep lychees, longans and rambutans in a sealed plastic bag in the fridge.

Fresh longans with lavender panna cotta

Use English lavender, *Lavandula angustifolia* for best results in cakes, ice-cream, shortbread and icing as well as this gorgeous panna cotta.

750ml pouring cream

220g (1 cup) caster sugar

$^1/_3$ cup milk

2-3 tsp dried lavender

1 tbsp powdered gelatine

18 fresh longans or lychees, peeled

Combine cream, sugar and milk in a medium-sized saucepan and cook over low heat until almost boiling. Remove from heat and add lavender. Stir well and set aside for 30 minutes. Strain.

Place 2 tablespoons hot water in a cup, sprinkle gelatine over, then stand cup in a saucepan of simmering water and stir until gelatine dissolves. Bring strained cream mixture almost to the boil and pour dissolved gelatine into cream and stir well to combine.

Pour cream mixture into 6 x 150ml moulds that have been rinsed in cold water, cover and refrigerate until set.

To serve, unmould panna cotta by dipping moulds in hot water for a few seconds. Serve with fresh longans or lychees and biscotti on the side.

Serves 6

Lychees with pistachios and strawberries in rosewater syrup

$1^1/_2$ cups (330g) caster sugar

1 tbsp lemon juice

2 tsp rosewater

30 lychees, peeled

250g strawberries, hulled and sliced

100g shelled pistachios, toasted and chopped

300g mascarpone

1 tsp vanilla extract

2 tbsp icing sugar, sifted

Place sugar and $1^1/_2$ cups water in a saucepan and stir over medium heat until sugar dissolves, then bring to the boil and simmer for 5 minutes. Remove from heat and cool to room temperature, then stir in lemon juice and rosewater.

Combine lychees and strawberries in a large bowl, pour sugar syrup over and toss gently.

Combine mascarpone, vanilla and icing sugar and beat with a wooden spoon until thick.

Divide fruit mixture among 6 glasses, drizzle with syrup, top with a scoop of mascarpone and sprinkle with pistachios.

Serves 6

Lychee and melon salad with ginger syrup

$^1/_4$ seedless watermelon (about 1.4kg), peeled and cut into 2 cm pieces

$^1/_2$ rockmelon, peeled, seeded and cut into 2cm pieces

12 lychees, peeled

2 tbsp mint, chopped

Ginger syrup

5cm piece ginger, peeled and chopped

1 vanilla bean, split lengthwise

$^2/_3$ cup fresh orange juice

$^1/_2$ cup honey

2 tbsp caster sugar

For the ginger syrup, combine ginger, scraped seeds from vanilla bean and the bean, orange juice, honey, sugar and 1$^1/_2$ cups of water in a saucepan and stir over low heat until sugar dissolves. Bring to the boil and simmer for 15 minutes or until mixture is syrupy. Remove from heat and stand for 15 minutes. Strain syrup, then refrigerate until cooled.

Combine watermelon, rockmelon and lychees in a large bowl, add syrup and toss gently to combine.

Serve fruit salad and syrup in 4 shallow bowls and top with mint.

Serves 4

Sticky mangoes with lychee sorbet

A delicious, low-kilojoule dessert.

2 cups dry white wine

2 tbsp honey

1 stick cinnamon

12 black peppercorns

1 strip lemon peel

2 sprigs thyme

4 small ripe mangoes, peeled and sliced

Sorbet

$^3/_4$ cup water

2 tbsp caster sugar

1 tbsp ginger, grated

2 x 565g cans lychees in syrup

1 tbsp white rum

For the sorbet, combine water, sugar and ginger in a small saucepan and stir over low heat until sugar dissolves. Bring to the boil and simmer for 5 minutes. Strain and cool to room temperature.

Drain lychees, reserving $^1/_2$ cup of liquid. Puree lychees and reserved liquid in a food processor until smooth. Strain and combine with sugar syrup and rum. Stir well and freeze in an ice-cream maker, according to manufacturer's instructions.

Combine white wine, honey, cinnamon, peppercorns, lemon peel and thyme in a pan and stir over medium heat until honey dissolves. Bring to the boil and simmer, covered, for 10 minutes. Then strain and cool wine syrup to room temperature. Pour over sliced mango and mix gently. Cover and refrigerate for at least 1 hour.

To serve, spoon mango and syrup into 4 bowls or glasses and serve scoops of lychee sorbet on top.

Serves 4

Fresh rambutans with orange granita

Orange-flower water is available at health food shops and Middle-Eastern food stores.

Granita

75g (1/3 cup) caster sugar

$^1/_2$ cup water

2 cups orange juice, strained

2 tsp orange-flower water

16 rambutans, peeled

For the granita, combine sugar and water in a saucepan and stir over low heat until sugar dissolves. Bring to the boil, then simmer for 3 minutes. Remove from heat, add orange juice and stir to combine. Cool to room temperature.

Add orange-flower water, stir well, pour into a 20cm x 30cm shallow metal try and freeze for 45 minutes or until partially set.

Use a fork to break up crystals, then freeze a further 2 hours, breaking up crystals every 30 minutes.

To serve, place peeled rambutans in shallow bowls, break up granita and spoon over.

Serves 4

Pineapple and longans with palm sugar caramel

$^1/_2$ pineapple, peeled, cored and thinly sliced

12 longans, peeled

1 mango, peeled and cut into pieces

1 tbsp white rum

120g palm sugar

2 tbsp water

$^1/_2$ cup coconut cream

2 tbsp toasted flaked almonds

Combine pineapple, longans and mango in a shallow bowl, drizzle with rum and toss gently. Combine palm sugar and water in a saucepan and stir over low heat until sugar dissolves. Add coconut cream and simmer for about 5 minutes until slightly thickened. Cool and drizzle over fruit. Top with flaked almonds.

Serves 4-6

Grand Marnier and chocolate mousse pots with fresh rambutans

375g cooking chocolate, broken into pieces

3 eggs

300ml pouring cream, whipped

1-2 tbsp Grand Marnier

16-24 rambutans (depending on size), peeled

For the chocolate mousse, melt chocolate in the microwave or in a bowl over a saucepan of simmering water. Beat eggs lightly and add to chocolate and stir to combine. Cool slightly and add cream and Grand Marnier and stir until smooth. Divide mixture evenly between 8 x $^1/_2$-cup mousse pots and smooth tops. Cover with plastic wrap and refrigerate until ready to serve.

To serve, top each pot with 2 or 3 rambutans.

Serves 8

Rambutan and pawpaw salad with vanilla coconut yoghurt

1 large ripe pawpaw, peeled, seeded and cut into small wedges

16 rambutans, peeled, halved and seeded

Vanilla coconut yoghurt

45g (1/2 cup) desiccated coconut, toasted

300ml plain yoghurt

2 tsp vanilla extract

2 tbsp caster sugar

1/4 tsp ground nutmeg

Combine pawpaw and rambutans in a bowl and toss gently, then cover and refrigerate for 30 minutes.

For vanilla coconut yoghurt, combine all the ingredients in a small bowl and mix well.

Serve cold fruit salad with vanilla yoghurt on the side.

Serves 4

Mandarins

Originating in the tropical and subtropical regions of Asia and Malaysia, mandarins have been grown in China and Japan for thousands of years. It's believed the name is derived from the yellow robes, called mandarins, that were worn by Chinese civil servants.

Called tangerines, in some markets, they are an excellent source of vitamin C. There are many varieties, all with a different juicy flavour. Imperial mandarins appear early in the season and have a flattish, round shape, a distinctive aroma and are easy to peel, with few seeds. Ellendales are larger and have a loose, vibrant-orange skin and sweet flavour. Honey murcots (known as honey tangerines in the US) have become very popular recently, as they are a good juicing fruit. Hickson, sunburst and fremont are other succulent varieties.

Select fruit that has a rich, glossy skin and feels slightly heavy for its size, signifying juiciness. A puffy skin indicates it is easy to peel, but avoid fruit with soft spots or irregular colouring.

Store them in the crisper or at room temperature in a cool place.

Chocolate and mandarin swirl cake

80g dark cooking chocolate, chopped

150g soft butter, chopped

220g caster sugar

2 eggs

300g self-raising flour, sifted

125ml milk

1 tsp orange-flower water

2 tbsp mandarin juice

finely grated rind of 2 mandarins

Glaze

120g dark chocolate

60g butter, chopped

Preheat oven to 180C.

Place chocolate in a bowl and melt in the microwave or over a saucepan of simmering water.

Beat butter and sugar in an electric mixer until pale and fluffy. Add eggs, one at a time, beating well after each. Fold in flour and milk alternately and divide mixture into two bowls. Add orange-flower water, mandarin juice and rind to one half and melted chocolate to the other and stir to combine.

Drop large spoonfuls of each mixture alternately into a greased and baking-paper-lined 11cm x 21cm loaf tin. Then, using a bread and butter knife, cut through mixture using a swirling motion. Bake for about 50-60 minutes or until a cake tester comes out clean. Rest in tin for 5 minutes before turning onto a cake rack to cool.

For the glaze, melt chocolate and butter in a bowl and stir until smooth, then pour immediately over cake.

Slice when glaze is set.

Serves 6-8

Mandarin, radish and olive salad

6 large mandarins, peeled and sliced 1cm thick

zest of $\frac{1}{2}$ orange

3 eschalots, finely sliced

1 bulb fennel, trimmed and very finely sliced

160g (1 cup) kalamata olives

3 large red radishes, finely sliced

$\frac{1}{2}$ cup flat-leaf parsley, torn

$\frac{1}{3}$ cup mint leaves, chopped

100ml extra virgin olive oil

1 large green chilli, chopped

juice of $\frac{1}{2}$ lemon

salt and cracked black pepper

Combine all the ingredients in a salad bowl and toss gently to combine.

Serve with barbecued chicken.

Serves 4

Mango

Mangoes vary tremendously in size and shape. Some are small and round, some are so large they are called coconut mangoes and others are long and slender. Several varieties have a crimson blush on the cheek, kissed by the sun, while others remain green when ripe.

The Kensington pride or Bowen mango is the most common in Australia. R2E2 varieties have a longer shelf life after picking and firm fibrous flesh, so are suitable for export. The new-variety calypso has a small seed, firm fibreless flesh and a distinctive high blush on the skin.

The fruit is very low in fat and an excellent source of vitamins A and C and potassium.

Firm green mangoes with their refreshing tang are like a different fruit. They are excellent in chutneys and add piquancy to summer salsas. Both ripe and green types are very good tenderisers – include them in marinades.

There are many ways to cut and eat mangoes; the most popular is to slice off the cheeks on either side of the large, flat seed, score the flesh in each curved cheek and then scoop out with a spoon.

Choose the fruit by its fragrance, as skin colour does not indicate ripeness. It should yield to gentle pressure near the stem end if ripe and ready to eat. Buy unblemished fruit and store at room temperature until ripe then in the crisper for two to three days. Alternatively, peel and remove the stone from firm fruit, slice and freeze in bags; you can also freeze the pulp in ice-cube trays to add to chilled orange juice.

Even when picked slightly under ripe, mangoes ripen well if stored in the fruit bowl at room temperature, though it may take a few days. Use half-ripe mangoes for chutneys and pickles, as they hold their shape during cooking.

Mumbai, India

Mango and pineapple with toffee shards

Serve this light and refreshing dessert over the festive season when mangoes are at their peak. It is an excellent finale to a seafood barbecue. The toffee shards can be made ahead and stored in an airtight container.

2 ripe mangoes

1 small ripe pineapple

440g (2 cups) caster sugar

25g roasted almonds, chopped

1 egg white

caster sugar, for dipping

375ml chilled moscato or other dessert wine

Peel and seed mangoes and cut into bite-sized pieces. Peel and core pineapple and cut into bite-sized pieces. Cover fruit and refrigerate until cold.

Combine caster sugar and 100ml water in a small heavy-based saucepan and stir over low heat until sugar dissolves. Bring to the boil and cook over medium heat, without stirring, until caramel coloured. Pour a thin layer of the toffee on a baking-paper-lined oven tray and sprinkle with almonds. Cool and break into shards.

Lightly beat egg white with a fork and brush a little around the tops of 6 serving glasses. Spoon a shallow layer of sugar onto a saucer and dip rims of glasses. Combine fruit and divide among glasses, drizzle with wine, then top with two toffee shards. Serve immediately.

Serves 6

Mango crab chilli and coriander tartlets

25-30 small cooked pastry cases (5cm diameter)

120g cooked crabmeat

1 tbsp lime juice

salt flakes and cracked black pepper

Salsa

1 ripe mango (about 200g), peeled
   and flesh chopped

1-2 small fresh red chillies, finely chopped

2 green onions, finely chopped

1 tsp lime juice

2 tsp brown sugar

few drops of sesame oil

2 tbsp coriander, chopped

For the mango salsa, combine all the ingredients in a bowl and mix gently.

Combine crab and lime juice in a bowl and season with salt and pepper.

To serve, spoon some of the crab into pastry cases and top with mango salsa.

Makes about 25

Mangoes with sweet sticky rice

2 cups (400g) sticky rice

2 cups coconut cream

2 tsp rice flour, mixed with a little water
    to form a paste

large pinch of salt

1 cup (220g) caster sugar

2 ripe mangoes, peeled and cut into wedges

Soak rice in cold water overnight or in warm water for 2 hours. Drain. Steam rice for about 20 minutes or until tender.

Meanwhile, heat coconut cream in a medium-sized saucepan over low heat and stir in flour paste and salt. When thick, add sugar and stir until dissolved. Do not add sugar before flour has thickened the cream or it will lose its sheen and turn grey.

When cooked, remove rice from steamer and pour coconut cream over. Stir well and set aside, covered, for 15 minutes.

Serve with wedges of ripe mango or other summer fruits.

Serves 6

Tropical fruit skewers with white rum and sago pudding

(pictured page 83)

1 large ripe mango, peeled, seeded and cut
    into 3-4cm pieces

$^1/_2$ ripe pineapple, peeled, cored and cut
    into 3-4cm pieces

1-2 bananas (depending on size), peeled
    and cut into thick slices

1 ripe papaya, peeled and cut into 3-4cm pieces

50ml white rum

$^1/_4$ cup honey

60g butter, melted

175g (1 cup) sago

1 litre coconut milk

220g caster sugar

1 tsp vanilla extract

Thread fruits onto 12 short bamboo skewers that have been soaked in water for 30 minutes, then place in a large shallow glass or ceramic dish. Combine rum, honey and butter and mix well. Pour mixture over fruit skewers, turn to coat and stand at room temperature for 20-30 minutes.

Meanwhile, rinse sago under cold water and drain. Combine coconut milk, sugar and 2 cups water in a saucepan and stir over medium heat until sugar dissolves. Add sago and bring to the boil, stirring constantly. Reduce heat to low and cook, stirring frequently, for 15-20 minutes or until sago is soft and transparent, then stir in vanilla. Spoon into six bowls.

Drain skewers and reserve rum mixture. Place skewers on a foil-lined tray and pour a little reserved rum mixture over. Grill under a hot grill until just heated through.

Serve skewers drizzled with remaining rum mixture, accompanied by sago pudding.

Serves 6

Melons

Melons are 90 per cent water and so are very low in kilojoules.

Watermelons belong to the cucurbit family, as do marrow, squash, cucumber, rockmelon and honeydew. They are characterised by a hard, white rind that is inedible raw and may be thick or thin depending on variety. Skin colour varies from dark to pale-green with stripes and they can be round or oval shaped.

These days, most watermelons contain just a few white immature seeds scattered through the rosy, aromatic flesh. Some new varieties are smaller too, similar in size to a lawn bowl and ideal for 2-3 serves.

The exotic champagne melon has sweet yellow flesh, shiny green skin and looks similar to a small watermelon. It is very tasty in fruit salads, but supplies can be erratic.

Rockmelon, with its orange flesh and smooth or ridged skin, is sometimes called netted melon because of the netting on its skin, and is occasionally labelled muskmelon on account of its wonderful aroma when ripe. Rockmelons are available all year, but are sweetest during summer.

Honeydew melon has smooth, hard, creamy-green skin with pale-green flesh and is bland when under-ripe, so press the stem end lightly before purchasing: it should yield to gentle pressure if ripe. Cantaloupes are smaller and rounder than rockmelons, with smooth or scaly skin that is tough and clearly marked in sections. Charentais have aromatic, deep-orange flesh and are one of the most popular cantaloupes.

When tapped lightly, watermelons should sound hollow, indicating maturity, and they should have a fragrant aroma. A rich colour is a good indication of sweetness.

Select melons with smooth, blemish-free skin. They should feel heavy for their size, indicating good juice content. Choose rockmelons with definite netting on the skin and the background colour should be beige – a ripe melon will also have a slightly paler side where it has rested on the ground before picking. They don't ripen any further after harvest like honeydew melons, which will do so if stored at room temperature for a few days.

Cut melons are best kept in the fridge in an airtight container or plastic wrap. The perfume from rockmelons can invade other unwrapped foods.

Angouleme markets, France

Honiara Central Market, Solomon Islands

Prawn, papaya and honeydew melon salad

1 honeydew melon, peeled, seeded and cut into
    2cm pieces

1 papaya, peeled, seeded and cut into 2cm pieces

16 cooked king prawns, shelled and deveined,
    with tails intact

100g snowpeas, trimmed, blanched in boiling
    water for 10 seconds, then refreshed in cold water

2 tsp fish sauce

2 tsp lime juice

1 tsp caster sugar

1 tbsp crisp fried eschalots (available from
    Asian food stores)

Combine melon, papaya, prawns and snowpeas in
a large bowl.

Whisk fish sauce, lime juice and sugar in a small
bowl until sugar dissloves.

Pour dressing over salad and toss gently to
combine. Serve salad topped with crisp eschalots.

Serves 4 as a light lunch or entree.

Rockmelon and tamarillos with ginger and honey yoghurt ice

220g (1 cup) caster sugar

4 tamarillos

1 vanilla bean, split lengthwise

1 rockmelon, peeled, seeded and cut into
    2cm pieces

Ginger and honey yoghurt ice

600ml plain yoghurt

$^1/_4$ cup honey

1 tbsp ginger, grated

Combine sugar and 2 cups of water in a saucepan
and stir over medium heat until sugar dissolves,
then bring to the boil.

Cut a small cross in the base of each tamarillo,
then place in the pan with sugar syrup, scraped
seeds of vanilla bean and the bean. Simmer
tamarillos for 5 minutes, until tender, then
remove from heat and cool in syrup. When cool
enough to handle, remove tamarillo skins and
discard vanilla bean. Return fruit to syrup and
refrigerate until cold.

For the ginger and honey yoghurt ice, combine
yoghurt, honey and ginger in a bowl and stir
well. Freeze in an ice-cream maker, according to
manufacturer's instructions.

Serve rockmelon and tamarillos wth a little of the
tamarillo syrup drizzled over and accompanied by
scoops of frozen yoghurt.

Serves 4

Barbecued chicken with watermelon salsa

2 cloves garlic, finely chopped

2 tsp lemon rind, grated

2 tbsp lemon juice

2 tbsp light olive oil

4 chicken breast fillets

lemon wedges, to serve

Melon salsa

$^1/_4$ small watermelon (about 1kg), peeled, seeded and chopped

10 cherry tomatoes, quartered

1 lebanese cucumber, seeded and cut into 1cm pieces

16 kalamata olives, pitted and halved

$^1/_2$ tsp caster sugar

1 tbsp red-wine vinegar

1 -2 small red chillies, finely chopped

2 tbsp extra virgin olive oil

Combine garlic, lemon rind, juice and olive oil in a small bowl and season to taste, then brush over chicken.

For the melon salsa, combine all the ingredients, season to taste and toss gently.

Barbecue chicken over medium heat, brushing frequently with marinade and turning once, until cooked through. Serve chicken with watermelon salsa, lemon wedges and baby salad leaves.

Serves 4

Honeydew wedges with chilled nectarine syrup

440g (2 cups) caster sugar

2 large ripe nectarines, stoned and cut into 8

1 vanilla bean, split lengthwise

1 tbsp kirsch

2 ripe honeydew melons, peeled, seeded, cut into wedges and refrigerated

Combine sugar and 2 cups water in a saucepan and stir over medium heat until sugar dissolves, then bring to the boil. Add nectarines, scraped seeds of vanilla bean and the bean and simmer, covered, for 30 minutes, until fruit is a pulp. Cool to room temperature.

Discard vanilla bean, strain mixture through a sieve and discard pulp. Stir in kirsch and refrigerate until cold.

Serve melon wedges in glasses with chilled syrup.

Serves 8

Watermelon and ricotta salad with barbecued sausages

$^1/_4$ small watermelon, cut into 2cm pieces

2 large kiwifruit, peeled and cut into wedges

$^1/_2$ small red onion, finely sliced

60g baby rocket leaves

1 tbsp sherry vinegar

2 tbsp hazelnut oil

$^1/_2$ tsp Dijon mustard

salt and cracked black pepper

200g ricotta cheese

8 beef sausages

Combine watermelon, kiwifruit, red onion and rocket leaves in a large bowl.

Whisk sherry vinegar, hazelnut oil, mustard, salt and pepper in a small bowl until smooth.

Pour dressing over salad and toss gently. Divide salad between 4 serving plates and crumble over ricotta cheese.

Barbecue sausages and serve with watermelon salad and jacket potatoes (optional).

Serves 4

Baked salmon with watermelon and avocado salad

4 salmon fillets (about 200g each)

olive oil

4 sprigs thyme

4 slices lime

salt and cracked black pepper

$^1/_4$ small watermelon, cut into 2cm pieces

1 ripe avocado, peeled and cut into 1cm pieces

80g baby spinach leaves

1 tbsp red-wine vinegar

3 tbsp extra virgin olive oil

1 clove garlic, very finely chopped

lime cheeks, to serve

Preheat oven to 200C.

Brush both sides of salmon fillets with a little olive oil and place in a single layer on a large piece of foil. Top each with a sprig of thyme and slice of lime and season. Bring edges of foil together and seal well. Bake for 6-10 minutes, until just cooked.

Combine watermelon, avocado and baby spinach leaves in a large bowl.

Whisk vinegar, extra virgin olive oil, garlic, salt and pepper until smooth. Pour over salad and toss gently.

Remove salmon from foil, discard thyme and lime slices and serve with watermelon salad and lime cheeks.

Serves 4

Watermelon and strawberries with chilled wine and toffee pistachio sticks

165g ($^3/_4$ cup) caster sugar

75g pistachio nuts, toasted and chopped

$^1/_4$ small watermelon, cut into bite-sized pieces

250g strawberries, hulled and halved

375ml dessert wine, chilled

Combine caster sugar and $^1/_2$ cup water in a small saucepan and stir over low heat until sugar dissolves. Increase heat and boil, without stirring, until mixture is a caramel colour, then pour onto a foil-lined tray. Sprinkle with pistachio nuts. Cool then break into pieces.

Combine watermelon and strawberries and divide among 4 serving dishes. Drizzle with dessert wine and top with toffee sticks.

Serves 4

Melon and blueberry salad with vanilla ricotta and almonds

$^1/_4$ small seedless watermelon, cut into 2cm pieces

$^1/_2$ rockmelon, peeled and cut into 2cm pieces

125g blueberries

300g ricotta cheese

2 tbsp icing sugar

2-3 tsp vanilla extract

25g ($^1/_3$ cup) flaked almonds, toasted

Combine watermelon and rockmelon in a large bowl with blueberries and toss gently.

Combine ricotta, icing sugar and vanilla extract in a bowl and mix well.

Serve fruit salad in 4 shallow bowls, top with ricotta and sprinkle with toasted flaked almonds.

Serves 4

Place d'Aligre Market, Paris

Olives

The symbol of world peace, the olive originated in the Middle East and has been cultivated for more than 6000 years. It is believed that olives and olive oil are largely responsible for the low incidence of heart disease in the Mediterranean where the trees can live for up to 1000 years. Although they have a reputation for being slow growing, they thrive in the poorest soil.

There are many varieties with a wide range of colours, shapes and sizes: kalamatas are said to be one of the finest black table olives and in demand in Greece. Manzanillo is a beautiful spreading tree that produces medium-sized fruit that can be pickled green or black. Verdale has the most silvery foliage of all olive trees and is often grown for its ornamental value; the fruit is best pickled but can be pressed for oil in areas where the summers are very hot. Frantoio, pichilone, gordal, picual and arbequina are other common varieties.

Aromatic extra virgin olive oil must have a maximum acidity of no more than 1 per cent, virgin olive oil acidity may not be higher than 1.5 per cent and olive oil, (often labelled pure olive oil in supermarkets), is blended from lesser quality virgin olive oil. The deeper the colour of the oil, the fuller the flavour, but both colour and flavour depend on the quality of the fruit, the variety and growing conditions.

Fresh olives can be bought from the produce markets during autumn, but if harvesting from your own trees pick green olives when they are pale-green and black olives when they are deep-purple and preserve as soon as possible. After pickling, it is not necessary to store them in the fridge.

If using olives in slow-cooked dishes, add them towards the end of cooking to preserve their texture and flavour.

Preserved green olives

2.5-3kg firm green olives

3 litres water

1 cup salt

Pour water into a large preserving jar, add salt and stir until dissolved.

Add olives and place a plate or weight on top to keep submerged.

Pour liquid off each day and add fresh salt water. Repeat this process for one week, then once a week for another 4-7 weeks or until the bitterness has gone from the olives. The best way to tell this is to taste the olives regularly.

(To speed this process up olives can be cracked with a wooden mallet or the base of a heavy glass before placing in the salt solution.)

Once the bitterness has gone the olives are ready to be eaten or stored in sterilised jars covered in olive oil or brine.

To marinate the olives, add olive oil and a choice of flavourings such as garlic, oregano, fennel seeds, bay leaf and chilli.

Olive and herb cheesecake

2 tbsp melted butter

150g grated parmesan

500g ricotta

1 cup basil

$^1/_2$ cup mint

$^1/_2$ cup flat-leaf parsley

$^1/_4$ cup oregano

100ml pouring cream

2 eggs

salt

$^3/_4$ tsp dried chilli flakes

20 large kalamata olives, stoned and chopped

Preheat oven to 190C.

Cover the base of a 22cm spring-form pan with baking paper, grease the base and sides with butter and sprinkle with 2-3 tablespoons of the parmesan.

Place half the ricotta, herbs and cream in a food processor and blend until smooth. Add remaining ricotta and eggs, one at a time, pulsing briefly after each one. Add remaining parmesan, salt and chilli flakes and pulse until combined.

Spoon mixture into prepared tin and scatter with chopped olives.

Bake for 25-30 minutes or until brown on the edges, but soft in the centre.

Serve immediately, as the cheesecake will sink on cooling.

Serves 4-6

Oranges

Although valencias and navels are by far the most common varieties grown in Australia, more seville and blood oranges are appearing in the markets each winter. But buy them when you see them, as they only have a short season.

Large, sharp-tasting sevilles have a rough, shiny skin, several seeds and a tough membrane so are most suited to cooking. They're also labelled bitter oranges or sour oranges in the shops. Perhaps their greatest claim to fame is that they are the preferred variety for the manufacture of traditional bitter marmalade.

Italy and Spain are by far the world's largest producers and consumers of blood oranges, which are small with few seeds and a flavour reminiscent of raspberries and cherries. Some have dark-pink splashes on the skin as well as the flesh, but the intensity of colour depends on the amount of sunlight the oranges receive while growing, as well as temperature conditions. They have more red pigment when grown in colder areas.

Navel oranges are characterised by their rich orange colour and slightly pebbly skin and are so named because of the dimple on their base. They have virtually no seeds and are easy to peel.

Valencias are the most popular juicing orange and have a smoother skin than navels, often with a green tinge. Bright-orange colouration is a result of crisp, cold weather at ripening time rather than ripeness, and the green colouration on valencias in no way affects the flavour.

Choose firm fruit and avoid any with brown patches or soft spots. It should feel heavy for its size, indicating juiciness. As with all citrus, the fruit is picked ripe and will not ripen any further after harvesting. Best stored in the crisper of the fridge.

Chunky orange and coriander marmalade

3 large seville oranges

2 lemons

1 tbsp coriander seeds

cold water, to cover

1.5kg white sugar (approximately), warmed

Halve oranges and lemons and slice thinly, retaining seeds and cores. Place seeds, cores and coriander seeds in muslin and tie securely with string. Place fruit and muslin bag in a bowl and add water to cover. Place a plate on top of fruit to keep it in the water and leave overnight.

Turn fruit and muslin bag into a large, heavy-based pan and cook over low heat until fruit is soft and half the liquid has evaporated (about 60-90 minutes). Remove muslin bag, squeezing juice back into fruit. Measure pulp.

For each cup of pulp add 1 cup of warm sugar and stir over medium heat until sugar is dissolved, then bring to the boil. Boil rapidly for 15-25 minutes or until setting point is reached.

Cool for 5 minutes then stir to distribute fruit evenly and pour into warm sterilised jars. Seal when cool.

Makes about 8 cups

*To test for setting point, use a sugar thermometer or place a small amount of marmalade on a chilled saucer: if it jells, the jam is ready for bottling.

Orange and lemon poppyseed muffins

2 cups self-raising flour

$1/2$ cup caster sugar

1 cup milk

$1/3$ cup vegetable oil

2 eggs

3 tbsp poppyseeds

1 tbsp lemon zest

1 tbsp orange zest

Preheat oven to 200C.

Combine flour and sugar in a large bowl. Combine milk, oil and eggs in a separate bowl and whisk lightly, then stir in poppyseeds, lemon and orange zest. Make a well in the centre of the flour mixture, pour in the liquid mixture and mix lightly. Spoon batter into 6 greased muffin tins ($1/2$ cup capacity) until two-thirds full then bake for 20-25 minutes or until golden and cooked.

Turn onto a wire rack to cool.

Serve with unsalted butter.

Makes 6

Blood orange ice-cream

(pictured page 95)

400ml fresh blood orange juice
165g ($^3/_4$ cup) caster sugar
250ml (1 cup) pouring cream

Combine orange juice and sugar in a medium-sized saucepan and stir over low heat just until sugar is dissolved. Remove from heat and cool. Add cream and stir until smooth. Chill.

Transfer mixture to an ice-cream maker and churn, according to manufacturer's instructions.

Alternatively, pour mixture into a freezer tray and freeze until crystals form around the edge. Remove and break crystals up with a fork. Return to freezer and repeat this process twice, then freeze ice-cream.

Serve with fresh fruit or biscotti.

Serves 4-6

Orange butter cake

280g butter, softened
250g caster sugar
finely grated rind of 2 oranges
5 eggs
185g ($1^1/_2$ cups) ground almonds
220g self-raising flour, sifted
1 tsp vanilla extract
$^3/_4$ cup fresh orange juice

Orange icing
50g cream cheese
2 tbsp soft butter
2 tsp fresh orange juice
finely grated rind of 1 orange
2 cups icing sugar mixture, sifted

Grease and flour a 22cm or 24cm square cake tin.

Combine butter and sugar until light and creamy. Add the orange rind and stir well. Add eggs, one at a time, beating well after each addition. Add ground almonds and stir. Mix in sifted flour and stir in vanilla extract and orange juice until smooth.

Spoon cake mixture into tin and bake at 18oC for about 1 hour or until a cake skewer inserted in the centre comes out clean.

Remove and rest cake in tin for 5 minutes before turning onto a cake rack to cool.

For the orange icing, combine all the ingredients in a mixing bowl or food processor and beat until smooth. Spread over cake.

Caramel oranges

220g (1 cup) caster sugar
1 cup water
1 cup fresh orange juice
zest of $^1/_2$ orange
1 tbsp Cointreau or Grand Marnier
4 oranges, peeled and sliced
250ml (1 cup) low-fat cream
few drops of vanilla extract

Combine caster sugar and water in a saucepan and stir over low heat until sugar is dissolved. Bring to the boil and cook, without stirring, until mixture is a golden colour. Remove from heat and when bubbles subside carefully pour in orange juice (take care as mixture will spit) and then stir over low heat until smooth. Remove from heat and add orange zest and Cointreau or Grand Marnier and stir well. Place oranges in serving dishes and pour sauce over.

Combine cream and vanilla in a small bowl and stir. Serve with caramel oranges.

Serves 4

Blood orange tart

When blood oranges are out of season make this intensely flavoured tart with navels or combine equal quantities of lime and lemon juice and adjust the sugar to taste.

Pastry

225g (1½ cups) plain flour

125g butter, chopped

1 tbsp icing sugar

1 egg yolk

icing sugar, for dusting

blood oranges, peeled and sliced to serve

Filling

2 tsp blood orange zest

1 cup blood orange juice (about 4 oranges)

220g (1 cup) caster sugar

¾ cup thick cream

6 eggs

Preheat oven to 200C.

Process flour, butter, icing sugar and a pinch of salt in a food processor until mixture resembles coarse breadcrumbs. Add 2 tablespoons iced water and egg yolk and process until mixture just comes together. Shape pastry into a flat disc, cover with plastic wrap and refrigerate for 30 minutes.

Roll out pastry on a lightly floured surface and line a round 28cm tart tin with removable base. Prick base with a fork and refrigerate for 30 minutes. Line pastry with baking paper, fill with dried beans or rice and bake blind for 10 minutes. Remove paper and weights, reduce heat to 180C and bake pastry for another 10 minutes or until dry and pale golden. Cool.

For the filling, stir zest, orange juice, sugar and cream in a bowl until well combined. Add eggs, one at a time, beating well after each. Pour orange mixture into tart shell and bake at 190C for 40-45 minutes or until filling is just set.

Serve warm or at room temperature dusted with icing sugar and accompanied by orange slices.

Serves 8

Orange, lemon and olive salad

4 oranges, peeled and thinly sliced

1 small red onion, peeled and thinly sliced

½ lemon, peeled and thinly sliced

¾ cup large kalamata olives

2 tbsp salted capers, rinsed

salt and cracked black pepper

¼ cup extra virgin olive oil

¼ cup flat-leaf parsley, coarsely chopped

Combine oranges, onion and lemon in a medium-sized bowl and add olives and capers. Season with salt and pepper and drizzle with olive oil. Scatter with parsley.

Serve with barbecued salmon or ocean trout fillets, french fries and lime cheeks on the side.

Serves 4

Citrus salad with wine and thyme syrup

2 ruby oranges

2 navel oranges

4 black or green figs, halved

double cream, to serve (optional)

Wine syrup

250ml fruity white wine, such as riesling

330g caster sugar

thinly peeled rind of $\frac{1}{2}$ lemon

1 tbsp fresh thyme leaves

For the wine syrup, place wine, sugar, lemon rind and 1 cup water in a saucepan and stir over low heat until sugar dissolves, then bring to the boil and simmer over medium heat for 8-10 minutes or until syrupy. Discard rind, stir in thyme and cool to room temperature.

Using a small knife, cut rind and pith from citrus, then cut fruit into wedges and place in a large bowl with figs. Pour wine syrup over and toss gently to combine. Divide salad among bowls and serve immediately topped with double cream, if using.

Serves 6

Other citrus

Pomelos are the largest fruit of the citrus family. Some varieties are round while others taper slightly at the stem end. They have pink or yellow succulent flesh that can be juicy or slightly dry and they vary from seductively sweet to tart and tangy.

The thick, slightly rough skin is normally light-green to bronze-yellow with tiny green spots that are the rind oil glands. The rind is easy to peel and encases up to 18 segments. Pomelos and grapefruit are closely related but, their flavour and structure are quite different. The core of a pomelo is open and spongy and the irregular segments, with semi-sweet flesh, are easily separated.

Cumquats are technically not a citrus fruit, as they have just 3-6 segments whereas citrus have 8-15, but they are generally classified in the citrus group. The slow-growing attractive trees, with their bright foliage and highly perfumed white blossoms, can be clipped for topiary. Large, round cumquats have sweet rind and juicy sour flesh and can be eaten fresh from the tree, although they are too tart for many people. The oval varieties are good for making liqueurs and marmalades. Snip the fruit from the tree rather than pulling them off, as it can tear the skin.

Brilliant coloured and tangier than an orange, with a distinctive flavour of their own, tangelos have lots of juice and are becoming very popular. They are a grapefruit-mandarin hybrid and can be easily identified by their pear-shaped neck. This fruit is easy to peel and has few, if any, pips. The juice is a unique combination of the tartness of a grapefruit and the sweetness of a mandarin, and develops a fuller, more mellow flavour as the season progresses.

Choose firm fruit and avoid any with brown patches or soft spots. It should feel heavy for its size, indicating good juice content. As with all citrus, the fruit is picked ripe and will not ripen any further after harvesting. Best stored in the crisper.

Pomelo, prawn and coriander salad

2 tbsp vegetable oil

2 brown eschalots, finely sliced

1 clove garlic, very finely chopped

1 pomelo, segmented and pith removed

300g cooked prawns, peeled and deveined

2 tbsp peanuts, roasted and chopped

1 large red chilli, very finely sliced

2 tsp fish sauce

2 tsp palm sugar

1 lime, juiced

2 tbsp coconut cream

$^1/_3$ cup coriander leaves

$^1/_3$ cup mint leaves

2 tbsp flaked coconut, toasted

Heat oil in a small pan and add eschalots and garlic. Stir-fry for 2-3 minutes or until fragrant. Drain.

Place the garlic, eschalots and pomelo in a large bowl. Add prawns, peanuts and chilli. Whisk fish sauce, palm sugar, lime juice and coconut cream in a small bowl until sugar is dissolved. Pour over prawn mixture and toss gently to combine. Serve salad topped with coriander leaves, mint and toasted coconut.

Serves 2

Pan-fried salmon with asparagus and tangelos

4 salmon fillets (about 180g each) boned

4 tbsp extra virgin olive oil

2 bunches asparagus, halved

juice and zest of 2 tangelos

2 tsp ginger, grated

2 tbsp balsamic vinegar

2 tsp lemon juice

salt and cracked black pepper

4 tangelos, peeled and thickly sliced

Brush salmon fillets on both sides with 1 tablespoon of olive oil and pan-fry over high heat for about 3 minutes, skin-side down. Turn and cook for another 2-3 minutes or until cooked as desired. Remove and keep warm.

Bring a large saucepan of lightly salted water to the boil and cook asparagus for 3-4 minutes or until tender but crisp. Drain.

For the dressing, place the juice and zest of tangelos in a small bowl and add ginger, vinegar, lemon juice, remaining olive oil, salt and pepper and whisk until smooth. Place salmon in the centre of serving plates and surround with asparagus and tangelo slices. Drizzle over dressing.

Serve with hot garlic bread.

Serves 4

Tangelo puddings with custard

These easy puddings can be made with oranges or mandarins when tangelos are not in season.

2 tbsp tangelo or orange marmalade

75g caster sugar

75g butter

1 large egg

$\frac{1}{2}$ tsp vanilla extract

1 tbsp honey

75g self-raising flour, sifted

1 tbsp tangelo juice

1 tsp tangelo zest

Preheat oven to 180C.

Grease 4 x 150ml ovenproof moulds and spoon 2 teaspoons of marmalade into the base of each.

Combine sugar, butter, egg, vanilla and honey in a medium-sized bowl and beat with an electric mixer for 4 minutes. Fold in flour and stir in tangelo juice and zest. Spoon mixture into prepared moulds to $\frac{3}{4}$ full and cover each firmly with buttered foil. Place puddings in a baking dish and pour in boiling water to come halfway up the sides of moulds.

Bake for 1 hour or until puddings spring back to the touch.

To serve, turn puddings out onto serving plates and accompany with thick cream or custard.

Serves 4

Little marmalade puddings with orange-flower tangelos

2 large tangelos

2 tsp orange-flower water

300ml thick cream

Puddings

2 tbsp tangelo or orange marmalade

75g caster sugar

75g butter

1 large egg

$\frac{1}{2}$ tsp vanilla extract

1 tbsp honey

75g self-raising flour, sifted

1 tbsp tangelo juice

1 tsp tangelo zest

Preheat oven to 180C.

For the puddings, grease 4 x 150ml dariole moulds and spoon 2 teaspoons of marmalade into the base of each. Combine sugar, butter, egg, vanilla and honey in a medium-sized bowl and beat with an electric mixer for 4 minutes. Fold in flour and stir in tangelo juice and zest. Spoon mixture into prepared moulds to $\frac{3}{4}$ full and cover each firmly with buttered foil. Place puddings in a baking dish and pour in boiling water to come halfway up the sides of moulds.

Bake for 1 hour or until puddings spring back to the touch.

Peel and cut each tangelo into 4 slices about 1cm thick. Place in a bowl and drizzle with orange-flower water.

To serve, turn puddings out onto serving plates and place 2 tangelo slices on the side. Accompany with thick cream.

Serves 4

Tangelos and prunes in herb syrup with honeyed yoghurt

500ml dry red wine

220g caster sugar

3 sprigs thyme

1 bay leaf

$^1/_2$ tsp fennel seeds

peel from one lemon

2 tbsp honey

1 vanilla bean, split

5 large tangelos, peeled and cut into 1cm slices

16 pitted prunes

300ml plain Greek-style yoghurt mixed with
    2 tbsp honey

Combine wine, sugar, herbs, fennel seeds, lemon rind, honey, vanilla bean and 1 cup water in a large saucepan and stir over medium heat until sugar dissolves, then simmer for 10 minutes. Add tangelo slices and prunes and simmer a further 1-2 minutes.

Using a slotted spoon, remove tangelos, prunes and herbs. Strain syrup, return to pan and simmer until reduced and slightly thickened.

Pour warm syrup over fruit and serve with honeyed yoghurt.

Serves 4

Red salad with tangelo dressing

Serve with barbecued lamb chops or roast chicken and desiree potatoes.

1 bulb fennel

2 red radicchio, washed and dried

2 blood oranges

1 tangelo

1 cup opal basil leaves

1 bunch purple or green asparagus, trimmed,
    blanched and cut into 4cm lengths

1 red onion, very thinly sliced

75g ($^1/_2$ cup) unsalted cashews, toasted

10 kalamata olives

Dressing

2 tbsp extra virgin olive oil

1 tsp white-wine vinegar

3 tbsp tangelo juice

1 tsp tangelo zest

6 fresh mint leaves, finely chopped

sea salt and cracked black pepper

Trim fennel and reserve fronds for garnish. Discard tough outer layers and cut bulb into very thin slices. Tear radicchio leaves into bite-sized pieces. Peel oranges and tangelo, removing all white pith, and cut into segments. Combine all vegetables and basil in a large serving bowl, cover and chill.

For the dressing, combine all the ingredients, mix well and season to taste.

To serve, add cashews and olives to salad, pour dressing over and toss gently. Garnish with some reserved fennel fronds.

Serves 4-6

Brandied cumquats

500g cumquats

500g white sugar

600ml brandy

Place cumquats in a large, sterilised preserving jar and add sugar and brandy. Stir every few days until sugar is dissolved then leave, covered, to mature for about 8 weeks before using. Add chopped cumquats to ice-cream, puddings, cakes and pies.

Makes about 6 cups

Passionfruit

Gloriously perfumed with tart-sweet pulp, passionfruit needs only the simplest of treatment. Spoon it over pawpaw, ice-cream, yoghurt or banana to make a delicious dessert or snack. There are many purple varieties, but Nelly Kelly, with its dry leathery skin, is said to be the most prolific home garden vine.

Banana passionfruit are longer in shape with more pulp than purple passionfruit, but they lack that special sweet/acid balance. Less common, slightly bigger yellow passionfruit have skin that is not wrinkled. This type thrives in tropical areas, but the pulp is less flavoursome and not as perfumed. Panama, easily identified by its shiny red/mauve skin, is a hybrid that grows well in tropical areas.

The juice of passionfruit is very acidic, so when making creams, custards and ice-cream add the pulp or juice after the custard or cream has cooled so it doesn't curdle. To make passionfruit juice, pulse the pulp very briefly in a food processor then strain to remove seeds. In recipes calling for a large amount of juice it can be diluted with orange juice, yet still keep the passionfruit flavour.

Choose large, purple passionfruit with undamaged, slightly wrinkled skin. They should be heavy for their size, indicating good juice content, with plenty of bright-orange pulp. Avoid small dry withered fruit. Smooth-skinned varieties can be stored in the fruit bowl and eaten before the skin starts to crinkle or stored for longer periods in the crisper of the fridge.

Passionfruit and cherry pudding

This is an easy, delicious dessert to serve when cherries and passionfruit are in season. Try it with strawberries if cherries are not available.

$^{1}/_{2}$ cup passionfruit pulp (about 8-10 large passionfruit)

30g plain flour, sifted

$^{1}/_{2}$ tsp baking powder

50g caster sugar

pinch of salt

4 eggs

1 cup milk

500g cherries, pitted

whipped cream, to serve

Preheat oven to 180C.

Lightly butter six 1-cup ramekins or a 6-cup capacity round ceramic dish, sprinkle with a little sugar and shake away excess.

Using the pulse button, process passionfruit pulp for 30 seconds, then strain and discard seeds.

Combine flour, baking powder, sugar and salt in a large bowl, add eggs and whisk until smooth. Stir in milk and passionfruit juice and mix until smooth.

Divide cherries among ramekins or place in dish. Pour batter over cherries and bake for 30-35 minutes (if using large dish cook an extra 5-10 minutes) or until cooked and golden. Serve warm with whipped cream.

Serves 6

Hot scones with passionfruit curd

Scones

450g self-raising flour

2 tsp baking powder

1 tsp salt

2 tsp icing sugar

50g butter, melted

180ml chilled water

180ml chilled milk

Preheat oven to 200C.

Sift dry ingredients into a large mixing bowl. Add butter, water and milk and mix with a spatula until a soft dough is formed. (It is important not to overmix or scones will be tough.)

Roll out dough and cut into desired shapes. Place on a lightly floured baking tray and bake for 10-12 minutes or until golden and cooked.

Serve hot with butter and passionfruit curd.

Makes 10-15

Passionfruit Curd

6 egg yolks

110g caster sugar

120ml passionfruit juice, (about 12 passionfruit), strained

150g unsalted butter, chopped

For the curd, whisk egg yolks, sugar and passionfruit juice in the top of a double saucepan or a heatproof bowl over a pan of simmering water until well combined. Add butter, piece by piece, whisking constantly until each piece has melted. Stir until mixture thickens enough to coat the back of a wooden spoon. Do not boil. Remove from heat, cool slightly, then cover with plastic wrap and refrigerate.

Passionfruit and semolina Easter cake

165g caster sugar

5 eggs, separated

100g fine semolina

50g ground almonds

2 tbsp lemon juice

2 tsp lemon rind, finely grated

Filling

150g ricotta

55g caster sugar

150ml whipped cream

$^3/_4$-1 cup passionfruit curd

icing sugar, to decorate

Preheat oven to 180C.

Whisk sugar and egg yolks until thick and pale. Fold in the semolina, almonds, lemon juice, rind and a pinch of salt. Whisk egg whites until stiff peaks form and fold into semolina mixture. Pour into a buttered and floured 20cm springform pan and bake for 30-40 minutes or until a cake skewer inserted in the centre comes out clean. Stand in pan for 5-10 minutes before turning out onto a wire rack to cool.

For the filling, beat ricotta, sugar and cream together until smooth and well combined. Cut cake in half horizontally, spread passionfruit curd over bottom half of cake and then ricotta mixture. Top with the remaining layer of cake. Dust top with icing sugar.

Serves 6-8

Little passionfruit custards with passionfruit sauce and kiwifruit

60g butter, chopped

110g ($^1/_2$ cup) caster sugar

3 eggs

2 egg yolks

finely grated rind of 1 lime

3 tbsp passionfruit juice

300ml light sour cream

6 tbsp plain flour, sifted

Sauce

125g butter, chopped

2 eggs

2 egg yolks

4-5 tbsp passionfruit juice

150g caster sugar

6 kiwifruit, peeled and sliced

Preheat oven to 180C.

For the custards, mix butter and sugar in a food processor until well combined. Add eggs and egg yolks, one at a time, processing briefly after each. Add lime rind and passionfruit juice and process briefly. Add sour cream and process until smooth. Remove to a bowl and fold in flour and whisk until smooth.

Pour mixture into 6 x 150ml greased ovenproof moulds and place in a baking dish and add enough hot water to come halfway up the sides of the moulds. Bake for 20-25 minutes or until custards are just set. Remove and rest for 10 minutes before turning out.

For the sauce, place butter in a heatproof bowl over a saucepan of simmering water and when melted add eggs, egg yolks, passionfruit juice and caster sugar and stir constantly over low heat until mixture thickens enough to coat the back of a wooden spoon.

To serve, place pudding in the centre of shallow serving bowls, spoon sauce around puddings and serve with the kiwifruit.

Serves 6

Pawpaw

Call it papaya or pawpaw, it really doesn't matter, as both names belong to the same plant species. In Australia, red-fleshed cultivars are often known as papaya to distinguish them from the larger, yellow-fleshed fruits known as pawpaw. They are both *Carica papaya*. They can be eaten ripe as a fruit or green as a vegetable, particularly in South-East Asia. The flesh has a sweet-tart exotic taste, but is firmer and more astringent when green and often served grated or shredded in salads.

Pawpaws continue to mature after picking and will ripen quickly at room temperature during summer. They should give slightly to pressure when fully ripe so handle with care to avoid bruising. Once cut, cover with plastic wrap and store in the fridge. In winter some varieties may develop spotted skin known as 'winter freckle' but this does not detract from the eating quality.

They are extremely high in vitamins A and C and are a good source of calcium and iron. Low in kilojoules, pawpaw also contains papain, a natural enzyme that aids the digestion of proteins.

Prawn, tomato and papaya salad

1 large ripe papaya

1 large bunch rocket

16 cherry or grape tomatoes, halved

2 tbsp flat-leaf parsley, coarsely chopped

24 cooked prawns, peeled with tails intact

75ml balsamic vinegar

2 tbsp extra virgin olive oil

salt and cracked black pepper

Peel papaya and cut into slices then place on a serving platter with rocket, tomatoes and parsley. Arrange prawns on top of salad.

In a small bowel, whisk vinegar and olive oil, season with salt and pepper and drizzle over salad.

Serves 4-6

Coconut and lemon custards with papaya salad and kaffir lime leaves

Custards

125ml ($^1/_2$ cup) milk

125ml ($^1/_2$ cup) coconut milk

$1^1/_2$ x 5g gelatine leaves (titanium strength)

4 egg yolks

110g ($^1/_2$ cup) caster sugar

1-2 tbsp lemon juice

1 tsp lemon zest

250ml (1 cup) pouring cream

Salad

110g ($^1/_2$ cup) caster sugar

$^3/_4$ cup water

2 tsp lemon juice

3 red papaya, peeled, seeded and sliced

1 large very finely shredded kaffir lime leaf

For the custards, combine milk and coconut milk in a small saucepan and stir over low heat until almost boiling. Remove from heat. Soak gelatine leaves in cold water until soft. Whisk egg yolks and caster sugar until thick then stir into milk mixture with a wooden spoon. Cook over low heat, stirring constantly, for about 3 minutes or until mixture is thick enough to coat the back of a wooden spoon.

Remove from heat and add drained gelatine leaves and stir until dissolved. Cool and stir in lemon juice and zest.

Softly whip cream and fold into custard. Pour mixture into 6 x 150ml lightly greased moulds, cover with plastic wrap and refrigerate overnight or until firm.

For the salad, combine caster sugar and water in a saucepan and stir over medium heat until sugar is dissolved. Bring to the boil, reduce heat and simmer for 8-10 minutes until mixture is syrupy. Cool and stir in lemon juice.

To serve, dip custard moulds briefly into hot water and invert onto serving plates. Serve papaya on the side and drizzle with sugar syrup. Top custards with shredded kaffir lime leaf.

Serves 6

Peaches & nectarines

The fragrant peach is considered the tree of life in China, where it originated.

Nectarines are actually a variety of peach and have either white or yellow flesh. Classic white peaches are popular with stone fruit lovers due to their gorgeous aroma and flavour, but their soft flesh bruises very easily.

Freestone types are good for cooking, halved or sliced, as the flesh separates easily from the stone. Clingstones have flesh that adheres tightly to the stone so are ideal for poaching or roasting whole. New varieties of sweet low-acid peaches and nectarines can be picked and transported while still hard, which is an advantage – enjoy them crisp like an apple.

Buy peaches with a strong perfume, which indicates a delicious flavour as their sweetness doesn't increase after harvesting. Choose firm, plump fruit with some give near the stem end – a red blush is not always an indication of ripeness. Always place them on top of your shopping basket, as they bruise easily. Don't buy fruit that has green skin because these have been picked before maturity.

Keep classic varieties in the fruit bowl to enhance their fragrance and the newer low-acid varieties in the crisper of the fridge. The skin can easily be removed from peaches by cutting a small cross in the base and plunging fruit into a saucepan of boiling water for a few seconds. Remove with a slotted spoon, plunge into cold water, then peel.

Cahors Market, France

Grilled honey nectarines with raspberries and Greek-style yoghurt

6 nectarines, halved, stones removed

¹/₃ cup honey

200g fresh raspberries

finely grated rind of ¹/₂ orange

190g (²/₃ cup) Greek style yoghurt or vanilla custard

Drizzle honey over cut surfaces of nectarines and place on a foil-lined tray under a hot grill for 5 minutes or until fruit is soft and caramelised. Transfer to a serving platter and drizzle over juices. Scatter with raspberries and sprinkle with orange rind.

Serve fruits with Greek-style yoghurt or bought vanilla custard.

Serves 4

Nectarine and coconut crumble

700g large white nectarines (about 5)

1 tsp lemon zest

1 tbsp fresh lemon juice

150g (²/₃ cup) caster sugar

Topping

75g (¹/₂ cup) self-raising flour

50g unsalted butter, chopped

65g (¹/₃ cup, firmly packed) brown sugar

20g (¹/₄ cup) desiccated coconut

Preheat oven to 180C.

For the topping, place flour in a medium-sized bowl and rub in the butter until mixture resembles coarse breadcrumbs. Add brown sugar and coconut and stir well.

Seed nectarines and cut each into 6 wedges. Combine nectarines, lemon zest, lemon juice, sugar and 2 tablespoons of cold water in a large bowl. Heat a non-stick frying pan over medium heat until hot and add nectarine mixture and stir for 2-3 minutes until nectarines have softened slightly.

Transfer nectarine mixture to a lightly greased 6 cup ovenproof dish and sprinkle with topping. Bake for 25-30 minutes or until topping is golden and nectarines are cooked.

Serve hot or warm with good quality vanilla ice-cream.

Serves 4

Nectarine, mango and honeydew salad with red-wine vinegar dressing

4 large ripe nectarines

¹/₂ honeydew melon, peeled and sliced

1 large ripe mango, peeled and cut into wedges

80g baby rocket leaves

¹/₄ cup light olive oil

1 tbsp red-wine vinegar

pinch of caster sugar

1 tsp Dijon mustard

salt and cracked black pepper

8 slices prosciutto

crusty bread, to serve

Combine nectarines, honeydew melon and mango in a medium-sized bowl. Add rocket leaves and toss gently to combine.

Whisk olive oil in a small bowl with red-wine vinegar, caster sugar, Dijon mustard, salt and pepper to taste. Add half the dressing to the salad and toss gently.

Divide salad among 4 plates and top each with prosciutto then drizzle with remaining dressing and serve with crusty bread.

Serves 4

Poached peaches with five-spice custard

6 ripe peaches, peeled

110g caster sugar

Custard

$^{1}/_{4}$ tsp ground cardamom

$^{1}/_{4}$ tsp ground cloves

$^{1}/_{4}$ tsp ground cinnamon

$^{1}/_{4}$ tsp ground star anise

1 cup milk

1 cup pouring cream

$^{1}/_{2}$ vanilla bean, split

5 egg yolks

165g caster sugar

Place peaches and 110g caster sugar in a large saucepan and add water to cover. Bring to the boil and simmer for 5-10 minutes depending on ripeness of fruit. Remove peaches from syrup and cool.

For the custard, place cardamom, cloves, cinnamon and star anise in a small pan and stir over low heat for 2-3 minutes until aromatic. Combine milk, cream, vanilla bean and the spices in a heavy-based saucepan and bring to simmering point. Whisk egg yolks and sugar until thick and pale and then stir in milk mixture. Return egg mixture to saucepan and cook over low heat, stirring constantly, until mixture thickens enough to coat the back of a wooden spoon.

Strain into a bowl and serve custard – warm or cold – with peaches.

Serves 6

Peaches in rosé syrup with basil and cinnamon wafers

(pictured page 113)

This recipe is ideal for the festive season, as it can be doubled or tripled easily and be made well ahead of time.

1 bottle rosé (750ml)

330g (1$^{1}/_{2}$ cups) caster sugar

1 cinnamon stick

8 peaches

24 small basil leaves

Cinnamon wafers

2 sheets x 25cm spring-roll wrappers

$^{1}/_{4}$ cup grapeseed oil

50g caster sugar

$^{1}/_{2}$ tsp ground cinnamon

1 tbsp ground almonds

vanilla ice-cream, to serve

Combine wine, sugar and cinnamon stick in a large saucepan and stir over low heat until sugar dissolves. Bring to the boil and simmer for 5 minutes.

Add peaches and simmer over medium heat until just tender (time will vary according to ripeness of fruit). Remove peaches and peel when cool enough to handle. Bring syrup to the boil and boil over high heat until reduced by one-third. Cool syrup to room temperature, return peaches to syrup, cover and refrigerate until ready to serve.

Serve peaches in a large bowl sprinkled with basil leaves. Accompany with cinnamon wafers and ice-cream.

Cinnamon wafers

Preheat oven to 180C.
Brush pastry sheets with oil. Combine sugar, cinnamon and almonds in a small bowl and sprinkle mixture evenly over pastry sheets. Cut each sheet into 8 triangles, place on lightly oiled baking trays and bake for 6-8 minutes or until crisp.

Keep in an airtight container.

Serves 8

Poached nectarines with mascarpone and almond bread

220g (1 cup) caster sugar

2 strips orange rind

1 cinnamon stick

8 whole nectarines

200g mascarpone

almond bread, to serve

Combine 3 cups water with caster sugar, orange rind and cinnamon stick in a large saucepan and stir over low heat until sugar dissolves. Bring to the boil and simmer, uncovered, for 2-3 minutes. Add nectarines and simmer for 5-8 minutes or until tender (depending on ripeness).

Using a slotted spoon, remove nectarines to a bowl and boil liquid, uncovered, for about 5 minutes or until reduced and syrupy. Cool to room temperature.

Serve 2 nectarines in each serving dish with syrup poured over and a dollop of mascarpone. Pass almond bread separately.

Serves 4

Creme caramel with fresh peaches

165g ($^3/_4$ cup) caster sugar

3 eggs

2 egg yolks

55g ($^1/_4$ cup) caster sugar, extra

2 tsp vanilla extract

$1^1/_2$ cups pouring cream

2 cups milk

3 large ripe peaches, stoned and sliced

thick cream, to serve

Preheat oven to 160C.

Combine sugar and $^1/_4$ cup water in a saucepan and stir over low heat until sugar dissolves. Increase heat and boil, without stirring, until mixture is a caramel colour. Pour into 6 x 175ml ramekins or small ovenproof dishes.

Whisk eggs, yolks, extra sugar, vanilla and a pinch of salt until combined. Combine pouring cream and milk in a saucepan and bring just to the boil. Whisk cream mixture into egg mixture, then pour evenly among prepared ramekins.

Place ramekins in a large baking dish and pour enough boiling water to come halfway up the sides of dishes. Bake for 35-40 minutes, until custard is just set. Remove ramekins from baking dish, cool to room temperature, then cover and refrigerate for at least 4 hours or overnight.

Carefully run a knife around edge of ramekins, turn out onto serving plates and serve with peaches and cream.

Serves 6

Caramelised amaretto peaches with thick cream and macaroons

330g ($1^1/_2$ cups caster sugar)

160ml water

80ml water

4 white peaches, stoned and quartered

1 tbsp unsalted butter

juice of $^1/_2$ lemon

2 tbsp amaretto liqueur

thick cream

macaroon biscuits, to serve

Combine caster sugar and 160ml water in a large saucepan or frying pan and stir over low heat until sugar dissolves. Bring to the boil and cook, without stirring, until mixture is a pale-caramel colour. Remove from heat and add 80ml water (taking care, as mixture will spit). Stir, then return to heat and add peaches in a single layer and cook for 3-5 minutes until they begin to soften, turning and stirring occasionally. Remove from heat and place peaches in 4 serving bowls.

Add butter to caramel with lemon juice and amaretto liqueur and stir until smooth. Pour syrup over warm peaches and serve with thick cream and macaroon biscuits.

Serves 4

Mercado De Encarnación, Seville

Pears

Succulent pears appear in autumn as the weather cools and are perfect raw or cooked.

Choose cinnamon-coloured beurre bosc for long slow cooking. These elegant pears have a long tapering neck and slightly granular flesh that won't become mushy when poached or baked unless overripe.

Shiny green josephine pears have virtually no neck and are squat. They are also classic cooking pears, but choose slightly under-ripe fruit and you'll be rewarded with a superior result. Juicy crisp corellas, named after the glorious parrots, have a red blush on the skin and a delicious, almost tropical flavour; williams (or bartletts), with their white buttery flesh, are used widely for preserving.

Closely related to apples, there are countless varieties to choose from although Williams (which ripen more quickly) and the larger packhams are the most plentiful. Beautifully shaped red sensations have a buttery texture and skin that changes from maroon to bright crimson when the fruit is fully ripe.

Juicy nashis are a more recent variety, originating in Asia. Perfectly round and pale-green, they have very crisp, crunchy, juicy flesh.

Pears are brought to the markets mature, but unripe. It is best to buy them a few days before you want to eat them and leave them in the fruit bowl to ripen at room temperature. Select blemish-free pears, because they ripen from the inside out, the easiest way to test for ripeness is to press the stem end gently, which should give slightly under moderate pressure. They can be stored in the fridge until ready to use. Ripening can be hastened by storing in a brown paper bag with an apple or banana, just as you would with an avocado.

Pears can be substituted for apples in many recipes, and if you are preparing a dish ahead of time with either fruit, sprinkle slices with a little lemon or lime juice to prevent discolouration.

Buttered pears with walnuts and Cointreau

(pictured page 119)

60g butter, chopped

3 beurre bosc pears, halved and cut into
    5mm thick slices

4 tbsp honey

2 tbsp Cointreau

2 tsp orange zest

2 tbsp orange juice

90g (³/₄ cup) walnuts, roasted and
    coarsely chopped

thick cream, to serve

Melt 40g butter in a large frying pan, add half
the pear slices and cook for 2-3 minutes on
each side or until golden. Remove pears and
cook remaining slices, then remove from pan.
Add remaining butter, honey, Cointreau, orange
zest, orange juice and walnuts to pan. Bring
to the boil, stirring continuously, then remove
from heat.

Divide pears among 4 serving bowls, drizzle
with sauce and serve with thick cream.

Serves 4

Salad of Atlantic salmon with crisp nashi, snowpeas and asparagus

Buy deep-fried eschalots at Asian food stores and
store in an airtight container in the fridge.

1 tbsp vegetable oil

salt flakes and cracked black pepper

4 salmon fillets (about 180g each), pin boned

2 bunches asparagus, trimmed and halved

100g snowpeas, trimmed and blanched

4 nashi, thinly sliced

1 cup watercress sprigs

2 witlof, leaves separated

1 cup mixed coriander, basil and mint leaves

deep-fried eschalots, to serve

Dressing

2 tbsp lime juice

1¹/₂ tbsp extra virgin olive oil

3 tsp soy sauce

1 clove garlic, finely chopped

2 tsp ginger, grated

pinch of dried chilli flakes

1 tsp palm (or brown) sugar

For the dressing, combine all the ingredients in a
small bowl and whisk to combine.

Brush salmon lightly with vegetable oil and
season to taste. Heat a large, non-stick frying pan
until hot, add salmon, skin side down, and cook
over medium heat for 2-3 minutes or until skin is
crisp, then turn and cook for another 2-3 minutes
(for medium rare) until cooked to your liking.
Remove and rest for 2-3 minutes then break into
bite-sized pieces.

Boil asparagus in lightly salted water for about
3 minutes. Refresh under cold water and drain.

Combine asparagus, snowpeas, nashi, watercress
and witlof in a large bowl. Add herbs and salmon
and toss gently. Pour dressing over salad and toss
to combine. Top with deep-fried eschalots.

Serves 4

South Melbourne Market

Nashi pears baked in verjuice with cinnamon ice-cream

100ml verjuice

200ml fresh orange juice

thinly peeled rind of 1 orange

$^1/_2$ cup caster sugar

6 nashi pears, peeled

Cinnamon ice-cream

150ml pouring cream

2 cups milk

2 cinnamon sticks

$^1/_2$ tsp ground cinnamon

2 x 1cm-wide strips lemon peel

3 egg yolks

$^3/_4$ cup caster sugar

$^1/_2$ tsp vanilla extract

For the ice-cream, combine cream, milk, cinnamon sticks, ground cinnamon and lemon peel in a saucepan and bring just to a simmer. Remove from heat and stand 30 minutes. Strain. Beat egg yolks, sugar and vanilla until thick and pale, then whisk in strained milk. Transfer mixture to a clean saucepan and cook, stirring constantly, over low heat until mixture thickens enough to coat the back of a wooden spoon. Do not boil. Cool to room temperature. Freeze in an ice-cream maker, according to manufacturer's instructions.

Preheat oven to 180C.

For the pears, combine verjuice, orange juice and rind, sugar and $^3/_4$ cup water in a saucepan and stir over medium heat until sugar dissolves.

Place pears in an ovenproof dish, pour verjuice mixture over, cover and bake for 30-45 minutes (depending on ripeness), until pears are tender. Remove pears from liquid and cool.

Boil verjuice mixture over high heat for 5-8 minutes, until reduced to about 1 cup. Cool.

Serve pears with a little of the verjuice syrup poured over and a scoop of ice-cream.

Serves 6

Poached pears with chocolate sauce

6 pears

$1^1/_2$ cups caster sugar

$1^1/_2$ cups water

juice of $^1/_2$ lemon

6 vanilla ice-cream slices

Chocolate sauce

100g good quality dark cooking chocolate, chopped

150ml pouring cream

100g caster sugar

2 tbsp unsalted butter

$^1/_2$ tsp vanilla extract

Peel pears carefully, leaving stems on.

Combine sugar, water and lemon juice in a large saucepan and bring to the boil over medium heat, stirring until sugar is dissolved. Simmer for 5 minutes. Add pears and simmer for 8-15 minutes or until pears are tender (depending on ripeness of fruit).

Remove pears and cool.

For chocolate sauce, combine chocolate and cream in a bowl over a saucepan of simmering water. Stir until smooth. Add sugar, butter and vanilla and stir until sugar is dissolved. Remove from heat and cool slightly before pouring on pears.

To serve, place pears on a slice of ice-cream and pour over chocolate sauce.

Serves 6

Caramel roasted pears with thick cream and shortbread

6 small buerre bosc pears

1 lemon, juiced and zested

1 vanilla bean, split

3 tbsp sugar

1½ cups thick cream

shortbread biscuits, to serve

Caramel

165g (¾ cup) caster sugar

3 tbsp water

100ml pinot noir

1 tbsp balsamic vinegar

Preheat oven to 200C.

Core pears and place in an ovenproof dish with lemon juice, zest and vanilla bean. Sprinkle with sugar, cover with foil and bake for 15 minutes.

For the caramel, combine sugar and water in a small saucepan over medium heat and stir until sugar dissolves. Bring to the boil, without stirring, until mixture turns a caramel colour. Remove from heat and add pinot noir and vinegar (taking care, as mixture will spit). Stir well over low heat until smooth then pour over pears and bake, uncovered, for a further 30-40 minutes or until pears are soft and cooked.

Pour sauce over pears and serve with thick cream and shortbread biscuits.

Serves 6

Pan-fried pears and quail with white wine and sage

4 jumbo quail, boned and butterflied

4 large sage leaves

4 thin slices spicy pancetta

2 tbsp extra virgin olive oil

3 tbsp dry white wine

80g butter

2 buerre bosc pears, peeled cored and each cut into 8 pieces

50g brown sugar

salt and cracked black pepper

100ml white wine

1 large bunch rocket leaves

Wrap each quail with a slice of pancetta, then secure a sage leaf on top with a toothpick. Heat a large frying pan over medium heat and add olive oil. Cook quail, breast side down, for 3-5 minutes; turn and cook a further 3-4 minutes or until cooked as desired.

Meanwhile, melt butter in a large frying pan over medium heat, then add pears and sugar and stir to combine. Add salt and pepper and toss gently. Add white wine and cook until wine evaporates. Add pears and juices to quail and return to a simmer, then remove from heat and rest, covered, for 3-4 minutes. Serve quail and pears with rocket scattered over and drizzled with pan juices.

Serves 4

Baked pears with vanilla, cloves, cinnamon and marsala

6 small buerre bosc pears, peeled and cored with stalks intact

1 vanilla bean, split

3 whole cloves

1 cinnamon stick

600ml marsala

50g butter

150g (⅔ cup) caster sugar

thick cream, to serve

Preheat oven to 180C.

Place pears in a large baking dish and add vanilla bean, cloves and cinnamon. Pour over marsala. Dot with butter and sprinkle with sugar.

Cover dish with baking paper and foil and bake for 45 minutes; turn pears and continue to bake, basting occasionally, for a further 30-40 minutes or until cooked and tender.

Remove spices and serve pears with pan juices and thick cream.

Serves 6

Pear, parmesan and pecan salad with sultanas

6 corella pears, cored and thinly sliced

juice of $\frac{1}{2}$ lemon

4 tbsp extra virgin olive oil

salt and cracked black pepper

$\frac{1}{3}$ cup (55g) sultanas

5 tbsp red-wine vinegar

sprigs from 1 bunch watercress

100g toasted pecan nuts, coarsely chopped

2 tbsp sour light cream

100g shaved parmesan

Combine pears and lemon juice in a medium-sized bowl, add 1 tablespoon of extra virgin olive oil, salt and pepper and toss gently to coat.

Combine sultanas and 4 tablespoons red-wine vinegar in a small bowl, stir and set aside for 5 minutes then drain.

Scatter watercress sprigs over a large plate and top with pears. Sprinkle with pecans.

Combine sour cream, remaining olive oil, 2 tablespoons water and remaining red-wine vinegar in a small bowl and mix until smooth. Pour dressing over pears, toss gently and scatter with parmesan.

Serves 4-6

Persimmons

Persimmons have been grown in China for thousands of years, before spreading to Japan and South-East Asia. There are two main types, astringent and non-astringent. Astringent varieties cannot be eaten straight from the tree; they must be harvested while still firm and then left to become completely soft. The translucent, gold flesh then becomes jelly-like and will be delicately sweet. Unripe fruit is very bitter. Many have a pointed shape while others can be flattened or squarish.

Non-astringent varieties (also known as Japanese and Chinese persimmons) can be eaten crisp like an apple, straight from the tree, but their flavour will improve if left to mature. The thin skin is delicate and bruises easily. They are often labelled sweet persimmon or fuyu fruit. This variety is round like a tomato and has a mild refreshing flavour.

Persimmons should have no brown patches – look for ones with a fresh, green calyx. Most of these are seedless and can be stored in the fruit bowl for a few days. Persimmons make excellent dried fruit. They can be peeled and dried whole or cut into slices and then dried.

Sweet persimmon and king prawn salad with pecans and balsamic dressing

$^1/_2$ cup (50g) pecan nuts, toasted and coarsely chopped

4 sweet persimmons, peeled and thinly sliced

200g baby rocket leaves

1 large ripe avocado, peeled and sliced

16 large cooked king prawns, shelled and deveined, tails intact

$^1/_2$ cup (100g) ricotta cheese

2 tbsp balsamic vinegar

4 tbsp extra virgin olive oil

salt and cracked black pepper

pinch of caster sugar

Place pecan nuts, persimmons and rocket leaves in a large bowl with avocado. Add king prawns, toss gently and divide salad mixture evenly between 4 serving plates. Crumble over $^1/_2$ cup ricotta cheese.

Combine balsamic vinegar, olive oil, salt and pepper and caster sugar in a small bowl, whisk well and drizzle over salads.

Serves 4 as an entree

Sweet persimmon wedges with rosewater creme caramel

Creme caramel is always popular, and this variation is perfect with the tangy persimmons. Also great with fresh strawberries when persimmons are not in season.

165g caster sugar

$^1/_4$ cup water

3 eggs

2 egg yolks

55g caster sugar, extra

1 tbsp rosewater

pinch of salt

$1^1/_2$ cups pouring cream

2 cups milk

4-6 sweet persimmons, depending on size

Preheat oven to 160C.

Combine sugar and water in a saucepan and stir over low heat until sugar dissolves. Increase heat and boil, without stirring, until mixture is a caramel colour. Pour into six 175ml ramekins.

Whisk eggs, yolks, extra sugar, rosewater and salt until combined.

Combine cream and milk in a saucepan and bring just to the boil.

Whisk cream mixture into egg mixture, then pour evenly among prepared ramekins.

Place ramekins in a large baking dish and pour enough hot water to come halfway up the sides of the dishes. Bake for 30 minutes or until custard is just set. Remove ramekins from baking dish, cool to room temperature, then cover and refrigerate for at least 6 hours or overnight.

To serve, remove stalk and peel persimmons then cut into wedges. Carefully run a knife around the edge of ramekins and turn out onto serving plates. Serve persimmon wedges on the side.

Serves 6

Pineapples

There are many varieties of sweet tropical pineapple and hundreds of uses for its juicy flesh, but they are not usually sold by variety in the markets. They are more often classified as smooth-leafed or rough-leafed: the small rough ones are particularly sweet with deep-golden flesh while the smooth ones are very juicy when ripe, but not as sweet.

Pineapples contain bromelin, an enzyme that breaks down protein. Don't try to make gelatine-based desserts with raw pineapple – it needs to be cooked first to neutralise the enzyme before you can make jellies and custards.

Your nose is the best judge when buying pineapple, as they should have a rich tropical aroma and will not ripen any further after picking. They may soften and turn golden, but do not get sweeter. Store them at room temperature briefly and eat as soon as possible. Peeled sliced pineapple can be stored in the fridge for 2-3 days.

To prepare a pineapple, cut off the ends, stand upright and slice off the spiky skin. Then quarter and remove the tough core from each wedge.

Pork and pineapple skewers with lemongrass rice

400g pork fillet, cut into 2cm pieces

1 red capsicum, deseeded and cut into 2cm pieces

$^1/_2$ medium-sized pineapple, peeled, cored and cut into 2cm pieces

2 red onions, peeled and cut into 4 wedges

1 x 250ml tin mild satay sauce

300g (1$^1/_2$ cups) long-grain rice

2 sticks lemongrass (white part only), bruised

Soak 12 long bamboo skewers in cold water for 10-15 minutes. Divide pork, capsicum, pineapple and red onion evenly and thread onto skewers. Place skewers in a large ceramic dish and pour satay sauce over, turning to coat. Rest, covered, in the fridge for 20-30 minutes.

Heat a greased barbecue plate and lightly spray skewers with cooking oil to prevent sticking. Cook, turning occasionally, for 8-10 minutes or until cooked as desired.

Meanwhile, cook rice and lemongrass in 3 cups boiling water for 12 minutes. Rest covered for 3-4 minutes. Remove lemongrass and serve with pineapple skewers.

Serves 4

Honey roasted pineapple with macadamia nuts

(pictured page 127)

6 slices fresh ripe pineapple, 1cm thick

1 vanilla bean, split lengthways

1 cup warm honey

$^1/_2$ tsp ground cardamom or ginger

50g ($^1/_3$ cup) macadamia nuts, toasted and chopped

thick cream to serve

Cut pineapple slices in half crosswise and place in a single layer in a shallow ovenproof dish. Scrape seeds from vanilla bean into honey and add vanilla bean. Pour honey mixture over pineapple, sprinkle with cardamom and roast at 180C for 10 minutes. Turn slices to coat in juice and roast for another 10-15 minutes or until pineapple is soft. Cool.

Serve pineapple with some of the juices poured over and sprinkle with macadamia nuts.

Serve with thick cream.

Serves 4

Pineappple and winter fruit pudding

4 slices fresh pineapple, peeled, cored and
    quartered

2 small pears, peeled, cored and cut in 6 pieces

2 small apples, peeled, cored and cut into 6 pieces

4 thick sticks rhubarb, cut into 4cm pieces

1 cup firmly packed brown sugar

1 vanilla bean, split

zest of 1 orange

Topping

80g soft butter

125g caster sugar

1 tsp vanilla extract

1 egg

1 tsp ground cinnamon

280g self-raising flour, sifted

pinch of salt

1 cup milk

Preheat oven to 180C.

Combine pineapple, pears, apples and rhubarb in a large bowl and add sugar, vanilla bean, orange zest and mix well. Transfer to an ovenproof dish and bake for 40 minutes, until fruit is cooked.

Strain fruit, reserving juices, discard vanilla bean and cook juices over medium heat until reduced by half. Spoon fruit into a large pie dish and pour reduced juices over fruit.

For the topping, beat butter and sugar in a medium-sized bowl until thick and pale then add vanilla, egg and cinnamon. Fold in flour and salt. Stir in milk until smooth and spoon topping over fruit. Bake for 25-35 minutes or until golden and cooked.

Serves 4-6

Caramelised pineapple with spiced syrup and ice-cream

300g (1^1/$_3$ cups) caster sugar

thinly peeled strip of lemon rind

1 star anise

2 cloves

1 vanilla bean, split lengthways

1 pineapple

1 tbsp butter

ice-cream, to serve

Combine 220g (1 cup) sugar with lemon rind, spices, scraped seeds from vanilla bean and the bean with ^{1}/$_2$ cup of water in a small saucepan and stir over medium heat until sugar dissolves. Remove from heat and cool.

Peel pineapple, cut small grooves in spiral to remove eyes, then cut into 1cm thick slices. Sprinkle slices of fruit with remaining sugar. Melt butter in a non-stick pan and cook pineapple in batches until lightly caramelised. Transfer to a flat dish, pour over cooled syrup and cool to room temperature.

Serve with vanilla ice-cream.

Serves 4-6

Plums

The final burst of summer is the perfect time to buy plump, juicy plums as early in the season they can be marred by tart skin and sour flesh. There are many varieties, but plums can be divided into two main groups, those that are sweet and juicy for eating fresh and those with tougher skin and drier flesh that cook beautifully.

European types are used for drying and preserving, while Japanese plums, which are actually varieties from China, can be used in cooking or eaten fresh. These include all the blood plums and are generally heart-shaped or round.

Choose plums that yield to gentle pressure (a sign of ripeness) to ensure best flavour. The fruit should not have wrinkled or split skin. Store them in the crisper of the fridge or in an unsealed plastic bag in the fridge.

If the skin is too tart for your liking, peel by splitting along the natural groove of the fruit and pouring boiling water over them for a few minutes, then dip in cold water before removing the skin.

Quick little plum tarts with almond cream

2 tbsp flaked almonds

120g soft butter

130g ($^2/_3$ cup) brown sugar

4-6 very ripe plums, cut into 6 wedges

2 sheets puff pastry, thawed

250ml thickened cream, whipped lightly

Preheat oven to 200C.

Place almonds on a baking sheet lined with foil and toast for about 5 minutes, until golden. Remove and cool.

Cream butter and brown sugar with an electric mixer until thick, then spread mixture evenly between 4 x 10cm non-stick, lightly greased tart tins and place plum wedges on top to cover.

Using thawed pastry, cut rounds to cover tops of tart tins, place over plums and press edges to seal. Cut a small slit in the centre of each tart for steam to escape and bake for 15-18 minutes or until pastry is golden brown and cooked.

To serve, run a small sharp knife around the edge of pastry, place a plate on top of each tart and invert quickly and remove tin.

Combine cream with the toasted almonds and serve a dollop on the side of each tart.

Serves 4

Vanilla poached plums

250ml (1 cup) red wine

165g (³/₄ cup) caster sugar

1 vanilla bean, split

1 strip lemon rind

8 large plums, halved

Combine red wine, sugar, vanilla bean and lemon rind with 1¹/₂ cups water in a large saucepan and stir over medium heat until sugar is dissolved. Cook for 3 minutes. Add plums and simmer for 5-8 minutes or until plums are tender. Remove from heat and cool in liquid.

Serve at room temperature with juices spooned over and accompanied by vanilla ice-cream.

Serves 4

Upside-down plum cake (tarte tatin)

Base

125g butter

1¹/₂ cups brown sugar

8-12 plums, halved and stoned

Cake

125g soft butter

1 cup caster sugar

2 eggs

1¹/₂ cups self-raising flour, sifted

1 tsp vanilla extract

¹/₃ cup milk

Preheat oven to 190C.

Grease a 24cm springform pan and line base with baking paper.

Combine butter and brown sugar in a saucepan over low heat and stir until sugar is dissolved. Pour the mixture into the base of the cake tin and arrange plums on top.

For the cake, place all the ingredients in a large bowl and beat with electric beaters until well combined. Spoon the mixture over the plums. Bake for 50-60 minutes or until cooked when tested with a cake skewer.

Invert the cake onto a serving platter and serve with vanilla ice-cream.

Serves 6-8

Ginger-roasted plums with vanilla yoghurt

Ginger preserved in syrup is available at large supermarkets

2 tsp soft butter

8 firm ripe plums

¹/₃ cup caster sugar

¹/₄ cup ginger syrup

¹/₄ cup water

6 pieces ginger in syrup, coarsely chopped

1 cup vanilla yoghurt, to serve

Preheat oven to 190C.

Smear soft butter over the base of a shallow ovenproof dish. Lightly score plums along the natural groove and place in the buttered dish.

In a small bowl, combine sugar, ginger syrup and water and mix well. Pour sugar mixture over plums, cover with foil and roast for 25-30 minutes (depending on ripeness) or until tender.

Serve warm plums with some of the cooking juices poured over, topped with chopped ginger and vanilla yoghurt on the side.

Serves 4

Pomegranates

Pomegranates (also called Chinese apples) have a festive air about them and are easily identified in the markets by their glossy garnet skin and small crown. The crimson juice that bursts from the jewel-like seeds makes a stunning addition to many dishes. Yet this robust fruit with its leathery skin is often overlooked because people aren't sure about how to eat them.

The tough rind encases numerous ruby-red seeds, which are divided by walls of spongy, bitter pith. To remove the seeds, cut away the top and bottom of the fruit and then carefully detach the seeds from the membrane. If the glossy seeds don't appeal, pomegranate juice can be made by briefly whizzing the seeds in a food processor, but be careful not to over process or the juice can become tannic. The seeds can also be pushed through a sieve or muslin bag.

The tart, tangy juice is used in flavourings and colourings and has long been the source of grenadine syrup, which is used in cocktails. Pomegranate syrup adds a mild astringency to dishes and is simple to make by boiling the fresh juice with a little caster sugar and lemon juice until reduced to a thick concentrate.

Buy large, bright, shiny fruit that is smooth and feels heavy for its size. Avoid any with dull, wrinkled skin and check the crown; there should be no signs of rot and the skin should not be broken.

When hairline cracks appear in the waxy skin, the fruit is perfectly ripe. Pomegranates will keep for several weeks in the fridge.

Pomegranate marinated chicken with lemon and couscous

3 cloves garlic, finely chopped

1 tsp cumin seeds, toasted

1 tsp sweet paprika

$^1/_2$ tsp dried chilli flakes (or to taste)

$^1/_4$ cup mint

$^1/_4$ cup coriander, chopped

2 tbsp lemon juice

$^1/_2$ cup pomegranate juice (about 1 large ripe pomegranate)

$^1/_4$ cup olive oil

sea salt and cracked black pepper

4 chicken marylands

seeds of 1 pomegranate

couscous and lemon wedges, to serve

Preheat oven to 200C.

Combine garlic, cumin, paprika, chilli flakes and herbs in a food processor until smooth. Add lemon and pomegranate juice, olive oil, sea salt and pepper to taste and process until smooth.

Pour marinade over chicken and turn to coat. Cover and refrigerate for at least 2-3 hours or overnight.

Roast chicken skin-side down, covered, for 30 minutes, then turn and roast uncovered for a further 20 minutes or until cooked. Rest in a warm place for 5 minutes.

Serve with lemon wedges and couscous.

Serves 4

Roasted leg of lamb with pomegranate and herb sauce and crisp potatoes

1 leg of lamb (about 2.5kg)

3 tbsp extra virgin olive oil

salt and cracked black pepper

2 tsp mixed dried herbs

6 small desiree potatoes, peeled and halved

Sauce

2 medium-sized pomegranates

100ml pomegranate molasses

150ml extra virgin olive oil

1 tbsp oregano, chopped

3 eschalots, peeled and finely chopped

2 tsp caster sugar

Preheat oven to 200C.

Rub lamb with 1 tablespoon olive oil, salt and pepper and sprinkle with mixed herbs. Heat 2 tablespoons of oil in a large ovenproof dish over medium heat and brown lamb on all sides. Place in oven and roast for 45 minutes. Add potatoes and roast for a further 30-45 minutes, turning potatoes occasionally, until lamb is cooked as desired and potatoes are crisp and tender. Remove and rest covered in a warm place for 10 minutes.

For the sauce, cut pomegranates in half and squeeze seeds and juice into a bowl. Add pomegranate molasses, olive oil, oregano, eschalots, sugar and salt and pepper and stir well. Serve lamb with pomegranate sauce, roasted potatoes and green salad leaves.

Serves 6

Summer salad of tomato, radish and cucumber with pomegranate dressing

1 cos lettuce, trimmed and sliced

3 ripe tomatoes, coarsely chopped

6 red radishes, sliced

2 Lebanese cucumbers, sliced

6 green onions, sliced

1 cup watercress sprigs

1 cup flat-leaf parsley, torn

$^1\!/_2$ cup mint leaves, coarsely chopped

1 round of pita bread, toasted

Dressing

2 tsp pomegranate molasses

$^1\!/_2$ tsp salt

2 cloves garlic, finely chopped

cracked black pepper

$^1\!/_2$ cup extra virgin olive oil

$^1\!/_4$ cup lemon juice

good pinch of sugar

$^1\!/_2$ tsp sumac

For the dressing, combine all the ingredients in a small bowl and whisk to combine.

Place vegetables and herbs in a large salad bowl and toss gently. Break bread into bite-sized pieces and add to salad. Pour over dressing and toss gently.

Serves 6

Roasted spatchcock with pomegranate, chilli and date salad

4 spatchcock (halved with backbone removed)

juice of 1 lemon

6$^1\!/_2$ tbsp extra virgin olive oil

2 tsp butter

salt and cracked black pepper

2 tsp paprika

$^1\!/_2$ bunch coriander leaves, coarsely chopped

$^1\!/_2$ bunch mint leaves

6 fresh dates, seeded and cut into quarters

1 large pomegranate, juiced and $^1\!/_2$ the seeds reserved

Preheat oven to 200C.

Place spatchcocks on a tray, drizzle with half the lemon juice and 2 tablespoons of olive oil, season with salt and pepper and turn to coat. Cover with plastic wrap and refrigerate for 30-60 minutes. Turn spatchcocks skin-side-up and sprinkle each half with paprika. Reserve marinating liquid.

Heat a lightly oiled, non-stick pan over medium-high heat, add butter and 2 teaspoons olive oil and sear spatchcocks, skin-side-down, until browned, then remove to a lightly greased oven tray and place skin-side-up. Roast for 10 minutes then baste with remaining marinade and roast a further 10-12 minutes or until cooked and tender.

For the salad, combine coriander, mint, dates and chilli in a medium-sized bowl.

In a small bowl, whisk pomegranate juice, remaining olive oil and remaining lemon juice, salt and pepper.

Pour about one-third of the dressing over salad and toss to combine.

To serve, place 2 spatchcock halves on top of one another, drizzle with remaining dressing, top with salad and sprinkle with pomegranate seeds.

Serves 4

Quince

In some European and Asian countries, quinces are eaten raw and dipped in salt as a snack, but many people find them far too mouth-puckering in their natural state. Closely related to the apple and pear, the fragrant quince is botanically a pome, a member of the rose family. Once cooked, it turns an alluring rose-pink and the grainy flesh becomes soft and delicately sweet with a musky aroma.

Quinces are not commonly sold by variety, but you can always ask your greengrocer for the smaller smyrna variety, as they are better suited to slow cooking. The other main variety is the pineapple quince, named because it smells not unlike pineapple when fresh.

Quinces have a hard skin, but still bruise easily so need to be handled with care. They do not soften as they ripen and should be checked for brown spots and any small holes, which often indicate the presence of a tiny grub. Because of their high pectin content, they are ideal for making jams and jellies – for best results choose slightly under-ripe specimens, lime-yellow but not golden. The fuzzy down disappears as the fruit ripens, and the fruit discolours on cutting so if you are pan-frying wedges to serve with meat, first drop the peeled slices into a dish of acidulated water (water with lemon juice).

Keep at room temperature for up to a week and, if storing in the fridge for longer, in a sealed plastic bag to prevent the aroma permeating the other foodstuffs.

quince

Roasted quince with spiced syrup and vanilla bean ice-cream

(pictured page 139)

500g sugar

3 large quinces, peeled and halved

1/2 crumbled cinnamon stick

10-12 coriander seeds

thinly peeled rind of 1/2 orange

thinly peeled rind of 1/2 lemon

1 star anise

vanilla bean ice-cream, to serve

Combine sugar with 1 litre water in a saucepan and stir over medium heat until sugar dissolves. Place quince in a single layer in a large baking dish, scatter with cinnamon stick, coriander seeds, orange rind, lemon rind and star anise. Cover tightly with foil and roast at 180C for 2 hours, basting occasionally. Remove foil and baste well. Roast for a further 30-45 minutes, basting frequently, until fruit is a deep-pink and tender. Using a slotted spoon, transfer quince to 6 bowls. Pour syrup into a saucepan and boil over high heat until reduced to 1 1/2 cups. Spoon syrup over quince and serve with a scoop of vanilla bean ice-cream.

Serves 6

Poached quince with buttermilk puddings and vanilla syrup

750g caster sugar

2 large quinces (about 1kg), peeled and cut into 1cm-thick slices

1 vanilla bean, split lengthways

Buttermilk puddings

20g powdered gelatine

2 1/2 cups pouring cream

1 cup caster sugar

400ml buttermilk

2 tsp vanilla extract

Combine sugar and 1 litre water in a large saucepan and stir over medium heat until sugar dissolves. Add quince and vanilla bean and simmer gently, partially covered, over very low heat for 90-120 minutes or until quince is tender and a deep-pink colour, then remove from heat. Using a slotted spoon, transfer quince to a heatproof bowl. Simmer cooking juices over medium heat for 10-15 minutes or until thick and syrupy, then remove from heat and strain through a fine sieve over quince.

For the buttermilk puddings, sprinkle gelatine over 1/4 cup of very hot water and stir until gelatine dissolves. Combine cream, sugar and buttermilk in a double saucepan or heatproof bowl over a pan of simmering water and stir until mixture is warm and sugar has dissolved. Remove from heat and stir in vanilla extract and gelatine mixture until well combined.

Pour into six 200ml dariole moulds that have been rinsed with cold water and refrigerate, covered, for 4 hours or overnight until set.

To serve, turn puddings out onto plates and serve with quince and vanilla syrup to the side.

Serves 6

Quince tarte tatin

125g unsalted butter

125g caster sugar

250g plain flour

4 egg yolks

1 tsp vanilla extract

Filling

2 large quinces, peeled, cored and sliced

275g caster sugar

80g unsalted butter

Preheat oven to 190C.

For the pastry, combine butter, sugar and flour in a food processor until mixture resembles coarse breadcrumbs. Add egg yolks, vanilla extract and 1 tablespoon of chilled water and process until mixture just comes together. Turn out on a lightly floured work surface and knead lightly until smooth. Wrap in plastic wrap and refrigerate for 30 minutes.

Roll out to about 1 centimetre thickness and cut a circle to fit the top of a 22-24cm frying pan with an ovenproof handle. Rest pastry on a baking sheet in the refrigerator until ready to use.

For the filling, poach quince with 110g sugar in enough water to cover for 15-20 minutes. Drain. Melt butter in the frying pan and add remaining caster sugar. Arrange quince slices in pan, packing them in tightly. Heat gently on low heat on top of stove for about 20 minutes or until caramelised. Let cool a little.

Place pastry on top of quince and bake for 15-20 minutes or until crust is golden and cooked through. Cool in pan before inverting onto serving dish.

Serve warm or at room temperature with custard or mascarpone.

Serves 6

Quince and apple crumble

1kg quinces, peeled, cored and cut into wedges

330g (1^1/$_2$ cups) caster sugar

750g granny smith apples, peeled, cored and cut into wedges

Topping

75g (^{1}/$_2$ cup) self-raising flour

100g (^{1}/$_2$ cup) brown sugar

1 tsp lemon zest

^{1}/$_4$ tsp ground nutmeg

45g (^{1}/$_2$ cup) rolled oats

100g butter

Preheat oven to 180C.

Combine quince, sugar and ^{3}/$_4$ cup water in a large saucepan and simmer, partly covered for about 1 hour or until tender and pink. Add apples and stir to combine. Simmer fruit, uncovered, for about 10 minutes or until apples are cooked.

Combine all topping ingredients except butter in a medium-sized bowl. Rub butter into mixture until it resembles coarse breadcrumbs.

Spoon fruit and juices into a shallow, lightly greased ovenproof dish and spread topping mixture evenly over the top.

Bake for 30 minutes or until topping is golden-brown.

Serves 6

Rhubarb

Rhubarb is a vegetable that is usually cooked as a fruit and is an old-fashioned favourite enjoying a resurgence with top chefs. Its earthy flavour marries well with other fruits, creamy desserts, crumbles, pastries and spices.

Field-grown rhubarb is usually a deeper red, tougher, juicier and more sour than that grown in greenhouses which has a softer texture. Look for slender, plump stalks that are deep pink and crisp. Reject green stalks, which lack sweetness and the tart earthiness of the magenta stems.

Keep stems in a plastic bag or an airtight container in the fridge and use within a few days.

Rhubarb freezes well so, when it is cheap, chop into lengths and freeze in sealed bags or an airtight container. Cooked rhubarb keeps in the refrigerator for 5-6 days.

Before using remove the toxic leaves, which contain high levels of oxalic acid, and trim the base of each stalk. It is high in acid, so use stainless-steel saucepans and ceramic ovenproof dishes.

Use just a little water when cooking, as rhubarb has plenty of moisture of its own.

Kingston Farmers Market, Highett

Stewed rhubarb with apple and cinnamon

3 granny smith apples, peeled and thinly
    sliced

³/₄ cup water

1 cinnamon stick

1 strip lemon peel

2 bunches rhubarb, trimmed and cut into
    4-5cm lengths

¹/₂ cup caster sugar

light cream, to serve

Place apples, water, cinnamon stick and lemon peel in a large saucepan and bring to the boil over medium heat. Reduce heat and simmer for 8-10 minutes, stirring occasionally. Add rhubarb and cook a further 5-6 minutes or until rhubarb is just tender. Remove cinnamon stick and lemon peel and serve warm or at room temperature with cream.

Serves 6

Rhubarb and strawberry compote with Russian Pashka

2 bunches rhubarb (about 600g each), leaves
    discarded

2 tbsp water

110g (¹/₂cup) caster sugar

250g (1 punnet) strawberries, hulled and halved

Russian Pashka

750g ricotta cheese, well drained

125g unsalted butter, softened

100ml cream

3 eggs

110g (¹/₂ cup) sugar

85g (¹/₂ cup) raisins

150g glace apricots, chopped

150g glace figs, chopped

150g flaked almonds, toasted

2 tsp rose flower water

2 tsp orange rind, finely grated

1 tsp vanilla essence

olive oil

For the pashka, beat the ricotta, butter and cream in a large bowl until very smooth. Beat the eggs and sugar until thick and pale. Gradually beat egg mixture into cheese mixture until well combined. Fold in remaining ingredients until evenly distributed. Spoon the mixture into a lightly oiled 1.5 litre mould. Cover with plastic wrap, place a plate on top and then a weight. Refrigerate overnight.

Cut rhubarb into 3-4cm pieces and place in a saucepan with water and sugar. Bring to a simmer over low heat and cook, covered, for about 3 minutes or until rhubarb is tender. Add strawberries and simmer for a further 3-4 minutes. Remove from heat and cool.

Turn pashka out onto a serving platter and cut into slices.

Serve with rhubarb on the side.

Serves 8

Rhubarb custards with coconut macaroons

800g rhubarb, washed and chopped

220g (1 cup) caster sugar (or to taste)

2 cups homemade or bought custard

1 cup pouring cream, whipped

1/2 cup mascarpone

1 tbsp caster sugar, extra

coconut macaroons, to serve

Preheat oven to 200C.

Cook rhubarb with sugar in a saucepan over low heat, stirring occasionally, for about 5 minutes or until just tender, but still holding its shape. Cool.

Combine custard, cream and mascarpone and stir until smooth. Layer individual ramekins or souffle dishes with rhubarb and custard mixture. Sprinkle each with extra sugar and bake for 5-10 minutes or until tops are golden.

Serve warm or at room temperature with macaroons.

Serves 8

Poached rhubarb and chocolate brownies with honey mascarpone

2 bunches rhubarb

1 orange

2-3 tbsp honey

1 tbsp water

Brownies

440g (2 cups) caster sugar

4 eggs

225g (1 1/2 cups) plain flour, sifted

1/4 tsp salt

2 1/2 tbsp cocoa powder

150g butter, melted

1 tbsp Tia Maria

90g (3/4 cup) toasted cashew nuts, chopped

1 cup mascarpone

3 tbsp honey

Preheat oven to 160C.

For the brownies, beat sugar and eggs in a large bowl until thick and pale, then fold in sifted flour and salt. Combine cocoa and butter and stir until smooth, then fold cocoa mixture into a greased, square 25cm cake tin and bake for 45-55 minutes, or until cooked when tested with a skewer.

Cool in tin.

Cut leaves from rhubarb and discard. Cut stalks into 3-4cm pieces. Finely grate the rind from the orange and then juice the fruit. Combine rhubarb, 1 teaspoon orange rind, 1/4 cup orange juice and honey in a large saucepan with 1 tablespoon water. Bring to a simmer over medium heat. Cover and cook for 5-8 minutes, stirring occasionally, or until rhubarb is tender but still holding its shape. Cool.

Combine mascarpone and honey in a bowl and stir well.

Cut brownies into squares, place in the centre of serving plates and top with a dollop of mascarpone. Serve rhubarb on the side.

Serves 8

Starfruit

Properly named carambola, thirst-quenching starfruit or 'five-corners' is ideal as a garnish or in fruit salads. In many Asian countries, the half-ripe fruit are dipped in salt before eating. The thin, waxy skin becomes yellow when ripe and the fruit is very juicy with a mild, sweet flavour.

Starfruit bruise easily, so handle with care. Choose firm fruit with a clean, crisp appearance and store at room temperature, where they will continue to ripen.

The fruit only needs to be washed, not peeled. Buy green starfruit for cooking (when acting as a souring agent) or eating as a snack. Carambola are a good source of vitamin C and potassium. And they are fabulous sliced and piled on pavlova.

Starfruit with coconut-sugar sauce and sago pudding

60g unsalted butter

100g coconut-sugar (available from Asian food
   stores), cut into pieces

400ml pouring cream

6 ripe starfruit, sliced

sago pudding

175g(1 cup) sago

1 litre coconut milk

220g (1cup) caster sugar

1 tsp vanilla extract

For the pudding, rinse sago under cold water and drain. Combine coconut milk, sugar and 2 cups water in a saucepan and stir over medium heat until sugar dissolves. Add sago and bring to the boil, stirring constantly. Reduce heat to low and cook, stirring frequently for 15-20 minutes or until sago is soft and transparent, then stir in vanilla.

Melt butter in a saucepan over medium heat, add coconut sugar and stir until sugar dissolves. Add cream and simmer, stirring frequently, over low heat for 5 minutes or until sauce is thickened. Strain and cool.

To serve, pour a little coconut-sugar sauce into 6 shallow bowls, top with starfruit and serve sago pudding on the side.

Serves 6

Tropical fruit salad with vanilla bean ice-cream

During summer this light and luscious recipe can be varied according to the tropical fruits available. For a quick, healthy dessert serve with low-fat ice-cream.

2 starfruit, sliced

2 kiwifruit, peeled and sliced

1 red papaya, seeded and cut into wedges

12 lychees, peeled and seeded

1 ripe mango, peeled, seeded and sliced

2 large white peaches, peeled and sliced

juice of 2 limes

vanilla bean ice-cream, to serve

Combine all the fruit in a large bowl, drizzle over lime juice and toss gently to combine.

Serves with scoops of vanilla bean ice-cream.

Serves 6

Tamarillos

Tart and tangy egg-shaped tamarillos hang from a small, attractive tree. This exotic fruit has satin skin that is usually crimson or golden, but the red variety is most favoured because of its bold tropical flavour and jelly-like flesh dotted with purple-black seeds.

The more mellow-flavoured golden variety is appearing increasingly in the markets. This fruit can be eaten fresh or cooked, but the astringent skin is not edible so peel with a sharp knife. Alternatively, snip off the stalk, cut a small cross in the base, cover with boiling water for a minute or two, refresh under cold water and slip off the skin.

Choose shiny vibrant fruit that yields to gentle pressure. The stem should be firmly attached; avoid any with black spots. Store in a fruit bowl and refrigerate when ripe. A slightly loose calyx means the fruit is ripe and ready to eat.

Vanilla-scented tamarillos with vanilla panna cotta

6 ripe tamarillos
110g ($^1/_2$ cup) caster sugar
vanilla bean, split

For the panna cotta
750ml pouring cream
220g (1 cup) caster sugar
125ml milk
1 tbsp powdered gelatine
2 tbsp hot water
1 tbsp vanilla extract
2 tbsp amaretto

Cut a small cross in the base of each tamarillo. Place fruit, sugar and vanilla bean in a large saucepan and add water to cover. Bring to the boil and simmer for 3-5 minutes or until fruit is just tender. Remove and, when cool enough to handle, peel and cut in half.

For the panna cotta, combine cream, sugar and milk in a medium-sized saucepan over low heat, bring almost to the boil and stir until sugar dissolves. Remove from heat. Sprinkle gelatine over hot water in a small cup, then stand cup in a saucepan of simmering water and stir until gelatine dissolves. Pour dissolved gelatine into cream mixture and stir well to combine. Cool slightly, add vanilla extract and amaretto and stir well again. Divide cream mixture between 6 x 150ml moulds that have been rinsed in cold water, cover and refrigerate until set. To remove panna cotta, dip moulds in hot water for a few seconds. Serve with tamarillos and a little of the juices poured over the dessert.

Serves 6

Pink peppercorn pavlova with tamarillos and raspberries

4 egg whites
330g (1$^1/_2$ cups) caster sugar
1 tsp vanilla extract
1 tsp white vinegar
1 tbsp cornflour, sifted
2 tsp schinus pink peppercorns, crushed *
2 red tamarillos
2 yellow tamarillos
375ml (1$^1/_2$ cups) pouring cream, whipped
2 punnets fresh raspberries

Preheat oven to 180C.

To make the pavlova, using an electric mixer, beat egg whites and a pinch of salt until soft peaks form, then add $^1/_4$ cup of sugar and beat for about 3 minutes until sugar dissolves. Add remaining sugar, $^1/_4$ cup at a time, beating until it dissolves before adding the next addition. Beat until mixture is smooth and glossy. Add vanilla and vinegar and beat until combined. Fold in cornflour and peppercorns and spread mixture into a 15x20cm rectangle on a greased baking-paper-lined oven tray.

Reduce temperature to 120C and bake pavlova for 1 hour. Turn oven off and leave to cool in oven.

Cut a small cross in the base of tamarillos and plunge into boiling water for a minute. Remove and refresh in iced water. Drain and peel skins. Slice.

To serve, spoon whipped cream over pavlova and top with tamarillo slices and fresh raspberries.

Serves 4-6

* Schinus pink peppercorns have a sweet, pine-like flavour and are available from specialist spice shops. Pink peppercorns in brine are not suitable for this recipe.

Vegetables

Top left, garlic, Campo de Fiori, Rome
Bottom left, Bangkok Central Market
Above: Pak choy, Salamanca Market, Hobart
Right, Richard Lenoir markets, Paris

Artichokes

They look like thistles and the prickly choke is inedible, but artichokes are irresistible marinated in good olive oil and tossed through risotto or pasta.

Globe artichokes originally grew wild around the Mediterranean coastline, where the huge unopened flowers were used as decoration and for medicinal purposes.

Long claimed to be aphrodisiacs, there are two main types – those with round green leaves and those with purple spiky ones although they taste similar. The heart of the artichoke and base of the leaves become very tender and succulent when cooked, but avoid the hairy dry choke in the centre.

Globe artichokes should not be confused with Jerusalem artichokes, which are not actually artichokes but knobbly tubers belonging to the sunflower family.

Select globe artichokes that look bright and fresh, as shrivelled or brown mottled leaves become quite bitter once cooked. The stem should be firm and the leaves tightly closed – partially opened leaves indicate the artichoke was picked some time ago. It is best to purchase small- to medium-sized specimens, as the large ones are often woody. Store them unwashed in the crisper of the fridge and prepare just before using.

When preparing artichokes to eat, use a sharp knife to remove the tough outer leaves and, if they are pointy and prickly, snip off the tops as well. Remove the hairy choke in the centre and trim and peel the stem. Once cut, artichokes discolour, so place them in a bowl of acidulated water (water with lemon juice added). Alternatively, rub the cut surfaces with lemon.

Note: artichokes should not be cooked in aluminium or cast-iron pans or wrapped in foil, as they will become an unappetising grey colour with an unpleasant taste.

Mozzarella, artichoke and pancetta mini pizzas

(pictured page 153)

4 tbsp extra virgin olive oil

4 x 16cm pizza bases

4 tbsp tomato paste

200g buffalo mozzarella, sliced

340g jar marinated artichoke hearts, drained
    and coarsely chopped

8 slices spicy pancetta (about 160g), chopped

salt and cracked black pepper

2 cups baby rocket leaves

1 cup shaved parmesan

Preheat oven to 230C.

Place baking tray in oven. Brush individual pizza bases generously with extra virgin olive oil. Spread each with 1 tablespoon tomato paste. Sprinkle buffalo mozzarella over bases. Scatter with artichoke hearts. Scatter spicy pancetta over artichokes. Season with salt and pepper. Place individual pizzas on the hot oven tray and bake for about 10-12 minutes or until cooked. Remove and scatter tops with baby rocket leaves and shaved parmesan.

Serve hot.

Serves 4

Risotto with artichokes and fresh green peas

4 small young artichokes, prepared and trimmed

2 tbsp olive oil

2 cloves garlic, finely chopped

sea salt and cracked black pepper

5 tbsp butter

1 medium-sized onion, finely chopped

400g (2 cups) arborio rice

200ml ($^3/_4$ cup) dry white wine

1.5-1.8 litres hot chicken stock

300g fresh peas, podded to produce about 1 cup

80g parmesan, grated

extra shaved parmesan

Cut artichokes into quarters and slice thinly. Heat olive oil in a frying pan and add artichokes and garlic and cook over low heat for 5 minutes, stirring continuously. Add cold water to just cover artichokes, season with salt and pepper and simmer for about 10-12 minutes until water has evaporated.

Melt 3 tablespoons butter in a large, heavy-based saucepan and add onion. Stir over medium heat until onion is pale-yellow. Add rice and stir until coated with the butter. Add wine and stir.

Cook, stirring constantly until wine has evaporated. Stir in 2 ladles of chicken stock or enough to cover rice. Stir over medium heat until stock has been absorbed.

When rice is half cooked, add peas and artichokes. Continue cooking, stirring and adding stock a ladle at a time, until rice is cooked but firm to the bite, about 15-20 minutes. Stir in remaining butter and grated parmesan. Check seasoning.

Serve with extra shaved parmesan.

Serves 4

Braised lamb shanks and artichokes

8 globe artichokes

juice of 1 lemon

2 tbsp olive oil

8 lamb shanks, trimmed

1 brown onion, coarsely chopped

2 cloves garlic, chopped

1 carrot, peeled and coarsely chopped

1 stick celery, sliced

1$^1/_2$ cups chicken stock

1 sprig thyme

$^1/_4$ tsp ground cumin

150g chickpeas, soaked in water overnight,
  then drained

3 sprigs flat-leaf parsley, torn

$^1/_4$ preserved lemon rind, finely chopped

mashed potato, to serve (optional)

Preheat oven to 160C.

Trim artichokes, remove hairy chokes and place in a bowl of water with lemon juice to prevent discolouration. Heat olive oil in a large roasting pan or ovenproof dish and cook lamb shanks, in batches, until browned all over. Remove shanks and discard all but 2 tablespoons of fat from pan. Add onion, garlic, carrot and celery and cook over low heat until soft. Stir in stock, thyme and cumin and season to taste. Bring to the boil, replace lamb shanks and add chickpeas, then cover and braise for 60 minutes.

Drain artichokes, add to lamb and cook, covered, for a further 30-45 minutes or until lamb is very tender. Serve sprinkled with chopped parsley and preserved lemon and accompanied by mashed potato.

Serves 4

Artichoke, scallop and potato salad with lemon

1 thin-skinned lemon (eg: meyer), washed

1 tbsp sea salt

4 globe artichokes

750g kipfler potatoes, scrubbed

100g whole almonds, toasted

4 sprigs flat-leaf parsley, torn

1 tbsp extra virgin olive oil

12 large plump scallops, cleaned

Dressing

3 tsp honey

$^1/_2$ cup extra virgin olive oil

2-3 tbsp lemon juice

salt and cracked black pepper

Slice lemon as thinly as possible, remove seeds and place on a large plate in a single layer and sprinkle with salt. Stand for 20-30 minutes, then rinse and pat dry with paper towel.

Meanwhile trim artichokes, cut in half, remove hairy chokes and place in a bowl of water with lemon juice to prevent discolouration. Cook artichokes in lightly salted, boiling water for 15-20 minutes or until tender. Drain well.

Boil potatoes in lightly salted water until tender. Drain, and when cool enough to handle peel and cut in half lengthways.

For the dressing, combine all the ingredients and whisk until smooth. Place potatoes in a large bowl, add half the dressing and toss to combine.

Heat olive oil in a frying pan, cook scallops briefly over medium heat on both sides until just cooked then remove from pan.

Add lemon slices, artichokes, almonds, parsley, salt and pepper and remaining dressing to potatoes and combine.

To serve, spoon salad onto serving plates and top with scallops.

Serves 4

Asian greens

The golden rule is that if it has thick stalks it will be good steamed, stir-fried or boiled; if it has small, round leaves it will add crunch, colour and flavour to soups and steamboats. To remedy confusion over various names for Asian greens, the NSW Department of Primary Industries has introduced a national naming system.

Both gai lan (Chinese broccoli) and choy sum (Chinese flowering cabbage) cook to a brilliant green in just minutes in a steamer. Bok choy, now known as pak choy or baby pak choy under the DPI system, is probably the most popular Asian green. It has white, fleshy stems and bright-green leaves and is succulent when stir-fried, braised or eaten raw in salads.

Choy sum has long, pale-green stems, bottle-green leaves and small yellow flowers. It is sold in bunches of about 10 pieces and teams well with oyster sauce and sesame oil. Gai choy (mustard green or mustard cabbage) has broad green leaves attached to a thick central stalk, with fleshy stems and the strong tang of mustard. After blanching, it has a milder flavour with a slight bitterness, making it tasty in pork and beef broth.

Wombok (Chinese or Peking cabbage) is a pale cabbage, with curly overlapping leaves that are white-to-pale green and good for wrapping food.

Kang kong (Chinese or water spinach) has dark-green, slender leaves on thin green stems. Slice into 4-5cm lengths and blanch briefly in a little water or stir-fry for a minute or two and it will become soft and velvety.

Select Asian greens with the brightest, deepest colour and firm, fleshy stems. Avoid any with yellow or shrivelled leaves. Store in a plastic bag in the fridge and eat within a day or two.

Steamed pak choy

2 tsp ginger, grated

1 tbsp fish sauce

2 tsp soy sauce

1 tbsp peanut oil

1 bunch pak choy

Combine ginger, fish sauce, soy sauce and 2$\frac{1}{2}$ tablespoons water in a small bowl and stir well. Heat wok and add peanut oil, swirling to coat the sides. Add pak choy and toss to coat with oil. Pour in ginger mixture. Toss again and cover wok with a lid. Cook for 3-4 minutes, stirring occasionally.

Serve pak choy with juices.

Serves 2 as a side dish

Gai lan (Chinese broccoli) and barbecued pork stir-fry

Barbecued pork (char siew) can be bought from Chinese barbecue shops.

1 tbsp peanut oil

3 cloves garlic, finely chopped

2 tsp ginger, grated

2 small fresh red chillies, finely chopped, or to taste

1 bunch gai lan, cut into 4cm lengths

$\frac{1}{2}$ cup chicken stock

500g barbecued pork, sliced

2 tbsp oyster sauce, mixed with 1 tbsp water

Heat oil in wok and, when hot, add garlic, ginger and chillies and stir-fry until fragrant.

Add gai lan stems and stir 1-2 minutes, then add gai lan leaves and chicken stock, cover and cook for 2-3 minutes.

Add pork and stir until heated through. Remove from heat and drizzle with oyster sauce. Serve with steamed jasmine rice.

Serves 4

Quick chicken and pak choy stir-fry

300g dried egg noodles

2 tbsp peanut oil

2 cloves garlic, finely chopped

2 tsp ginger, grated

3 chicken breast fillets, cut into thin strips

leaves from 3 heads pak choy

3 tbsp soy sauce

1 tbsp oyster sauce

1 red chilli, finely chopped (or to taste)

120g (^{1}/$_2$ cup) toasted cashew nuts

4 green onions, thinly sliced

Cook noodles in plenty of boiling water for 4-5 minutes. Drain and rinse under cold water.

Heat peanut oil in wok and add garlic and ginger. Stir-fry until aromatic. Add chicken and stir-fry until chicken changes colour. Add pak choy and stir-fry until wilted. Add soy sauce, oyster sauce and chilli and stir to coat chicken and pak choy.

Serve chicken topped with cashews and green onions and accompanied by noodles or steamed rice.

Serves 4

Red curry of beef with baby pak choy

2 tbsp peanut oil

500g lean beef strips

2-3 tbsp Thai red curry paste

400ml light coconut milk

1 tbsp brown sugar

2 tbsp fish sauce

140ml light coconut cream

1 carrot, finely sliced

200g baby corn, halved lengthways

3 heads pak choy

2 kaffir lime leaves, very finely shredded

steamed rice or noodles, to serve

Heat 1 tablespoon peanut oil in a wok over high heat and stir-fry beef strips until brown. Remove and set aside. Add remaining tablespoon of peanut oil and when hot add Thai red curry paste and stir-fry for 2-3 minutes until fragrant. Add coconut milk, brown sugar, fish sauce and coconut cream and simmer for 5 minutes. Add carrot and baby corn and cook until tender. Return beef to wok, add pak choy and stir until wilted. Serve curry sprinkled with kaffir lime leaves and steamed rice or noodles.

Serves 4

King prawns with pak choy and jasmine rice

2 cups jasmine rice

2 tbsp peanut oil

16 large green (raw) king prawns, shelled and deveined, tails intact

4 cloves garlic, finely chopped

2 small red chillies, finely chopped

3 heads pak choy

2 tsp sesame oil

150ml chicken stock

3 tbsp oyster sauce

^{1}/$_2$ cup toasted cashew nuts, coarsely chopped

steamed rice, to serve

Combine rice with 4 cups of water in a large saucepan and bring to the boil over medium heat. Stir well and simmer, covered, over low heat for 12 minutes. Meanwhile heat peanut oil in a wok and stir-fry prawns for 2-3 minutes each side or until just cooked. Remove prawns and add garlic and chillies. When garlic starts to colour add leaves from pak choy and stir until wilted. Add cooked prawns, sesame oil, chicken stock and oyster sauce and stir to combine.

Spoon rice into 4 bowls and top with prawn mixture. Sprinkle with cashews.

Serves 4

Pak choy stir-fry with noodles, cashews and ginger

This is a super vegetarian dish, but you can add 2 pan-fried chicken breasts, cut into strips if desired.

400g fresh rice noodles

1/2 cup unsalted cashews

1 tbsp vegetable oil

2 cloves garlic, crushed

3 tsp ginger, grated

1 bunch Shanghai pak choy, chopped

1 bunch gai lan, chopped lan (Chinese broccoli)

2 tbsp soy sauce

2 tbsp sweet chilli sauce

4 tbsp crisp-fried eschalots (available from Asian food stores)

Place noodles in a large bowl and pour boiling water over them to cover, gently shaking the strips apart (2-3 minutes) with a pair of chopsticks. Drain.

Heat a large wok over high heat. Add cashews and stir-fry for 1 minute or until golden. Remove.

Add oil, garlic, ginger, pak choy and gai lan stems (reserving leaves) to wok and stir-fry for 3-4 minutes or until stems are tender. Add pak choy and gai lan leaves, soy and sweet chilli sauce, stir-fry for 2-3 minutes or until leaves have just wilted. Stir in noodles and cashews and toss to combine. Sprinkle with fried eschalots and serve immediately.

Serves 4

Stir-fried kang kong (water spinach) with ginger and prawns

1 tbsp vegetable oil

1 clove garlic, finely chopped

1 tbsp ginger, grated

1 large bunch kang kong (water spinach), cut into 4-5cm lengths

1 tbsp oyster sauce

2 tsp soy sauce

16 small cooked prawns, shelled and deveined

Heat oil in a wok and stir-fry garlic and ginger over medium heat for 1 minute. Add water spinach and stir-fry until spinach is just wilted. Stir in oyster sauce, soy sauce and prawns. Serve immediately.

Serves 4

Chicken and wombok (Chinese cabbage) salad with mint and coriander

500g chicken thigh fillets, trimmed

cracked black pepper

1-1 1/2 cups chicken stock, to cover

1/2 small wombok, finely shredded

1 small red onion, halved and finely sliced

1 carrot, peeled and shaved into ribbons

1 small red chilli, very finely chopped

2 tsp sugar

1 1/2 tbsp fish sauce

2 tbsp lime juice

1 tsp soy sauce

6 sprigs mint, torn

6 sprigs coriander, torn

Combine chicken fillets, pepper and chicken stock in a saucepan and bring to the boil over low heat. Simmer for 5 minutes then remove from heat and cool chicken in stock for 20 minutes. Drain stock and slice chicken into thin strips.

For the salad, combine chicken, wombok, red onion, carrot and red chilli in a large bowl. In a small bowl, combine sugar, fish sauce, lime juice and soy and stir well and pour dressing over salad. Add mint and coriander leaves and toss to combine.

Serves 4-6

Wombok (Chinese cabbage) and beef stir-fry with green chillies and vermicelli

80g rice vermicelli

vegetable oil, for frying

1 tbsp peanut oil

500g beef stir-fry strips (rump)

125g baby corn, halved

1 carrot, peeled and sliced diagonally

$^1/_4$ tsp Chinese five-spice powder

2 purple eschalots, sliced

2 cloves garlic, finely chopped

1 tbsp ginger, grated

$^1/_4$ small wombok, finely shredded

1 tbsp oyster sauce

2 tbsp soy sauce

1 tsp sesame oil

1-2 green chillies, very finely sliced

230g tin water chestnuts, drained and
    coarsely chopped

Separate 20g vermicelli and heat vegetable oil in a saucepan over medium heat. When oil is hot add vermicelli and fry briefly until puffed. Remove and drain on paper towel.

Heat peanut oil in a wok over high heat and add beef. Stir-fry for 3-4 minutes, until browned. Add corn and carrot and stir-fry for 2 minutes. Add five-spice powder, eschalots, garlic, ginger and stir. Add wombok and $^1/_2$ cup of water and stir. Add oyster sauce, soy sauce and sesame oil. Add green chillies and water chestnuts.

Cook remaining vermicelli in boiling water for 1-2 minutes, drain and add to the wok. Stir and serve immediately topped with fried vermicelli.

Serves 4

Stir-fried vegetables with crisp vermicelli

vegetable oil, for frying

60g rice vermicelli

1 small red capsicum, cut into 2cm pieces

1 small green capsicum, cut into 2cm pieces

1 carrot, peeled and thinly sliced on the diagonal

1 clove garlic, finely chopped

1 tbsp ginger, grated

100g button mushrooms, thinly sliced

100g snowpeas, trimmed

1 bunch baby pak choy, coarsely sliced

$^1/_3$ cup chicken stock

2 tbsp soy sauce

1 tsp oyster sauce

$^1/_2$ tsp sesame oil

3 tsp cornflour mixed with 2 tbsp water

6 green onions, sliced diagonally into 4-5cm lengths

$1^1/_2$ cups (110g) beansprouts

Heat oil in a wok or large pan over high heat and deep-fry vermicelli in batches until crisp and puffed. Set aside on on absorbent paper.

Drain all but 1 tablespoon of oil from wok and add capsicum and carrot and stir-fry for 2-3 minutes, then add garlic, ginger, mushrooms, snowpeas and pak choy and stir-fry until pak choy is wilted. Add chicken stock, soy sauce, oyster sauce and sesame oil and stir. Pour in cornflour mixture and stir until sauce thickens. Add green onions and beansprouts and stir. Serve immediately on top of crisp vermicelli.

Serves 4

Stir-fried choy sum with asparagus and baby corn

1 bunch baby choy sum

2 tbsp peanut oil

1 bunch green asparagus, trimmed and sliced in half diagonally

2 cloves garlic, finely chopped

2 tsp ginger, grated

125g baby corn, halved lengthways

2 tbsp shaoxing wine

2 tsp malt vinegar

2 tsp oyster sauce

$^1/_2$ tsp sugar

$^1/_4$ tsp salt

$^1/_4$ tsp sesame oil

$^1/_3$ cup chicken stock

3 green onions, cut into 3cm lengths

Cut stems from choy sum and set aside. Heat peanut oil in a wok over high heat and add choy sum stems and asparagus and stir-fry for 1 minute. Add garlic, ginger and corn and stir-fry for another minute. Add wine, vinegar, oyster sauce, sugar, salt, sesame oil and choy sum leaves and stir-fry until leaves wilt. Pour in stock and green onions and stir-fry for 30 seconds. Remove from heat and serve immediately.

Serves 4 as part of a shared meal

Stir-fried kang kong (water spinach) with cauliflower and snake beans

1 tbsp peanut oil

500g cauliflower florets

200g snake beans, cut into 4-5cm pieces

1 clove garlic, finely chopped

4 green onions, cut into 4-5cm lengths

1 tsp ground turmeric

1 small bunch kang kong (water spinach) cut into 4-5cm lengths

1 tbsp lime juice

1 tbsp soy sauce

4 sprigs coriander, torn

Heat oil in a wok over high heat and add cauliflower and snake beans and stir-fry for 2 minutes. Add garlic and green onions and turmeric and stir-fry for a further 1 minute. Add $^1/_4$ cup water and stir-fry until cauliflower is almost tender. Add kang kong and stir-fry for 1 minute. Add lime juice, soy sauce and stir. Remove from heat, scatter with torn coriander leaves and serve immediately.

Serves 4

Asparagus

Available all year, perfectly shaped asparagus spears are at their best in spring. Green asparagus is the biggest selling fresh variety, but recently white asparagus has become more popular – although it will always be a luxury item because of the painstaking hand-harvesting it requires.

Plump, purple asparagus is a variety of green asparagus and turns green on cooking. Chop, slice or shred it and use it raw in salads to preserve the unusual colour.

All three are prepared in the same way. Snap each spear at its natural breaking point and discard the end (which can be added to stock for extra flavour.) Use a vegetable peeler or small, sharp knife to peel the lower half of the remaining stem on white asparagus, which tends to be tougher.

Select stems that are straight with tips that are compact and tightly closed. If it is just harvested, they will be firm and brittle. Make sure the ends are not dry, wrinkled or split. Asparagus that is not fresh can taste bitter and grassy and may discolour when cooked.

Stand bunches in a couple of centimetres of water in the fridge or store wrapped in damp absorbent paper in the crisper. Use as soon as possible, as asparagus gets more fibrous the older it becomes.

Asparagus, Mercado de Triana, Seville

Steamed asparagus with herb butter sauce

2-3 bunches asparagus, trimmed

4 tbsp white-wine vinegar

6 peppercorns

¹/₂ bay leaf

1 sprig fresh tarragon

1 sprig fresh chervil

1 eschalot, chopped

2 egg yolks

1 tbsp water

100g butter, chopped

salt and cracked black pepper

Combine vinegar, peppercorns, bay leaf, tarragon and chervil with eschalot in a small saucepan and reduce over medium heat to two thirds the quantity. Beat egg yolks with water in a bowl and place bowl over a saucepan of simmering water. Add strained vinegar and stir. Add butter, piece by piece, stirring continuously until sauce is smooth and slightly thickened. Remove from heat and season to taste.

Steam or boil asparagus briefly until tender but still crisp.

Serve warm asparagus drizzled with herb and butter sauce.

Serves 4

Top left: Asparagus farm, Koo Wee Rup, Victoria
Left: Salamanca Market, Hobart

Asparagus, tomato and preserved lemon salad

1 bunch asparagus, cut into 3-4cm pieces

4 ripe tomatoes, coarsely chopped

$^1/_2$ red onion, chopped

$^1/_4$ preserved lemon, pith removed, rinsed
    and finely chopped

1 tbsp white-wine vinegar

$^1/_4$ cup extra virgin olive oil

1 tsp Dijon mustard

$^1/_4$ tsp ground cumin

$^1/_4$ tsp paprika

salt and cracked black pepper

$^1/_2$ cup flat-leaf parsley, chopped

grilled lamb chops, to serve

Blanch asparagus in lightly salted, boiling water for 2 minutes. Refresh under cold water and drain. Combine asparagus, tomatoes, onion and preserved lemon in a medium-sized bowl.

Whisk vinegar, extra virgin olive oil, Dijon mustard, ground cumin and paprika in a small bowl, season to taste and pour over vegetables and sprinkle with parsley.

Serve with grilled lamb loin chops.

Serves 4

Macaroni with ham and asparagus

400g macaroni

1 tbsp butter

1 tbsp extra virgin olive oil

1 brown onion, sliced

1 bunch asparagus, trimmed, blanched and
    cut into 2cm lengths

300g leg ham, coarsely chopped

1 cup light cream

$^1/_2$ cup grated parmesan

salt and cracked black pepper

extra shaved parmesan

Cook macaroni in lightly salted, boiling water until al dente. Drain.

Meanwhile, heat butter and olive oil in a frying pan over medium heat and cook onion until soft. Add asparagus and leg ham and cook for 2-3 minutes. Stir in light cream and parmesan, salt and pepper and simmer for 2 minutes or until sauce thickens slightly.

Pour sauce over drained pasta, toss to combine, and serve immediately with extra shaved parmesan.

Serves 4

Warm salad of roasted asparagus with sweet potato, pecans and cherry tomatoes

Serve this delightful spring salad accompanied by char-grilled baby lamb cutlets or barbecued lamb and rosemary sausages.

500g sweet potato, peeled and cut into
    1cm thick slices

3 tbsp extra virgin olive oil

2 cloves garlic, finely chopped

sea salt and cracked black pepper

1 punnet (250g) cherry tomatoes

$^3/_4$ cup (75g) pecan nuts

2 bunches asparagus, trimmed

2 tsp Dijon mustard

1 tsp honey

2 tbsp white-wine vinegar

Preheat oven to 210C.

Combine sweet potato with 1 tablespoon of oil, garlic, salt and pepper in an ovenproof dish and roast for 15-20 minutes, until almost tender. Scatter with tomatoes, pecan nuts and asparagus and roast for a further 8 minutes.

For the dressing, combine mustard, honey, vinegar and remaining oil in a small bowl and whisk until smooth.

Place warm vegetables on a serving plate and drizzle with dressing.

Serves 4

Avocado

Rich, buttery avocadoes are classified as a fruit and mature on the tree, but only ripen when harvested. They can take from 2-6 days to ripen at room temperature and are very high in antioxidants, heart-healthy fats and vitamin E.

Hass avocados grow year-round and are characterised by their pebbly green skin, which turns a dull purple when fully ripe. Pear-shaped fuertes have very smooth green skin with creamy, pale-yellow flesh and a more subtle flavour than nutty hass. Reed avocados are often called canon balls because of their size and shape. Their shiny green skin is easy to peel. Tiny cocktail avocados are also called salad avocados and are the small, unfertilised fruit and not a particular variety.

Check fruit before buying to make sure it is free of blemishes. When ripe it should yield to gentle pressure at the stem end. To speed ripening, place avocados in a paper bag with a banana or apple (which give off ethylene gas) and leave at room temperature. Keep ripe avocados in the crisper of the fridge for a couple of days only; unripe avocadoes will develop black spots if stored at low temperatures.

Cut the fruit in half and carefully twist the halves to separate. To remove the seed, slip the tip of a small spoon gently underneath and lever out, or strike the seed gently with a knife, rotate and lift out. Brush cut avocados with lemon or lime juice to prevent discolouration. They are not suited to cooking, as heat brings out the bitter tannins.

Lynne's guacamole

1 small clove garlic, chopped

1 small onion, chopped

1 tbsp coriander leaves

1 small tomato, seeded

2 large ripe avocadoes, peeled and seeded

$^1/_2$ tsp salt

$^1/_2$ tsp mild chilli powder

$^1/_2$ tsp caster sugar

3 tbsp lemon juice

Combine garlic, onion, coriander and tomato in a food processor briefly until just combined.

Add avocadoes and process briefly.

Add salt, chilli, sugar and lemon juice and process until combined.

Remove mixture to a bowl and serve with crackers or corn chips.

Makes about 2 cups

Avocado and warm goat's cheese salad with rocket

200g goat's cheese, cut into 3cm cubes

80g butter, melted

70g (1 cup) breadcrumbs

150g bacon rashers, chopped

2 tsp balsamic vinegar

2 tbsp extra virgin olive oil

salt and cracked black pepper

1 large bunch rocket leaves, trimmed

1 large ripe avocado, peeled and sliced

Toss goat's cheese in half the melted butter and then in breadcrumbs. Refrigerate for 20-30 minutes.

Cook bacon rashers in a non-stick pan over medium heat until crisp then drain on absorbent paper.

Heat remaining butter in a non-stick pan and cook cheese over medium heat until golden on all sides. Drain on absorbent paper.

Whisk balsamic vinegar with extra virgin olive oil, salt and pepper in a small bowl.

Place rocket leaves in a large, shallow serving bowl and add avocado. Pour dressing over and toss gently. Top with goat's cheese and scatter with bacon pieces.

Serves 4 as an entrée with crusty bread

Nachos

2 tbsp extra virgin olive oil

400g lean beef mince

1 brown onion, chopped

1 small red chilli, finely chopped

3 tsp ground cumin

2 tsp ground coriander

2 tbsp tomato paste

1 cup tomato passata (chunky tomato sauce)

1 x 400g tin kidney beans, drained

165g cheddar, grated

1 large ripe avocado, peeled and sliced

$^1/_2$ cup light sour cream

corn chips, to serve

Heat 1 tablespoon extra virgin olive oil in a large fry-pan and add beef mince and cook over high heat (stirring and breaking up any lumps with a wooden spoon) for 5-8 minutes or until well browned. Transfer to a bowl. Add remaining olive oil to the pan with onion, red chilli, cumin and coriander and cook over medium heat for 2-3 minutes. Add mince, tomato paste, tomato passata and drained red kidney beans and cook over low heat for 5 minutes. Place in an ovenproof dish and sprinkle with cheddar and place under a hot grill for 3- 5 minutes or until cheese is melted.

Garnish with avocado and dollops of light sour cream. Serve with corn chips.

Serves 4

Smoked trout, avocado and snowpea salad

(pictured page 169)

2 smoked trout (about 800g)

300g snowpeas, trimmed

3 small Lebanese cucumbers

1 stick celery, sliced

leaves from 2 baby cos lettuce, torn

1 avocado, peeled and sliced

sea salt and cracked black pepper

$^3/_4$ cup good mayonnaise, mixed with
    2 tbsp hot water

4 hard-boiled eggs, peeled and quartered

$^1/_2$ cup flat-leaf parsley, coarsely chopped

lime cheeks, to serve

Remove skin and bones from smoked trout and flake flesh into medium-sized pieces. Blanch snowpeas in boiling, lightly salted water for 30 seconds, drain and refresh under cold running water. Drain well and spread on paper towel to dry.

Thinly slice Lebanese cucumbers on the diagonal and place in a large bowl with celery. Add cos lettuce, trout and snowpeas to cucumbers with avocado. Season with salt and pepper and toss gently with mayo.

Divide salad among 4 serving plates and top with hard-boiled eggs. Scatter with flat-leaf parsley and serve with lime cheeks.

Serves 4

Beans

There are many varieties of this vegetable, and to retain their crispness all beans are best cooked as briefly as possible; except borlottis. These speckled beans must be boiled for 30-45 minutes to become tender, with salt added after cooking so as not to toughen the skins.

Beans are an excellent source of dietary fibre, iron and potassium and contain virtually no fat. When buying green beans, look for fresh, small specimens, as the quality is better when they are picked tiny and crunchy. Most regular green beans have had the strings bred out these days, making preparation much speedier.

Appetising butter beans, also called wax beans, are simply a pale-yellow variety of the green bean. They look spectacular when combined with green varieties in a salad. Broad beans, also known as fava or shell beans, are large, flat, pale-green beans and delicious when podded – shell to remove the outer skin before steaming briefly and serving with a knob of butter and cracked black pepper. Winged beans are known by many names including asparagus beans and are unique with their four serrated edges. They are delicious cooked briefly in stir-fries or sliced finely and served raw in Thai salads. These delicate beans are best eaten as soon as possible after purchasing.

Widely used in Asian cooking, sinuous snake beans have a denser texture than green beans and are fabulous in stir-fries because they retain their crunch. Sold in bundles, they can range in length from 20cm to 90cm. In South-East Asian cookbooks, you'll find them listed as yard-long beans or asparagus beans.

Roman beans, also known as flat, Italian or continental, are much wider than green beans with seeds giving the edge of the pod a wavy appearance.

Choose fresh beans that are crisp and bright, not wrinkled or discoloured. Look for crunchy beans that snap when bent. Avoid those sold in bags as the plastic makes them sweat.

Store for 2-3 days in the crisper of the fridge and trim just before cooking.

Cahors Markets, South West France

Thai chicken, wing bean and cucumber salad

100g trimmed sugar snap peas (snowpeas could be substituted in this recipe if wing beans are unavailable).

280g chicken thigh fillets, cut into
    bite-sized pieces

2 tbsp fish sauce

½ cup (75g) rice flour

vegetable oil, for deep-frying

3 lebanese cucumbers, thinly sliced diagonally

½ tsp sugar

12 wing beans, trimmed and sliced
    on the diagonal

1 cup loosely packed coriander leaves

1 cup loosely packed mint leaves

2 red eschalots, very thinly sliced

⅓ cup toasted peanuts, coarsely chopped

Dressing

50g piece palm sugar, shaved

1 clove garlic, chopped

2 tbsp fish sauce

2 tbsp lime juice

1 small red chilli, finely chopped

For the dressing, place palm sugar and garlic in a mortar and pestle and pound until crushed. Add remaining ingredients and stir well.

Combine chicken and fish sauce in a bowl and then dust chicken in flour, shake to remove excess and deep-fry in hot oil until golden and crisp. Drain on absorbent paper.

Place cucumber in a bowl, scatter with sugar and set aside for 10 minutes to soften slightly. Blanch wing beans in boiling water for 30 seconds, then remove and refresh under cold water. Drain.

Combine herbs, eschalots and cucumber in a bowl, toss with half the dressing and divide among 2 serving plates. Scatter with chicken pieces and top with wing beans. Drizzle with remaining dressing and sprinkle with peanuts.

Serves 2

Warm salad of snake beans, asparagus and sweet potato with blue cheese

1 orange sweet potato, (about 500g) peeled and cut into 2-3cm pieces

1 tbsp olive oil

1 bunch asparagus, trimmed and halved

300g snake beans, cut into 4-5cm lengths

1 corella pear, cored and cut into thin slices

2 cups baby mache (lamb's lettuce)

200g King Island blue cheese, cut into 1cm pieces

Dressing

100ml extra virgin olive oil

2 tbsp white-wine vinegar

1 clove garlic, halved

1 tsp Dijon mustard

sea salt

Preheat oven to 200C.

For the dressing, combine all the ingredients, season to taste and whisk well. Toss sweet potato with olive oil in a roasting pan and roast for 30 minutes or until lightly browned and tender.

Steam asparagus and beans until tender. Rinse under cold water and drain.

In a large bowl, combine sweet potato, asparagus, beans, pear and mache.

Discard garlic clove from dressing, whisk well, then pour over vegetables and toss gently to combine. Divide salad among 4 plates and scatter with blue cheese.

Serves 4

Bacon, bean and lentil salad with smashed peas

1 cup (200g) green lentils

1 brown onion, chopped

300g lean bacon, chopped

150g baby green beans, trimmed

150g snowpeas, trimmed

2 cups frozen peas, partly thawed

100ml extra virgin olive oil

2-3 tbsp lemon juice

$^1/_3$ cup torn mint leaves

$^1/_3$ cup basil, torn

salt and cracked black pepper

Combine lentils in a saucepan with onion, cover with water and simmer over medium heat for about 20 minutes or until lentils are tender. Drain and place in a large bowl.

Cook bacon in a non-stick pan over medium heat until crisp.

Boil baby green beans in a saucepan of boiling water for 2 minutes, add snowpeas and boil for 30 seconds, then add 2 cups frozen peas that have been squashed slightly with a potato masher. When water returns to the boil remove from heat and drain vegetables.

Add bacon and vegetables to lentils with extra virgin olive oil, lemon juice, mint and basil. Served seasoned with salt and pepper.

Serves 4

Pasta and bean soup

(pictured page 173)

2 tbsp extra virgin olive oil

1 carrot, chopped

2 sticks celery, chopped

1 brown onion, chopped

150g bacon rashers, chopped

1 x 400g tin tomatoes

1.5 litres chicken stock

3 cups podded fresh borlotti beans
(or 2 x 400g cans rinsed drained borlotti beans)

salt and cracked black pepper

100g dried stellette (or other small soup pasta)

2 tbsp flat-leaf parsley, chopped

1 tbsp sage, chopped

6 tbsp shaved parmesan

extra virgin olive oil, to drizzle

Heat oil in a large saucepan, add carrot, celery, onion and bacon and cook over medium heat for 5-8 minutes, stirring often. Add tomatoes and chicken stock and bring to the boil and simmer for 10 minutes. Add fresh borlotti beans and simmer for 10 minutes (if using tinned variety, simmer for 5 minutes). Remove $^1/_2$ cup beans and vegetables from the liquid with a slotted spoon and process in a food processor until smooth. Return to the saucepan and stir well. Season with salt and pepper and add pasta and simmer for 3-5 minutes. Stir in parsley and sage and serve each bowl topped with a tablespoon of shaved parmesan and drizzle of extra virgin olive oil. Serve with crusty bread.

Serves 6

Macaroni with green beans, asparagus, bacon and chilli

400g macaroni or penne pasta

1 bunch asparagus, cut into 2cm lengths

200g green beans, trimmed and sliced

2 tsp extra virgin olive oil

1 brown onion, sliced

3 rashers bacon, chopped

1 cup light cream

$^1/_2$ tsp dried chilli flakes

$^1/_2$ cup grated parmesan

extra shaved parmesan

Cook pasta in lightly salted, boiling water over medium heat until al dente. Blanch asparagus and green beans in lightly salted, boiling water for 2-3 minutes then drain. Refresh under cold water then drain again.

Heat olive oil in a large pan over medium heat and add onion and bacon. Cook for about 4-5 minutes until bacon is crisp.

Add light cream, chilli flakes and grated parmesan to pasta and stir to combine. Add beans and asparagus and toss well.

Serve in 4 warm pasta bowls topped with onion and bacon mixture and extra shaved parmesan.

Serves 4

Baby beans with herbs and walnut dressing

300g baby beans, trimmed

Dressing

2 green onions, chopped

$^1/_4$ cup chervil, chopped

$^1/_4$ cup tarragon, chopped

$^1/_4$ cup flat-leaf parsley, chopped

$1^1/_2$ tbsp verjuice

60g walnuts, toasted

$^1/_2$ cup extra virgin olive oil

salt and cracked black pepper

Cook beans in lightly salted, boiling water for about 3 minutes until just tender. Drain and refresh briefly under cold water. Drain again.

Combine green onions, herbs, vinegar, walnuts and half the oil in a food processor and process until combined. With motor running slowly drizzle in more oil until mixture is smooth and thick. Remove to a bowl and add salt and pepper.

Spoon dressing over beans and serve with roast chicken and boiled baby potatoes.

Serves 4

Braised chicken with sherry vinegar, tomato and broad beans

2 tsp sweet paprika

salt and cracked black pepper

1 size-12 chicken, cut into 8 pieces

2-3 tbsp olive oil

2 cloves garlic, finely sliced

4 brown eschalots, peeled and sliced

2 sprigs flat-leaf parsley

2 sprigs fresh oregano

1 sprig thyme

2 tbsp tomato paste

100ml sherry vinegar

400ml chicken stock

1 cup fresh or frozen podded broad beans

2 tsp butter

Rub paprika, salt and pepper all over chicken. Heat oil in a large, heavy-based frying pan and brown chicken on all sides over medium heat. Add garlic, eschalots, and herbs and cook for 5 minutes. Add tomato paste and vinegar and bring to the boil. Add stock, cover and cook over low heat for 10-15 minutes. Remove lid and cook over high heat until sauce is reduced and chicken is almost cooked, add broad beans and cook for 4-5 minutes. Add butter and stir.

Serve chicken with mashed potato and a watercress and witlof salad.

Serves 4

Vegetable soup with parmesan and parsley

2 tbsp extra virgin olive oil

1 brown onion, thinly sliced

1 leek, white part only, thinly sliced

500g pumpkin, peeled and chopped

1 carrot, chopped

1 litre vegetable or chicken stock

1 zucchini, cut into 1cm pieces

100g green beans, trimmed and sliced

salt and cracked black pepper

4 tbsp grated parmesan

4 tbsp flat-leaf parsley, chopped

Heat olive oil in a large saucepan, add onion
and leek. Cook over low heat for about 5 minutes
or until soft. Add pumpkin and carrot and stir
over medium heat for 3 minutes. Add stock and
simmer for 5 minutes, then add zucchini and
green beans, salt and pepper. Simmer for about
5 minutes or until vegetables are just cooked.
Serve in warm soup bowls and sprinkle each
with parmesan and parsley.

Serves 4

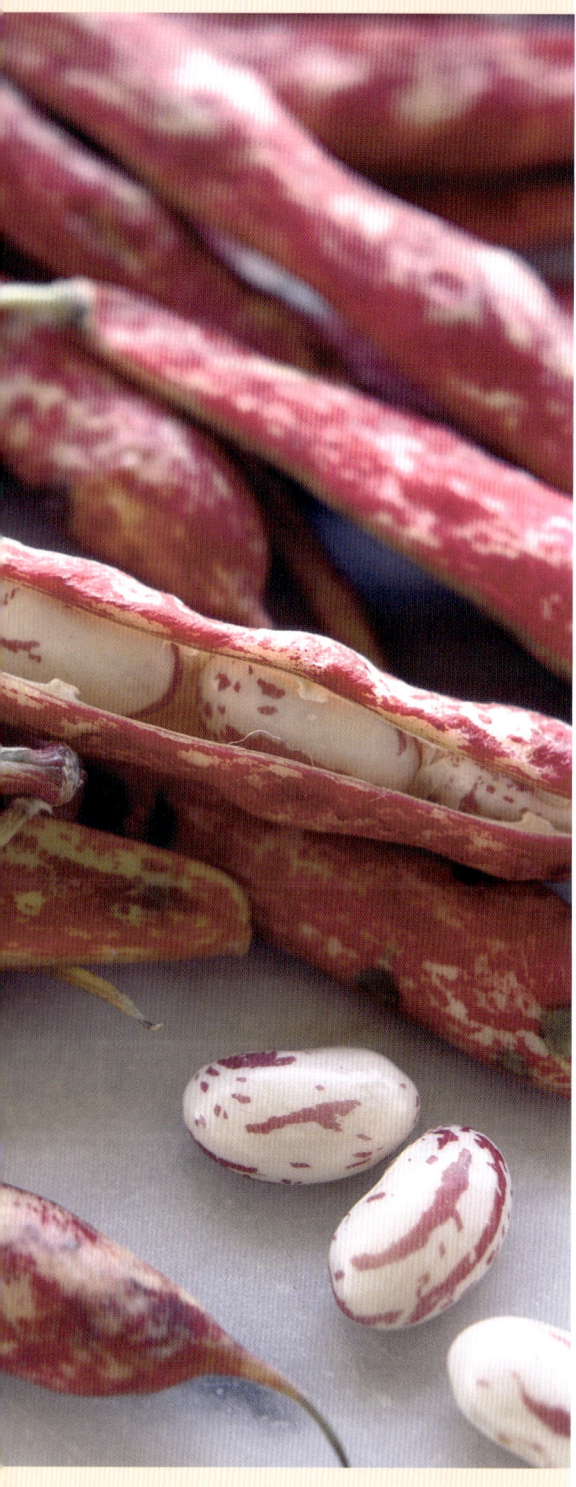

Bean salad with herb and lemon mayo

200g baby green beans, trimmed

200g butter beans, trimmed

150g flat roman beans, trimmed and halved

250g fresh borlotti beans, shelled

250g fresh broad beans, shelled

100ml extra virgin olive oil

salt and cracked black pepper

Dressing

200ml good mayonnaise

1/4 cup oregano leaves, chopped

1/4 cup mint leaves, torn

juice of 1/2 lemon

3 tbsp salted capers, rinsed

Cook green, butter and roman beans in lightly salted, boiling water for about 3 minutes then drain. Blanch borlotti and broad beans in lightly salted, boiling water for 2 minutes then drain.

For the dressing, combine all the ingredients in a bowl and stir to combine.

To serve, spread beans on a serving plate and top with dollops of dressing.

Serves 6

Salad Nicoise

200g roman beans, trimmed and cut
 into 4-5cm lengths

1 small red onion, very thinly sliced

1 punnet cherry tomatoes, halved

3 sticks celery, thinly sliced on the diagonal

12 quail eggs, hard boiled and peeled
 (or 3 regular eggs, hard boiled and quartered)

1 x 425g tin tuna in oil, drained

3/4 cup nicoise olives

1 1/2 tbsp baby salted capers, rinsed

4 sprigs flat-leaf parsley, torn

8 basil leaves, torn

Dressing

1 clove garlic, finely chopped

1 anchovy, mashed

1/2 cup extra virgin olive oil

1/4 cup lemon juice

salt and cracked black pepper

1/2 tsp sugar

For the dressing, combine all the ingredients in a small bowl and whisk until smooth.

Cook beans in lightly salted, boiling water for about 3 minutes until just tender. Drain.

Scatter beans, onion, tomatoes, celery, and eggs on a large serving platter. Flake tuna over vegetables. Top with olives, capers, parsley and basil and drizzle with dressing.

Serve with crusty bread.

Serves 4

Green and butter bean salad with tarragon and chervil

250g green beans, topped

250g butter beans, topped

2 eschalots, finely sliced

2 tbsp Dijon mustard

2 tbsp salted capers, rinsed

1/2 bunch chervil, chopped

1/2 bunch French tarragon leaves, chopped

100ml extra virgin olive oil

1 clove garlic, finely chopped

salt and cracked black pepper

4 tbsp white-wine vinegar

Cook beans in lightly salted, boiling water for 3-5 minutes then drain.

Mix remaining ingredients except vinegar in a large bowl. Add beans and toss to coat. Stir in vinegar and serve immediately.

Serves 4

Beef, capsicum, semi-dried tomato and two-bean salad

2 red capsicum, roasted, peeled and sliced

2 tbsp extra virgin olive oil

1 eggplant, cut into 5mm thick slices

salt and cracked black pepper

olive oil, for shallow frying

300g green beans, trimmed

4 small spring onions

400g cooked rare roast beef, thinly sliced

1 x 400g tin cannellini beans, rinsed and drained

100g kalamata olives

12 semi-dried tomatoes in oil

4 sprigs flat-leaf parsley, torn

Dressing

1 tbsp white-wine vinegar

2 tbsp extra virgin olive oil

1 tbsp oil from semi-dried tomatoes

1 clove garlic, finely chopped

Preheat oven to 200C.

Drizzle capsicum with olive oil and roast for about 20 minutes, turning occasionally. Remove and place in a plastic bag and rest for 10-15 minutes then peel, seed and slice.

Sprinkle eggplant slices with salt and pepper and shallow fry in hot olive oil over medium heat until golden then drain on paper towel.

Cook beans in lightly salted, boiling water for 3-4 minutes then drain. Place spring onions in a bowl, cover with boiling water, stand for 2-3 minutes, drain and quarter.

Combine beef, cannellini beans, eggplant, capsicum, green beans, onions, olives and tomatoes in a large bowl.

For the dressing, whisk all the ingredients together in a small bowl.

Pour dressing over salad and toss gently to combine. Top with torn parsley.

Serves 4

Beetroot

Beetroot was originally grown around the Mediterranean, the Greeks and Romans preferring the leaves. The earthy, sweet globes can be roasted, steamed or boiled, and leave the skins on to preserve the flavour and colour. They'll also be less messy to prepare.

More recently, beetroot has been making a resurgence in restaurants thanks in part to the miniature white, gold and red varieties. Their big advantage is that they don't bleed as much as the larger ones.

The leaves are high in vitamin A and iron and can be used in salads or substituted in recipes using silverbeet, a close relative. Beetroot is a good source of potassium and folate and is low in kilojoules. Look for firm, undamaged beetroot with fresh tops that are not wilted. Always buy them with the leaves (which should look fresh and crisp) attached. Avoid those that are too large, as they can be woody inside.

Cut off the leaves before storing in a plastic bag in the crisper of the fridge and wash just before using, as wet beetroot deteriorates rapidly. Leave a couple of centimeters at the root end so the beets don't bleed during cooking, which causes the colour to fade dramatically.

Char-grilled pork cutlets and baby beetroot, capsicum and cucumber salad with basil vinaigrette

4 pork cutlets, about 220g each

8 baby beetroot, trimmed

2 tbsp extra virgin olive oil

salt and cracked black pepper

1 red capsicum

1 yellow capsicum

100g sugar snap peas, trimmed

2 Lebanese cucumbers, halved

2 tbsp capers

1/2 cup baby basil leaves

Dressing

1 1/2 cups basil (firmly packed)

1/4 cup lemon juice

1/2 cup extra virgin olive oil

Preheat oven to 200C.

Place baby beetroot in a baking dish, drizzle with 1 tablespoon olive oil, cover with foil and roast for 40-50 minutes or until tender. Cool then peel.

Drizzle capsicum with remaining olive oil and grill over a gas flame or under a hot griller until skin is blackened. Cool in a plastic bag for 10 minutes then peel, deseed and slice into thick strips.

Blanch sugar snap peas in lightly salted, boiling water for 1 minute then drain and refresh under cold water. Halve two unpeeled cucumbers lengthways, scoop out seeds with a teaspoon then slice thickly on the diagonal. Place beetroot, capsicum, peas and cucumber in a bowl.

For the dressing, combine basil and lemon juice in a food processor until finely chopped then, with motor running, gradually add extra virgin olive oil in a thin, steady stream and add salt and pepper. Drizzle half the dressing over vegetables and toss gently to combine.

Cook 4 x 220g pork cutlets under a hot grill for 3-5 minutes each side or until cooked as desired.

Divide beetroot salad between 4 serving plates and top each with a cutlet. Drizzle remaining dressing on pork cutlets.

Serves 4

Salmon gravlax with beetroot, vodka and avocado cream

1/2 side Atlantic salmon (about 750g), pin boned

60g sugar

60g salt

500g raw beetroot, peeled and grated

30ml vodka

1 large ripe avocado

1 tbsp pouring cream

1 tsp lemon juice

salt and cracked black pepper

1 cup baby cress leaves, or mixed baby herbs

Place salmon in a large dish, skin-side down, and sprinkle with sugar and salt. Cover with grated beetroot and pour over vodka. Cover with plastic wrap and cure, refrigerated, for 24 hours. Turn fish and spoon any juices over, cover again and refrigerate for a further 24-36 hours.

Discard beetroot and liquid and rinse salmon briefly under cold water. Dry with paper towel.

Combine avocado, cream, lemon juice, salt and pepper in a food processor until just smooth.

To serve, thinly slice salmon on the diagonal and place in a single layer on chilled serving plates. Place a dollop of avocado cream in the centre of each plate and sprinkle salmon with herbs.

Serves 6

Salad of beetroot, watercress, pecans and goat's cheese

(pictured page 181)

3 medium-sized beetroot

18 green asparagus spears, trimmed

1 cup watercress sprigs

1 cup baby cress leaves

60g (1/2 cup) pecan nuts, toasted and chopped

3 tbsp extra virgin olive oil

3 tbsp walnut oil

1 1/2 tbsp red-wine vinegar

salt and cracked black pepper

150g soft goat's feta

6 sprigs chervil, coarsely chopped

2 tbsp chives, snipped

Cook beetroot in lightly salted, boiling water until tender. Remove and when cool enough to handle peel and cut into small wedges.

Cook asparagus in lightly salted, boiling water for 2-3 minutes, remove and drain. Place beetroot, watercress, cress leaves and pecans in a large bowl. Combine olive oil, walnut oil, vinegar, salt and pepper in a small bowl and whisk until smooth. Drizzle over salad and toss gently to combine.

Pile salad onto 6 serving plates and top each with 3 spears asparagus. Dot salads with feta and sprinkle with chervil and chives.

Serves 6

Roasted beetroot wedges with lemon and mint mayo

1.5kg small beetroot, trimmed

1 cup good mayonnaise

1 tsp Dijon mustard

1 clove garlic, finely chopped

2 tsp lemon juice

salt and cracked black pepper

3/4 tsp lemon zest

3 tbsp mint, chopped

Preheat oven to 200C.

Wrap beetroot in foil and bake in the oven for about 1 hour (depending on size) or until tender.

Combine mayonnaise with remaining ingredients in a bowl and stir well.

Cool beetroot and peel then cut into wedges.

Drizzle with mayo and serve with barbecued sausages.

Serves 6-8

Broccoli & broccolini

The word broccoli means 'little sprouts' in Italian and it is native to the eastern Mediterranean, where it was originally known as Italian asparagus. Available all year, it is very high in antioxidants, folate and dietary fibre. The densely clustered broccoli florets contain virtually no fat or carbohydrate and 100g will provide several days' supply of vitamin C.

Broccolini is a cross between Chinese kale and broccoli and belongs to the brassica family also, along with brussels sprouts and cauliflower. The stems, soft, dark-green leaves and flowering buds (with their slightly peppery taste) are all edible. Broccolini stalks don't need peeling and are best cooked quickly.

Calabrese broccoli, with its blue-tinged heads grown on dark-green plants, has a delicate flavour while sprouting broccoli has smaller heads on individual stems and is often sold in bunches. Broccoli rabe, a non-heading variety of broccoli similar to Italian rapa, has a milder, less bitter taste. Its leaves and stems are edible and it should be firm when fresh, with small stems, few buds and no open flowers.

Select closely bunched, compact heads of vibrant green or green-blue broccoli with stout stems. Avoid any that are yellowing or limp with woody, hollow stalks. Broccoli and broccolini are best stored unwashed in a plastic bag in the fridge.

Broccoli, pinenut and lemon zest with macaroni pasta

2 tbsp pinenuts

400g macaroni or penne pasta

500g broccoli, trimmed and broken into florets

2 tbsp extra virgin olive oil

2 cloves garlic, finely chopped

1 cup green onions, sliced

3 tsp lemon zest

sea salt and cracked black pepper

extra virgin olive oil, to drizzle

shaved parmesan, to serve

Place pinenuts in a small, dry frying pan and stir over low heat until golden. Remove from heat.

Cook pasta in plenty of lightly salted, boiling water until almost al dente then add broccoli. Cook for a further 2 minutes then drain.

Heat olive oil in a large frying pan and cook garlic and green onions over low heat for about 2 minutes. Add drained pasta, broccoli and lemon zest. Season with salt and pepper and add pinenuts. Toss gently and serve drizzled with extra virgin olive oil and shaved parmesan.

Serves 4

Broccoli bruschetta with walnuts and vincotto

olive oil, for brushing

8 thick slices sourdough bread

500g broccoli florets

3 tbsp extra virgin olive oil

1 clove garlic, finely chopped

2 tbsp black olive tapenade

1 tbsp vincotto *

50g walnuts, toasted and coarsely chopped

salt and cracked black pepper

200g fresh goat's curd

Brush sourdough bread with olive oil and toast on both sides.

Steam broccoli florets over a pan of simmering water for 6-8 minutes or until tender. Drain and reserve 2 tablespoons of cooking water.

Heat extra virgin olive oil in a small frying pan and add garlic and cook over low heat until pale golden. Add black olive tapenade and vincotto and whisk until well combined.

Place broccoli, 2 tablespoons water, vincotto mixture and walnuts in a large bowl, season with salt and pepper and toss to combine.

To Serve, spread fresh goat's curd over sourdough toasts and top with broccoli mixture.

Serves 4

* Vincotto is made by cooking freshly crushed grapes until syrupy. It has a deep raisiny flavour and is available at delicatessens. Substitute with balsamic vinegar if unavailable.

Broccoli frittata with three cheeses

150g broccoli florets

8 large free-range eggs

salt and cracked black pepper

200g ricotta cheese

60g cheddar, grated

1/2 red capsicum, chopped

oil, for greasing

50g grated parmesan

Steam broccoli florets over a pan of simmering water for 6-8 minutes or until just tender then coarsely chop.

Whisk eggs in a large bowl, season with salt and pepper and add broccoli. Stir in ricotta cheese, grated cheddar and red capsicum.

Coat base and sides of a large ovenproof non-stick pan with oil, heat pan and then add egg mixture and cook over medium heat without stirring until top is nearly set. Sprinkle with grated parmesan then place under a hot grill until top is browned.

Cut into wedges and serve.

Makes 8 slices

Chilli and ginger pork with broccolini

400g fresh rice noodles

1 1/2 tbsp vegetable oil

500g pork fillet, sliced

3 green onions, sliced

1 clove garlic, finely chopped

1 tsp sesame oil

2 tbsp ginger, grated

1/2 tsp chilli flakes

1 bunch broccolini, trimmed and halved

1/3 cup chicken stock

2 tbsp sweet chilli sauce

1/2 cup frozen peas

1/3 cup coriander leaves

Place noodles in a bowl and cover with boiling water and rest for 2-3 minutes or until just tender. Separate noodles, drain and set aside.

Heat a wok over high heat and add 2 teaspoons vegetable oil and half the pork and stir-fry for 1-2 minutes, until browned. Remove and repeat with another 2 teaspoons oil and remaining pork then remove. Add remaining oil to wok with green onions, garlic, sesame oil, ginger, chilli flakes and broccolini and stir-fry for 1 minute. Add stock, sweet chilli sauce and frozen peas. Toss well, cover and cook for 1 minute. Add pork and noodles and stir-fry for 1-2 minutes. Scatter with coriander leaves and serve.

Serves 4

Brussels sprouts

Brussels sprouts grow on stems in clusters
and resemble miniature wild cabbages, from
which they descended. They are high in sulphur
compounds and are a good source of vitamin C,
dietary fibre and folate. These are not usually sold
by variety, and are most popular during the winter
months.

Look for sprouts that are small, bright-green and
firm. The leaves should be tightly furled if fresh,
with no browning or split skin.

Store the compact buds in a plastic bag in the
crisper for a few days and use as soon as possible,
as they become bitter as they get older.

Best boiled or steamed until just tender, don't
overcook or the sulphur compounds break down
to give an unpleasant odour and bitter taste.

Chicken and vegetables with soy sauce and noodles

500g chicken breast fillets, cut into strips

2 tbsp soy sauce

2 tbsp sweet chilli sauce

2 tsp ginger, grated

1 clove garlic, finely chopped

8 tsp vegetable oil

6 brussels sprouts, trimmed and quartered

100g snowpeas, trimmed and halved

$\frac{1}{2}$ red capsicum, cut into strips

150g button mushrooms, quartered

noodles, to serve

Combine chicken breast fillets in a medium-sized bowl with soy sauce, sweet chilli sauce, grated ginger and garlic. Stir and set aside for 5 minutes.

Heat 3 teaspoons vegetable oil in a wok over medium heat and cook half the chicken (reserving marinade) for 3-4 minutes or until cooked. Remove and repeat using 3 teaspoons vegetable oil and remaining chicken. Add another 2 teaspoons vegetable oil, brussels sprouts, snowpeas, capsicum and mushrooms and stir-fry for 2-3 minutes. Add chicken, reserved marinade and 2 tablespoons water and stir-fry for 2-3 minutes or until heated through.

Serve immediately with noodles.

Serves 4

Brussels sprouts with herbs and bacon

300g Brussels sprouts, trimmed and halved

salt

100g bacon, chopped

1 tbsp butter

cracked black pepper

2 tsp thyme leaves

1 tbsp oregano leaves, coarsely chopped

1 tbsp flat-leaf parsley, coarsely chopped

Cook brussels sprouts in lightly salted, boiling water for 3 minutes then drain. Refresh under cold water and cut into quarters.

Cook bacon in a non-stick pan over medium heat for about 4-5 minutes, add butter and when butter has melted add sprouts and pepper. Toss gently over medium heat for 2-3 minutes until sprouts are golden and heated through. Top with herbs, stir and serve.

Serves 4

Cabbage

There are many varieties of round or oval cabbages, some with soft leaves others with firm heads tightly furled.

Sugarloaf has strong, waxy leaves and a pointy head while savoy is a sweet cabbage with loose, crinkled leaves. Cavalo nero, originally from Italy, is a dark, blackish cabbage with long curly leaves and is very tasty in soups and braises. It is also known as black Tuscan cabbage and resembles a miniature palm tree growing in the garden, where it can reach a metre high with stylish plume-like leaves. Its astringent, mild cabbage flavour is equally good as a side dish or in minestrone. It can be used to make cabbage rolls, where it provides a striking black coloured wrap.

White cabbage is firm with a large core and strong leaves ranging from pale-green to white. Red cabbage is the variety of choice for relishes and pickles. Cabbage is an excellent source of vitamin C and good source of dietary fibre.

Most varieties are available all year. Choose specimens that feel heavy for their size with no brown or wilted edges. Store in a plastic bag in the fridge and cook briefly.

Cavolo nero with swiss mushrooms, garlic and polenta

10 large stems cavolo nero

salt

1 tbsp butter

2 brown eschalots, finely chopped

250g swiss brown mushrooms, trimmed and sliced

4 cloves garlic, finely chopped

$^1/_4$-$^1/_2$ tsp dried chilli flakes

1.5 litres chicken stock

250g coarse polenta

150g butter, chopped

100g grated parmesan

shaved parmesan, extra

Remove stems from cavolo nero and discard. Cook leaves in lightly salted, boiling water for 5-8 minutes. Drain, coarsely chop.

Melt 1 tablespoon butter in a frying pan over medium heat and add eschalots and mushrooms and stir for 2 minutes. Add garlic and chilli flakes and cook for a further 2-3 minutes or until mushrooms are tender. Remove from heat and combine in a bowl with cavolo nero.

Place chicken stock in a large saucepan and bring to the boil. Pour polenta into stock in a slow steady stream while stirring. Stir continuously so mixture does not become lumpy. Reduce heat to low and simmer, stirring frequently, for about 30-40 minutes or until polenta comes away from the sides of the pan. Add butter and parmesan and stir until smooth. Add cavolo nero mixture and stir.

Check seasoning and serve in warm bowls topped with shaved parmesan.

Serves 6

Tuscan vegetable soup

1 tbsp extra virgin olive oil

3 rashers bacon, coarsely chopped

2 brown onions, peeled and coarsely chopped

1 stick celery, sliced

2 potatoes, peeled and chopped

2 small carrots, peeled and chopped

1/4 small savoy cabbage, shredded

1-2 tbsp tomato paste

3 cups chicken stock

3 1/2 cups water

3 sprigs flat-leaf parsley

2 sprigs thyme

1 x 400g tin cannellini beans, rinsed and drained

Heat olive oil in a large saucepan and cook bacon, stirring occasionally, for about 5-6 minutes. Add onions, celery, potatoes, carrots, cabbage, tomato paste, chicken stock, 3 cups water and herbs and bring to the boil. Reduce heat and simmer for about 45 minutes or until vegetables are very soft.

Place half the beans in a blender or food processor with remaining water and blend until smooth.

Add the puree and beans to soup, add salt and pepper, bring to the boil and simmer for 2-3 minutes.

Serve with hot sourdough toast.

Serves 6

Chicken marylands with red cabbage and pinenuts

4 chicken marylands

5 tbsp extra virgin olive oil

salt and cracked black pepper

1/3 cup white wine

salt and cracked black pepper

1/2 red cabbage (about 750g), coarsely shredded

2 tsp caster sugar

1 1/2 tbsp white-wine vinegar

50g pinenuts, toasted

mashed potato, to serve

Preheat oven to 200C.

Drizzle chicken marylands with 3 tablespoons olive oil and season with salt and pepper. Roast for about 40-50 minutes, turning occasionally, until brown and cooked. Remove and rest in a warm place for 8-10 minutes. Place defatted pan juices over medium heat and add white wine, salt and pepper. Stir over high heat until boiling then simmer for 1-2 minutes.

Heat 2 tablespoons olive oil in a large frying pan and add red cabbage. Toss over high heat until wilted then add caster sugar, vinegar and toasted pinenuts. Season to taste and stir until cabbage is tender but crisp

Place cabbage mixture in the centre of 4 serving plates, top with chicken and pour sauce over. Serve with mashed potato.

Serves 4

Prawn, cabbage, watercress and cannellini bean salad

24 large cooked king prawns, shelled and deveined, tails intact

2 cups finely shredded cabbage

1 grapefruit, peeled and segmented

1 x 400g tin cannellini beans, rinsed and drained

1/2 bunch watercress sprigs

1/3 cup olive oil

2 tbsp red-wine vinegar

1 tsp Dijon mustard

salt and cracked black pepper

1/2 tsp caster sugar

50g salmon roe

Place peeled king prawns in a large bowl, add cabbage, grapefruit, cannellini beans and the watercress sprigs and toss gently.

Whisk olive oil, red-wine vinegar, Dijon mustard, salt, pepper and sugar in a small bowl. Pour dressing over salad and toss gently to combine.

Serve salad on 4 plates topped with salmon roe.

Serves 4

Capsicum

Crisp, green and red capsicum were once prominent at markets in Australia, but today there is a multitude of colours including purple, orange, yellow and chocolate. Red types are sweeter than un-ripe green ones while purple, chocolate and black varieties revert to green when cooked so are best used raw in salads. Sometimes known as bell or sweet peppers, capsicum are members of the Solanaceae family along with chillies, potatoes and tomatoes.

Banana or horn-shaped capsicum are about half the size of normal ones with slightly thinner flesh and a mild, sweet flavour. Their shape makes them especially good for stuffing.

Some people find the skin indigestible and bitter but it can easily be removed.*

Select firm, fleshy specimens that are well shaped and glossy. Avoid wrinkled, dull-looking capsicum with soft spots and blemishes.

Store them in the crisper of the fridge for up to 7 days, but not in plastic wrap as they tend to sweat.

* To peel capsicum, sear them over a gas flame or barbecue or roast in a hot oven for 15-20 minutes until well blistered, then place them in a plastic bag until cool enough to handle and peel the skin away with a sharp knife.

Caponata-style salad

1 small red capsicum, deseeded and
   coarsely chopped

1 yellow zucchini, sliced

1 baby fennel, finely sliced

2 eschalots, chopped

1 green pear, cored and coarsely chopped

3 tbsp small black olives

2 tsp salted capers, rinsed and drained

2 tbsp flat-leaf parsley, chopped

1 tbsp oregano leaves

1 small red chilli, finely chopped

1 clove garlic, finely chopped

juice of 1 lemon

1½ tbsp extra virgin olive oil

salt and cracked black pepper

Place all the ingredients in a large bowl and toss gently until combined .

Goes well with barbecued sausages.

Serves 6

Risotto primavera (risotto with spring vegetables)

6 cups chicken stock

2 tbsp extra virgin olive oil

1 small onion, chopped

2 cups arborio rice

1 cup white wine

salt and black pepper

1 carrot, chopped

1 stick celery, chopped

½ red capsicum, chopped

½ green capsicum, chopped

½ cup fresh green peas

4 tbsp butter

4 tbsp parmesan cheese

6 basil leaves, torn

grated parmesan, to serve

Bring stock to the boil in a large saucepan, reduce heat and simmer.

Heat olive oil in a large pan over medium heat and add onion. Cook, stirring constantly, until onion has turned golden. Add rice and stir to coat with oil. Add wine and cook until evaporated. Season with salt and pepper. Add all vegetables.

Continue adding stock, 1 cup at a time, stirring until all the liquid is absorbed. It should take about 20 minutes for the rice to cook.

Remove saucepan from heat and stir in butter, parmesan and basil. Rest for 2-3 minutes before serving.

Serve with grated parmesan.

Serves 6

Roasted olive-stuffed capsicum

6 red banana capsicum, peeled
   (see note on page 194)
$^1/_2$ small onion, finely chopped
1 tbsp tiny capers
3 slices toasted bread made into crumbs
2 tbsp grated parmesan
finely grated rind of $^1/_2$ lemon
2 tbsp flat-leaf parsley, chopped
80g ($^1/_2$ cup) pitted black olives, chopped
$^1/_4$ cup extra virgin olive oil
sea salt and cracked black pepper
1 tsp dried oregano
1 tbsp extra virgin olive oil, extra

Preheat oven to 180C.

For the filling, combine all the ingredients except oregano and extra oil in a medium-sized bowl and stir well.

Remove stem end from capsicum and make a cut down one side. Remove seeds, fill with stuffing and roll up.

Place in a single layer in an oiled ovenproof dish, sprinkle with oregano and drizzle with olive oil. Roast for about 15-20 minutes.

Serve with grilled lamb cutlets or rump steak.

Makes 6

Sweet and sour capsicum

$^1/_4$ cup currants
2 tbsp red-wine vinegar
2 tbsp extra virgin olive oil
2 tbsp pinenuts
2 red capsicum, seeds removed and sliced
2 yellow capsicum, seeds removed and sliced
$1^1/_2$ tbsp caster sugar
1 tsp salt
2 tbsp oregano leaves, chopped

Combine currants and vinegar in a small bowl.

Heat olive oil in a large frying pan over medium heat and add pinenuts. Stir for 1-2 minutes or until golden then remove with a slotted spoon and set aside. Add capsicum, sugar and salt to the pan and stir. Simmer, covered, for 15-18 minutes or until capsicum are tender and cooked. Add currants and vinegar and pinenuts and stir. Top with oregano leaves.

Serves 4 as a side dish

Red capsicum mayo with grilled lamb chops and watercress salad

1 red capsicum
$2^1/_2$ tbsp extra virgin olive oil
1 cup good mayonnaise
pinch of sweet paprika
8 small lamb loin chops
2 cups watercress sprigs
2 tsp red-wine vinegar
salt and cracked black pepper
mashed potato, to serve

Preheat oven to 200C.

Rub capsicum with 1 tablespoon olive oil and roast in oven for 10 minutes then turn and roast for a further 10 minutes. Place in a plastic bag for 10 minutes. Remove skin and seeds.

Chop half the capsicum coarsely and mix with mayo and sweet paprika. Reserve other half for another use.

Grill lamb loin chops on a hot griddle or barbecue over medium heat for about 4 minutes each side or until cooked as desired.

Toss watercress sprigs with red-wine vinegar and $1^1/_2$ tablespoons extra virgin olive oil, salt and pepper to taste.

Serve lamb chops topped with capsicum mayo and accompanied by watercress salad and mashed potato.

Serves 4

Stir-fried chicken with rice, snowpeas, capsicum and coriander

1¹/₂ cups jasmine rice (300g)

2 tbsp vegetable oil

2 large chicken breast fillets (500g), chopped

1 brown onion, chopped

2 cloves garlic, finely chopped

1 large red chilli, finely sliced

1 red capsicum, sliced

100g snowpeas, trimmed and halved

2 tsp brown sugar

2 tbsp fish sauce

2 tbsp soy sauce

¹/₄ tsp sesame oil

¹/₄ cup Thai basil, torn

¹/₃ cup coriander leaves, torn

Combine jasmine rice with 3 cups cold water and cook, covered, over low heat for 10-12 minutes or until tender. Spread on a tray and refrigerate until cold.

Heat vegetable oil in a wok or large frying-pan over high heat and add chicken breast fillets and stir-fry until lightly browned. Add brown onion, garlic and red chilli. Add capsicum and cooked rice and stir-fry until chicken is cooked. Add snowpeas, brown sugar, fish sauce, soy sauce and sesame oil and toss to combine.

Remove from heat and add Thai basil leaves and coriander leaves. Toss gently and serve.

Serves 4

Chicken, carrot and capsicum rice-paper rolls

1 large chicken breast fillet (about 250g)

1 tbsp extra virgin olive oil

1 red capsicum

1 small butter lettuce

1 carrot, peeled

1 cup beansprouts

12 small sprigs mint

12 sheets rice paper

hoisin sauce, to serve

Heat extra virgin olive oil in a frying pan over medium heat and cook chicken for about 4-5 minutes each side or until browned and cooked through. Cool and cut into strips.

Cut capsicum into strips, separate leaves from the heart of the butter lettuce and cut carrot into matchsticks. Rinse beansprouts in cold water and drain. Rinse mint under cold water and drain.

Dip one sheet of rice paper briefly into warm water and drain on a tea towel. Top rice paper with a piece of chicken, a small lettuce leaf, capsicum and carrot strips, a few beansprouts and a mint sprig. Fold sides in and roll up firmly. Repeat to make 12 rolls.

Serve with hoisin sauce for dipping.

Makes 12

Quick chilli con carne

1 tbsp vegetable oil

1 brown onion, chopped

2 cloves garlic, finely chopped

500g lean minced beef

1 x 420g tin tomato soup

salt and cracked black pepper

1 tbsp mild chilli powder, or to taste

¹/₂ cup water

1 green capsicum, deseeded and chopped

2 x 420g cans red kidney beans, rinsed and drained

1 ripe avocado, peeled

4 tbsp light sour cream

corn chips, for dipping

Heat vegetable oil in a large saucepan and cook onion over medium heat for 3-4 minutes. Add garlic and minced beef and cook until meat browns, stirring often. Add tomato soup, salt and pepper, chilli powder and water and simmer for 10 minutes, stirring occasionally. Add green capsicum and red kidney beans and simmer for a further 10 minutes.

Slice peeled avocado. Serve chilli con carne in shallow bowls, topped with a dollop of light sour cream and avocado slices. Pass the corn chips.

Serves 4

Sydney Produce Market

Carrots

Carrots can be round, stumpy, small, large or tapering – the length depends largely on the temperature in which they are grown. Those from hot climates tend to be short and stubby, whereas cool-climate carrots are usually long and slender They are members of the umbelliferae family along with parsley, dill and coriander, and some heirloom varieties are pink, black, purple or white. Baby carrots, sometimes known as dutch carrots, usually need only rinsing (not peeling) if being used raw in school lunch boxes or on a vegetable platter with dips. New varieties of golf ball carrots are available at specialty shops – choose small specimens for a sweeter flavour.

Mature carrots can be peeled or scrubbed with a brush, but leave them chunky if you are slow cooking, for example in a braise.

Select firm, brightly coloured carrots that smell earthy, with fresh, crisp tops and no split ends or soft spots. Deeply coloured carrots contain more betacarotene.

Store in a plastic bag in the fridge – but not near melons, bananas or apples, as the ethylene gas from these fruits will cause carrots to go bitter.

Barley, carrot, herb and prawn soup

2 tbsp extra virgin olive oil

2 sticks celery, chopped

1 brown onion, chopped

1 carrot, chopped

1 cup (200g) pearl barley

3 sprigs thyme

4 sprigs flat-leaf parsley

1 clove garlic, chopped

6 cups chicken stock

2 tbsp tomato paste

1 x 400g tin chopped tomatoes

salt and cracked black pepper

12 large cooked king prawns, shelled
    and deveined with tails intact

Heat 1 tablespoon extra virgin olive oil in a large saucepan over medium heat and add celery, onion and carrot and cook for about 5 minutes, until onion is soft. Add pearl barley, thyme, parsley and garlic and stir over low heat for 2-3 minutes. Add chicken stock, tomato paste, tomatoes, salt and pepper and simmer, covered, over low heat for about 45 minutes or until barley is tender.

Discard herbs and remove ½ cup barley and vegetables with a slotted spoon and process in a food processor until smooth. Return barley mixture to saucepan, check seasoning and heat through.

Serve in 6 warm soup bowls, each topped with 2 prawns and drizzled with the remaining olive oil.

Serves 6

Carrot, radish and orange salad

2 oranges, peeled and sliced

8 red radishes, trimmed and thinly sliced

2 carrots, peeled and thinly sliced

⅓ cup (55g) sultanas

juice of ½ an orange

juice of ½ a lemon

2 tbsp extra virgin olive oil

1 tsp orange-flower water

salt and cracked black pepper

2 tbsp chives, snipped

Place oranges in a large bowl with radishes. Add carrots and sultanas.

Combine orange juice, lemon juice and 2 tablespoons extra virgin olive in a small bowl. Add orange-flower water, salt, pepper and a pinch of caster sugar and whisk until smooth. Add dressing to salad and toss gently. Scatter with chives.

Great served with barbecued whole baby snapper.

Serves 4

Carrot and almond cake

3 eggs

220g (2 cups) caster sugar

1 cup light olive oil

1 tsp vanilla essence

225g (1½ cups) self-raising flour

1 tsp bicarb soda

pinch of salt

2 tsp ground cinnamon

90g almonds, chopped

250g grated carrots (about 2 large carrots)

Cream-cheese icing

100g cream cheese, softened

90g icing sugar, sifted

2 tsp orange juice

3 tsp orange rind, grated

Preheat oven to 180C.

Combine eggs and sugar in a large bowl and stir until well mixed and sugar begins to dissolve. Add oil and vanilla essence and stir well. Sift flour, bicarb soda, salt and cinnamon together, and fold into cake mixture until smooth. Add almonds and carrot and stir until well combined.

Pour mixture into a greased and paper-lined 23cm-square tin and bake for about 45 minutes or until a skewer inserted in the centre comes out clean. Cool in tin for 20 minutes. Turn onto a cake rack to cool then top with cream cheese icing if desired.

Store in an airtight container.

For the cream cheese icing, combine all the ingredients in a medium-sized bowl and stir until smooth.

Stir-fried lamb with carrots and water chestnuts

(pictured page 201)

2 tbsp peanut oil

1 clove garlic, finely chopped

1 small red chilli, finely chopped

1 carrot, peeled and thinly sliced

1 brown onion, thinly sliced

1 tbsp green curry paste

500g lamb backstrap, thinly sliced

230g water chestnuts, coarsely chopped

4 green onions, sliced diagonally

1 tbsp fish sauce

2 tbsp water

⅓ cup coriander leaves

steamed jasmine rice, to serve

Heat 1 tablespoon peanut oil in a wok. Add garlic and chilli and stir-fry until fragrant. Add carrot and onion and stir-fry for 2-3 minutes.

Remove ingredients from wok, add remaining peanut oil and green curry paste and stir-fry for 1 minute. Add lamb and cook until brown and tender (this may need to be done in batches).

Return vegetables to wok with water chestnuts and green onions. Add fish sauce and water and stir until hot.

Serve immediately with coriander leaves and rice.

Serves 4

Cauliflower

Creamy cauliflower belongs to the brassica family and contains high levels of sulphur compounds (some of which are given off when cooking), so is best eaten raw or cooked very briefly. The majority are white, but there are pink, purple and pale-green varieties, all high in vitamin C.

The newer lime-green, pointed romanesco has characteristics of both broccoli and cauliflower. Mini cauliflowers are a little more expensive, but are great served whole and stay firm when cooked. Broccoflower is a cross between cauliflower and broccoli.

One of the best ways to cook cauliflower is to roast it with a drizzle of olive oil, as the flavour becomes luscious and concentrated. If you boil it add a squeeze of lemon to the water to keep it pearly white.

Cauliflowers should have a tightly packed head surrounded by fresh green leaves. A cream or brownish head indicates the cauli has been picked some time ago.

Store in a plastic bag in the fridge and use as soon as possible.

Melbourne wholesale fruit and vegetable Market

Cauliflower, raisin and onion salad

1 small cauliflower (about 600g), cut into florets

600g broccoli, cut into florets

²/₃ cup extra virgin olive oil

1 red onion, finely sliced

100g raisins

2 tbsp salted capers, rinsed and drained

50g pinenuts, toasted

2 tbsp oregano, chopped

100g kalamata olives

2 tbsp flat-leaf parsley, chopped

salt and cracked black pepper

Cook cauliflower in lightly salted, boiling water for about 6-8 minutes or until just tender.

Cook broccoli in lightly salted, boiling water for about 3 minutes or until bright-green and crunchy. Drain, refresh both vegetables under cold water, drain again and place in a serving dish.

Heat olive oil in a saucepan, add onion and cook over low heat until soft. Add remaining ingredients and cook over low heat, stirring occasionally, for 5 minutes or until raisins are plump. Pour onion mixture over cauliflower and broccoli, season with salt and pepper and toss gently to combine.

Serve at room temperature.

Serves 6 as an accompaniment

Farfalle with cauliflower, chilli, herbs and olives

500g cauliflower, cut into florets

300g farfalle pasta

100ml extra virgin olive oil

2 cloves garlic, finely chopped

1 large red chilli, finely chopped

2 anchovy fillets, finely chopped

¹/₂ cup flat-leaf parsley, torn

1 tsp thyme leaves

salt and cracked black pepper

1 cup grated parmesan

Cook cauliflower in lightly salted, boiling water over medium heat for about 15 minutes or until tender. Drain.

Cook pasta in lightly salted, boiling water over medium heat until al dente. Drain.

Heat olive oil in large pan over low heat and add garlic, chilli and anchovies and cook for 2-3 minutes. Add parsley, thyme and cauliflower and mash with a wooden spoon. Add salt and pepper and parmesan and stir well.

Serves 4

Roasted cauliflower with king prawns, currants and spicy dressing

1 cauliflower, trimmed and cut into florets

salt flakes and cracked black pepper

220ml olive oil

35g (¼ cup) currants

3 tbsp red-wine vinegar

2 tsp ground cumin

2 tsp ground coriander

1 tsp smoked paprika

1 clove garlic, very thinly sliced

¼ tsp dried chilli flakes

24 large green king prawns, peeled and deveined, tails intact

½ cup coriander leaves

¼ cup flat-leaf parsley

lime cheeks, to serve

Preheat oven to 180C.

Place cauliflower on a roasting tray and season well. Drizzle with 60ml (3 tablespoons) olive oil and toss to coat. Roast for 25-30 minutes or until cooked and golden.

Combine currants and vinegar and bring to the boil, then drain.

In a small pan, combine cumin, coriander and paprika and dry fry over low heat until fragrant. Add garlic, chilli flakes and 120ml (6 tablespoons) olive oil and cook over low heat until garlic is golden. Remove from heat and season.

Heat remaining oil in a large frying pan and stir-fry prawns over high heat until almost cooked. Add spicy dressing and cook until just heated through. Stir in currants and herbs and remove from heat.

Serve cauliflower and prawns warm or at room temperature accompanied by lime cheeks.

Serves 6

Cauliflower cheese

1 small cauliflower, trimmed and cut into florets

50g butter

4 tbsp plain flour

3 cups milk

salt

¼ tsp cayenne pepper

1 tsp Dijon mustard

1 cup (125g) grated gruyere cheese

1 tbsp grated parmesan

½ cup (50g) dried breadcrumbs

Preheat oven to 200C.

Cook cauliflower in plenty of lightly salted, boiling water for 5 minutes. Drain.

Melt butter in a small saucepan over low heat, stir in flour and cook for 1 minute then remove from heat and gradually stir in milk. Return to low heat and stir constantly until mixture thickens. Add salt, cayenne and mustard and stir until smooth.

Place cauliflower in a shallow, greased ovenproof dish and pour sauce over. Sprinkle with combined cheeses and breadcrumbs and bake for 15-20 minutes.

Serves 6

Celeriac

Beneath the bulbous skin is creamy flesh with a subtle, sweet flavour. Sometimes called celery root or knob celery, celeriac belongs to the parsley family – along with carrots, parsnips and celery. Unlike celery, which is available all year, celeriac arrives at the markets in autumn and is at its peak through winter.

Introduced to England from Egypt in the 18th century, celeriac is considered a delicacy in regional France, where it is frequently whisked into buttery, creamy mash. The delicately flavoured flesh is scrumptious grated raw and added to coleslaw and the young leaves give colour and pungency to salads.

Celeriac should be crisp and have a sweet, mild celery flavour if it has just been harvested. Fresh celeriac should be pale, not brown, and have a greenish tinge at the base of its mid-green leaves.

Select firm, small- to medium-sized specimens that feel heavy for their size, with a minimum of rootlets and knobs. It needs to be peeled thickly to remove all the lumps and bumps and, like artichoke, discolours when cut, so peel and then drop into a bowl of water with lemon juice added to it. It can be eaten raw or cooked but it's essential to peel it first.

Celeriac can be used in many recipes calling for celery. It's best grated or shredded when eaten raw, but it can be boiled, braised, sauteed and baked and is especially tasty in soups and braises.

Store it in the crisper of the fridge for up to a week.

Celeriac remoulade with king prawns

(pictured)

12 large cooked king prawns

1 small celeriac

1 lemon, halved

1 cup good mayonnaise

1 tbsp Dijon mustard, or to taste

salt and cracked black pepper

1 tbsp oregano, chopped

Peel and devein prawns, leaving tails intact. Cover and refrigerate.

Peel celeriac thickly, cut into quarters and place in a bowl of water with the squeezed lemon.

Combine mayonnaise and mustard in a medium-sized bowl and stir well to combine. Season to taste.

Remove celeriac from the water, drain and shred the pieces using the grater disc on a food processor and mix immediately with the mayonnaise.

To serve, add oregano to celeriac mixture and stir to combine. Pile three prawns onto each serving plate, with the celeriac remoulade beside the prawns.

Serves 4 as an entree

Celeriac Mash

2 tbsp extra virgin olive oil

6 green onions, trimmed and sliced

500g peeled celeriac, chopped

500g sebago potatoes, peeled and chopped

300ml chicken stock

salt and cracked black pepper

Heat olive oil in a saucepan and add green onions and cook over low heat for 3 minutes or until just wilted, then remove with a slotted spoon and set aside.

Add celeriac and potato to the same pan and cook, stirring, over low-medium heat for 5 minutes. Add stock and season to taste, bring to the boil then cover and simmer for 20-25 minutes. Uncover and boil until liquid is evaporated and vegetables are tender. Mash with a potato masher and stir in green onions.

Serve with barbecued lamb chops or grilled sausages.

Serves 4

Celery

While sticks of celery are often eaten as a snack or sliced in salads, the base of the bunch – the tender heart – is also a true delicacy and should not be overlooked. Use the tough outer sticks in stocks and soups and the heart in salads.

Asian or Chinese celery (kun choi) is smaller and darker, with a stronger flavour – it is popular in stir-fries and soups. Celeriac, its bulbous cousin, has creamy white flesh and makes heavenly mash and great chips. It is often called celery root. Lovage is a celery-flavoured herb whose slim stems add flavour to stocks and soups.

Celery should always look crisp, not limp, with fresh-looking leaves. Do not buy bunches with cracked stalks or any browning.

Store in an airtight container in the fridge or plastic wrap in the crisper. Don't wash the sticks until ready to use, as moisture encourages deterioration.

Roasted free-range chicken stuffed with celery, herbs and sourdough bread

1 tbsp butter

1 large stick celery, chopped

2 brown eschalots, chopped

leaves from 2 sprigs thyme

2 sprigs flat-leaf parsley, chopped

1 thick slice sourdough bread, torn into 1cm pieces

2 tbsp sour light cream

salt and cracked black pepper

1 medium-sized free-range chicken

2 tbsp extra virgin olive oil

1 tsp mixed dried herbs

Preheat oven to 200C.

Melt butter in a frying pan over medium heat and add celery, eschalots, thyme and parsley. Cook for 5-6 minutes, stirring occasionally, set aside.

Place bread on an oven tray and toast for 5-6 minutes until crisp. Combine bread and celery mixture in a bowl and cool. Add sour light cream, salt and pepper and mix well to combine. Spoon stuffing into cavity of chicken. Tie legs together with string.

Place olive oil in the base of a roasting pan and add chicken, turning to coat. Season with salt and pepper and sprinkle with mixed dried herbs.

Roast chicken for 75 minutes or until cooked and golden.

Remove and rest, lightly covered, in a warm place for 6-8 minutes before carving.

Serve with roast pumpkin and a watercress salad.

Serves 4

Celery, bacon and cheese gratin

Serve this creamy dish with roast leg of lamb or for lunch with a green salad and crusty Italian bread. It can also be cooked in individual ovenproof dishes (about 1½ cup capacity).

1 large bunch celery, trimmed

250g bacon, chopped

40g butter, chopped

3 brown eschalots, chopped

1 clove garlic, finely chopped

100g swiss gruyere cheese, grated

1¼ cups pouring cream

leaves from 2-3 sprigs thyme

salt and cracked black pepper

3 tbsp grated pecorino or parmesan

Preheat oven to 180C.

Cut celery on the diagonal into 3cm-thick slices.

Fry bacon in a heavy-based, non-stick fry pan over high heat, until browned and crisp. Remove bacon with a slotted spoon and leave fat to cool slightly. Add butter to pan and when melted add celery and cook for 5 minutes. Add eschalots and garlic and cook over medium heat for a further 5 minutes, stirring occasionally, until vegetables are cooked and lightly browned. Stir in bacon, gruyere, cream and thyme. Season.

Spoon mixture into a 6-cup ovenproof dish, sprinkle with pecorino or parmesan and bake for 15-20 minutes or until golden.

Serves 4

Chilli

Brilliantly coloured chillies, members of the capsicum family, are very rich in vitamin C. They are one of the most widely used seasonings in the world, used in cooking for centuries. There are hundreds of varieties, which are usually green until they mature, when they may turn red, purple, brown, yellow or black.

Capsaicin is the substance contained in the membrane and seeds that gives chillies their heat and causes the brain to release endorphins, creating a feeling of wellbeing. Remove the membrane and seeds before using if you want to add only a little heat to your dish.

Chillies are often labelled on a heat scale of one to 10. Habanero, the lantern-shaped chillies, can be orange, green or red and are at the top of the scale, so handle with care. Jalapeno (5) often found pickled in bottles or cans, are long, plump and much milder. Tiny bird's-eye chillies (8) give Thai food its hot reputation. The larger, long, Dutch red and green chillies (6) add a spicy flavour with just a little heat to soups, salads and braises.

Buy fresh chillies that are firm and not wilted. Ripe chillies should have the stem attached (a sign of freshness) and be quite glossy and smooth.

Fresh chillies can be stored in a fruit bowl for a few days if it is not humid or for longer in the crisper.

Street market, Amalfi

Chocolate chilli cakes with soft-choc centres and vanilla ice-cream

¹/₄ cup pouring cream

60g dark chocolate, coarsely chopped

100g soft unsalted butter

110g (¹/₂ cup) caster sugar

2 eggs

4 tbsp sour light cream

150g (1 cup) plain flour

³/₄ tsp mild chilli powder

¹/₄ tsp bicarb soda

¹/₄ tsp salt

vanilla bean ice-cream, to serve

Preheat oven to 175C.

Heat cream until boiling and pour over chopped chocolate, stirring until chocolate is melted and smooth. Line a small bowl with plastic wrap, pour chocolate mixture into bowl, cool, cover and freeze until very firm.

For the chilli cakes, beat butter and sugar until light and fluffy. Add eggs, one at a time, beating well between additions. Add sour cream and beat until smooth. Sift flour, chilli powder, bicarb soda and salt together. Stir into butter mixture and mix until well combined. Spoon mixture into 6 greased muffin tins and bake at 175C for 15 minutes. Cut firm chocolate into 6 pieces, roll each into a small ball and place 1 piece in the centre of each cake, pressing down gently into cakes. Bake for a further 15-18 minutes or until firm to touch. Cool cakes in tin for 5-8 minutes before turning out.

Serve warm cakes with vanilla bean ice-cream.

Serves 6

Tomato, chilli, calamari and chorizo salad with cannellini beans

3 tbsp extra virgin olive oil

1 brown onion, chopped

1 clove garlic, finely chopped

200g spicy chorizo sausage, sliced

1 x 400g tin cannellini beans, rinsed and drained

salt and cracked black pepper

1 x 400g tin tomatoes, chopped

2 tbsp tomato paste

50ml red wine vinegar

350g cleaned calamari, cut into thin strips, tentacles halved

1-2 large green chillies, finely chopped

¹/₂ bunch coriander leaves

¹/₂ bunch basil leaves, torn

¹/₄ bunch flat-leaf parsley leaves

3 green onions, finely sliced

juice of ¹/₂ lemon

Heat 1 tablespoon olive oil in a large frying pan over medium heat and cook onion for 4 minutes or until soft. Add garlic and chorizo and cook for 5 minutes, stirring frequently. Add cannellini beans, salt, pepper, tomatoes, tomato paste, vinegar and 100ml water and simmer until liquid is absorbed.

Heat remaining olive oil in a large frying pan over high heat. Add calamari and cook for 2 minutes or until opaque. Add green chilli and cook, stirring, for 30 seconds. Remove from heat and place in a bowl. Add coriander, basil, parsley, green onions and lemon juice. Spread beans on a serving plate and top with calamari.

Serves 4

Pan-seared prawns with chilli, chives, coriander and cannellini beans

This versatile recipe is delicious as a starter but you can also add a few more prawns and serve it as a light lunch with thick slices of sourdough smeared with cultured butter.

2 tbsp extra virgin olive oil

16 large green (raw) king prawns, peeled and deveined, tails intact

salt flakes and cracked black pepper

2 eschalots, peeled and very finely sliced

2 x 400g cans cannellini beans, rinsed and drained

2 witlof, trimmed and finely sliced

2 long red chillies, seeds removed and finely sliced lengthways

1 bulb fennel, trimmed and finely sliced

1/2 bunch chives, chopped

1/2 cup coriander leaves

Dressing

1/2 clove garlic, mashed

11/2 tbsp lime juice

3 tbsp extra virgin olive oil

salt flakes and cracked black pepper

Heat olive oil in a large pan and sear prawns over medium heat for about 2-3 minutes each side. Season. Add eschalots and cook over medium heat for 2-3 minutes. Add beans and remove from heat.

Spoon prawn mixture onto a large shallow serving platter. Scatter over witlof, chillies and fennel.

Combine dressing ingredients in a small bowl and whisk well. Pour over salad and top with chives and coriander.

Serves 4 as a starter

Crab and chilli bruschetta

This is a fabulous appetiser; the ingredients simply need to be combined while the bread is grilling.

6 thick slices sourdough bread

2 tbsp extra virgin olive oil

2 cloves garlic, halved

200g crabmeat

1 tbsp flat-leaf parsley, chopped

1 small red chilli, seeded and finely chopped

1 tbsp lime juice

salt and cracked black pepper

lime cheeks, to serve

Brush both sides of bread with olive oil and toast under a hot grill for 2-3 minutes each side or until golden. Rub one side of bread with cut garlic, then cut in half on the diagonal.

Combine remaining ingredients and toss gently.

Serve bruschetta topped with crabmeat mixture and lime cheeks on the side.

Serves 6

Spicy deep-fried quail

These delightful little nibbles are fast and easy to prepare; they need just 30 minutes for the flavours to develop.

8 quail

2 tbsp Chinese five-spice powder

2-3 small red chillies, seeded and finely chopped

1 tbsp salt

$^1/_3$ cup extra virgin olive oil

vegetable oil, for deep-frying

Remove legs, thighs and breasts from quail (or ask your butcher to do this). Combine five-spice powder, chilli and salt in a bowl and mix well. Brush quail portions with olive oil, toss in spice mixture, then cover and refrigerate for 30 minutes.

Deep-fry quail in batches in hot vegetable oil for about 2 minutes or until golden and cooked. Drain on paper towel.

Makes 24

Spaghetti with anchovies, chilli, crumbs and parmesan

400g spaghetti

3 tbsp extra virgin olive oil

6 anchovy fillets, chopped

$1^1/_2$ cups (105g) day-old breadcrumbs

$^1/_2$ cup flat-leaf parsley, chopped

$^1/_2$ cup (80g) pitted kalamata olives, chopped

1 large red chilli, finely chopped

salt and cracked black pepper

40g grated parmesan

Cook spaghetti in lightly salted, boiling water for 8-10 minutes or until al dente, then drain and return to saucepan.

Heat olive oil in a non-stick frying pan and add anchovy fillets. Stir over low heat for 1 minute then add breadcrumbs and stir until golden.

Combine crumb mixture, flat-leaf parsley, pitted kalamata olives and red chilli and stir through spaghetti.

Season with salt and pepper and divide among four pasta bowls.

Serve scattered with grated parmesan cheese.

Serves 4

Steamed broccolini with chilli, almonds and T-bone steaks

2 bunches broccolini, trimmed

3 tbsp extra virgin olive oil

1 large clove garlic, finely chopped

2 tbsp black olive tapenade

1 tbsp balsamic vinegar

1-2 large red chillies, very finely sliced

salt and cracked black pepper

50g toasted almonds, coarsely chopped

4 T-bone steaks, grilled

Steam 2 bunches of trimmed broccolini over a pan of simmering water or in a steamer for 4-6 minutes or until tender. Drain.

Heat olive oil in a small frying pan and add garlic and cook until aromatic. Add black olive tapenade, balsamic vinegar, chillies and 2 tablespoons water and whisk well.

Place broccolini in a large bowl, add garlic mixture, salt and pepper and toss gently to combine.

Scatter with almonds and serve with grilled T-bone steaks.

Serves 4

Sweet red chilli sauce with ripe mangoes and vanilla ice-cream

2 long red chillies, seeded and very thinly sliced

$^1/_2$ cup (110g) caster sugar

juice of $^1/_2$ lemon

2 large ripe mangoes

vanilla bean ice-cream, to serve

Place chillies in a saucepan with caster sugar, 300ml water and lemon juice. Bring to the boil over medium heat and then simmer gently for about 20 minutes or until syrupy. Transfer to a bowl and refrigerate.

Peel and slice two large, ripe mangoes and place on serving plates. Spoon sweet red chilli sauce over mangoes and serve with a scoop of ice-cream.

Serves 4

Chokoes

Chokoes belong to the cucurbit family along with pumpkin, gourds and zucchini. The tough green skin has deep creases (and often with soft prickles, depending on variety). The single nutty-tasting seed is edible, particularly when very young, as are the tender shoots and leaves popular in Asian cuisines. Native to central America, they appear in our markets year-round, although supplies can be erratic.

Chokoes can be roasted, fried, pickled, steamed or mashed, and the distinctive but rather bland flavour combines well with spicy ingredients.

Choose the smallest, shiny chokoes without any brown spots. If they are all large, the ones with the softest spines will be most tender.

Chokoes keep well in the fridge crisper, but if stored for too long they will start to sprout from the seed and become stringy. When cut, they exude a slippery sap that is hard to wash off your hands and can cause itchiness, so use rubber gloves to peel them or cut off each end and immerse in cold water for a few minutes before peeling.

Roasted chokoes with free-range chicken

1 x 1.8kg free range chicken

1 lemon

6 tbsp extra virgin olive oil

2 sprigs rosemary

2 sprigs sage

salt and cracked black pepper

2 chokoes, peeled and cut into quarters

1 bulb fennel, trimmed and cut into quarters

750g pumpkin, peeled and cut into chunks

2 carrots, peeled and cut into chunks

4 unpeeled cloves garlic

1 tsp dried rosemary

4-5 tbsp verjuice

Preheat oven to 200C.

Place chicken in roasting dish and squeeze lemon juice over chicken then drizzle with half the olive oil. Place lemon halves in chicken cavity with rosemary and sage. Tie chicken legs together with string. Season generously with salt and pepper. Roast for 75 minutes or until cooked.

Place vegetables in an ovenproof dish, drizzle with remaining olive oil, season and sprinkle with dried rosemary. Toss to coat. Roast vegetables in oven, turning occasionally, for 1 hour or until cooked.

Remove and rest chicken, covered with alfoil, in a warm place. Add verjuice to defatted pan juices and stir over high heat for 1 minute. Check seasoning.

Serve chicken with roasted vegetables and verjuice sauce.

Serves 4

Stir-fried choko with baby corn, carrot and pumpkin

1 choko, peeled and seeded

400g pumpkin, peeled and seeded

1-2 tbsp vegetable oil

2 cloves garlic, finely chopped

125g baby corn, halved

1 carrot, peeled and thinly sliced

2 tbsp soy sauce

1 tbsp mirin

1 tsp sesame oil

$^1/_2$ tsp dried chilli flakes

$^1/_3$ cup coriander leaves

Slice choko and pumpkin, about 5mm thick. Heat vegetable oil in a wok or large frying pan and add choko, pumpkin, garlic, corn and carrot and stir-fry over medium heat for 6 minutes or until vegetables are just tender. Add soy sauce, mirin, sesame oil and chilli flakes and stir.

Top with coriander leaves and serve.

Great with barbecued chicken skewers.

Serves 4

Cucumber

Cucumbers belong to the cucurbit family and, like melons, are more than 95 per cent water.

The most common varieties are green ridge or garden, which has glossy dark skin, rounded ends and is usually picked when 20cm long. The slender telegraph cucumber, also known as burpless, has fewer seeds and is harvested when 25-30cm long. Lebanese cucumbers, easily distinguished by their petite size and thin, shiny skin, are sweet and crunchy with tiny seeds; their big advantage is that they don't need peeling. Apple cucumbers are round and usually about 9cm in diameter, with pale, creamy-green skin and a mild taste. Pickling cucumbers or gherkins are dark-green with bumpy skin and very firm, dense flesh, making for crisp pickles.

For maximum flavour, buy cucumbers with firm skin and pickle or preserve as soon as possible. Look for shiny cucumbers that feel heavy for their size – those with yellow patches should be avoided, as they could be overripe. Store unwashed in the crisper of the fridge and avoid storing them with fruit, as they will soften quickly.

If a recipe calls for seeded cucumbers, simply cut the cucumbers in half lengthways and scoop out the seeds with a teaspoon.

Salad of king prawns with cucumber, watercress, papaya and chilli

(pictured page 221)

Fried eschalots are available at Asian food stores.

1 cup mini cabbage, finely shredded

$^1/_2$ cup peeled and julienned green papaya

1 large or 2 small Lebanese cucumbers,
    very finely sliced

1 cup watercress sprigs

16 cooked king prawns, peeled and deveined
    with tails in tact

$^1/_3$ cup mint leaves, coarsely chopped

$^1/_3$ cup coriander leaves, coarsely chopped

$^1/_4$ cup roasted peanuts, coarsely chopped

$^1/_4$ cup fried eschalots

Dressing

2 cloves garlic, chopped

2 long red chillies, chopped

1 tbsp grated palm sugar

$1^1/_2$ tbsp fish sauce

3 tbsp lime juice

For the salad, scatter cabbage and papaya on
a large serving platter. Scatter over cucumber
slices and watercress. Top with prawns. Sprinkle
over herbs and pour dressing over salad. Top with
peanuts and fried eschalots and serve immediately.

For the dressing, place garlic and chillies in a
mortar and pestle and pound to a paste. Add palm
sugar, fish sauce and lime juice and combine well.

Serves 4 as a starter

Cucumber, fennel and tuna salad with lemon caper dressing

400g small kipfler potatoes, peeled

200g small green beans, trimmed

2 lebanese cucumbers, thickly sliced on the diagonal

1 baby fennel, trimmed and finely sliced

250g cherry tomatoes, halved

100g small black olives

425g tuna, drained

$^1/_2$ cup flat-leaf parsley, chopped

Dressing

2 tbsp extra virgin olive oil

$^1/_2$ red onion, chopped

1 clove garlic, finely chopped

2 tbsp salted capers, rinsed

2 tbsp lemon juice

salt and cracked black pepper

Cook potatoes in lightly salted, boiling water for 12-15 minutes or until just tender. Add beans for last 2 minutes of cooking. Drain and refresh under cold running water.

Thickly slice potatoes and place in a large bowl with beans, cucumbers, fennel, tomatoes, olives and tuna.

For the dressing, combine ingredients in a small bowl and whisk until smooth. Pour over salad and scatter with parsley.

Serves 4

Char-grilled salmon fillets with dilled cucumbers, light sour cream and roasted potatoes

4 lebanese cucumbers, unpeeled

2 tsp salt

$^1/_4$ cup light sour cream

2 tsp lemon juice

1 tbsp dill, chopped

3 sprigs mint, leaves torn

2 tbsp chives, snipped

cracked black pepper

4 salmon fillets (about 230g each)

1 tbsp extra virgin olive oil

roasted jacket potatoes, to serve

Slice cucumbers lengthwise and scoop out seeds with a teaspoon. Cut into slices on the diagonal about 5mm thick. Toss with salt and place in a colander for 10 minutes. Pat dry with paper towel. Combine cucumbers in a bowl with sour cream, lemon juice, dill, mint leaves, chives and pepper.

Brush salmon fillets with extra virgin olive oil, salt and pepper and cook on a lightly oiled griddle pan over medium heat for 3-5 minutes each side or until cooked as desired.

Serve topped with dilled cucumbers and roasted jacket potatoes.

Serves 4

Pan-fried flathead fillets with spicy cucumber dressing

2 tbsp butter

2 tbsp extra virgin olive oil

4 flathead fillets (about 200g each)

self-raising flour

Dressing

200ml rice-wine vinegar

75g caster sugar

1 Lebanese cucumber, unpeeled, finely chopped

1 tbsp coriander, chopped

2 small red chillies, finely chopped

1 eschalot, finely chopped

1 tbsp roasted peanuts, coarsely chopped

hot chips (optional), to serve

Melt butter and olive oil in a large frying pan over medium-high heat. Dust flathead fillets in self-raising flour, shake off excess and pan-fry skin side down, for 2-3 minutes, until golden, then turn and cook a further 2-3 minutes or until just cooked through. Drain on absorbent paper and serve with spicy cucumber dressing and hot chips.

For the spicy cucumber dressing, combine rice-wine vinegar and caster sugar in a small saucepan and stir over low heat until sugar is dissolved. Remove from heat and cool. Add cucumber, coriander, red chillies, eschalot and roasted peanuts and stir well. Pour over fish and serve.

Serves 4

Eggplant

In Europe, eggplant is often salted before cooking to remove the bitter juices, but the improved varieties grown in Australia have lost most of the bitterness – unless they have been on the greengrocer's shelf for too long. Some say that salting also helps to reduce the amount of oil absorbed during cooking.

If you buy a very mature eggplant (the seeds will be dark-brown) slice and sprinkle it with salt, leave for 20-30 minutes then rinse and drain before cooking for improved flavour. There is no need to peel eggplant, although some believe taking the skin off removes bitterness.

Known as aubergine in Britain and France, melanzane in Italy and brinjal in India and Africa, the many varieties vary in size and colour, which can be pale-green, white, white streaked with purple, mauve, deep-purple or even orange. Thai eggplants are small and round and can be green, cream or mauve with green stripes. They have tough skins and add a bitter flavour to Thai salads, curries and soups. Japanese eggplants are long and slender, about 15-20cm, with either purple or light-mauve skin.

Pea eggplants – small, crunchy and bitter – are popular in Thai green curries, pickles and Vietnamese salads. They are sold in clusters at Asian stores.

Select eggplant that are medium-sized and heavy, the skin should be satin-like and shiny, not dull, and there should be no soft spots.

Store them in a cool place or in the crisper of the fridge for just a few days, as they will go brown if chilled for any length of time.

Eggplant is delicious grilled, barbecued, fried, baked, stuffed or stewed.

Sweet and sour eggplant salad (caponata)

I brought this recipe back from Menfi, Sicily, where they use huge glossy eggplants and luscious, almost overripe roma tomatoes during the hot summer months – but always tinned tomatoes during winter.

vegetable oil, for frying

1 large eggplant, cubed

salt

3-4 tbsp extra virgin olive oil

2 sticks celery, sliced

1 red onion, peeled and finely sliced

500g very ripe tomatoes, chopped

1 tbsp salted capers, rinsed

2 tbsp currants, covered with red-wine vinegar
    and brought to the boil, then drained

75g small green olives

1 tbsp toasted pinenuts

1 tbsp red-wine vinegar

1 tbsp caster sugar

cracked black pepper

Heat vegetable oil in a large frying pan over high heat and shallow fry eggplant cubes in batches. Drain on paper towel and season with salt.

Heat olive oil in a large frying pan over medium heat and cook celery and onion until just tender. Add chopped tomatoes and cook over low heat for about 10 minutes, stirring occasionally, until thick. Add remaining ingredients and stir well. Cook for 3-4 minutes. Add eggplant, stir to combine and set aside to cool before serving.

Serves 4

226

Eggplant involtini with ricotta, herbs and tomato

2 large eggplants, (about 500g each) sliced
    1cm thick lengthways

100ml extra virgin olive oil

250g ricotta cheese

1 egg, lightly beaten

salt and cracked black pepper

40g grated parmesan

35g ($^{1}/_{4}$ cup) currants

4 tbsp red-wine vinegar

$1^{1}/_{2}$ cups tomato passata (chunky tomato sauce)

40g ($^{1}/_{4}$ cup) pinenuts

$^{1}/_{4}$ cup oregano, chopped

$^{1}/_{4}$ cup flat-leaf parsley, chopped

$^{1}/_{4}$ cup day-old breadcrumbs

Preheat oven to 200C.

Brush eggplant slices with olive oil and place on baking trays in one layer. Roast for 10 minutes, turn and roast for a further 10 minutes or until just tender.

Reduce oven temperature to 170C.

Combine ricotta and egg in a bowl and add salt and pepper. Add half the parmesan and mix well.

Combine currants and vinegar in a small bowl and set aside for 5 minutes then drain. Add currants to ricotta mixture and stir well. Spoon about 1 tablespoon of the ricotta mixture onto each eggplant slice and roll up tightly.

Spray a medium-sized ovenproof dish lightly with cooking oil and spread half the tomato passata over the base of the dish. Place the eggplant rolls on the tomato passata, seam side down so they don't unroll. Spoon over remaining tomato passata and sprinkle with remaining parmesan.

Combine pinenuts, oregano, parsley and breadcrumbs in a small bowl. Sprinkle over eggplant and cover with foil. Roast for 20 minutes, then increase heat to 180C, remove foil and roast for a further 10-12 minutes or until top is golden.

Serves 6

Chilli-roasted spatchcock with roasted eggplant salad and tahini dressing

4 spatchcocks (halved with backbone removed)

juice of 1/2 lemon

4-5 tbsp extra virgin olive oil

salt and cracked black pepper

4 tbsp chilli jam

2 large eggplants, cut into quarters, lengthways

2 tsp butter

2 tsp olive oil (extra)

2 large Lebanese cucumbers, cut into 1-2cm pieces

1 punnet (250g) cherry tomatoes, halved

1 cup flat-leaf parsley, torn

1/2 red onion, very finely sliced

1 tsp sumac

200ml natural yoghurt

1/2 tbsp lemon juice

1 clove garlic, finely chopped

1 tbsp tahini paste

Preheat oven to 200C.

Place spatchcocks on a tray, drizzle with lemon juice and 2 tablespoons of olive oil, season with salt and pepper and turn to coat. Cover with plastic wrap and refrigerate for 30-60 minutes. Turn spatchcocks skin side up and brush each half with about 2 teaspoons of chilli jam. Reserve marinating liquid.

Brush eggplants with 2-3 tablespoons olive oil and roast for 20 minutes, turning once. Remove and cool.

Heat a lightly oiled, non-stick pan over medium-high heat. Add butter and 2 teaspoons olive oil and sear spatchcocks, skin-side down, until browned, then place skin-side up on a lightly greased oven tray. Roast spatchcocks for 10 minutes then baste with remaining marinade and roast a further 10-12 minutes or until cooked and tender.

Combine eggplants, cucumber, tomatoes, parsley and red onion in a bowl with sumac and toss gently to combine.

Combine yoghurt, 1 1/2 tablespoons lemon juice, garlic, tahini paste and salt and pepper in a small bowl and stir well.

To serve, divide eggplant salad evenly between 4 serving plates and place spatchcocks on top of salad. Serve a spoonful of yoghurt dressing on the side.

Serves 4

Lentil and eggplant salad with pan-fried salmon fillets

300g (1 1/2 cups) lentils, rinsed

1/4 cup extra virgin olive oil

1 small eggplant, chopped

1/2 red capsicum, chopped

1 rasher bacon, chopped

2 tbsp currants, plumped in hot water for 5 minutes, then drained

2-3 tbsp red-wine vinegar

1/4 cup flat-leaf parsley, chopped

4 salmon fillets (about 200g each)

3 tbsp extra virgin olive oil

salt and cracked black pepper

flat-leaf parsley, chopped (extra)

Cook lentils in a saucepan of simmering water for about 20-25 minutes or until just tender. Drain.

Heat 1/4 cup extra virgin olive oil in a large frying pan, add eggplant and red capsicum and cook over medium heat until eggplant is half-cooked. Add bacon and cook until crisp, and eggplant is tender. Remove from heat and stir in currants, red-wine vinegar and flat-leaf parsley. Add lentils, 2 tablespoons extra virgin olive oil, salt and pepper and stir to combine.

Meanwhile, brush 4 salmon fillets with remaining olive oil and pan-fry on both sides in a non-stick frying pan over high heat for 2-3 minutes each side or until cooked as desired.

Serve lentils on 4 serving plates, top with salmon and sprinkle with chopped flat-leaf parsley.

Serves 4

Endive

Endive's mildly bitter flavour complements other salad greens beautifully. It is sometimes sold as frisee or curly endive and belongs to the chicory family. In France, it's called *chicorée frisée* and some markets label it escarole. Baby endive is much smaller, with crisp, green leaves and a pale heart. Its slight bitterness goes well with creamy mustard dressings, chicken and bacon. Choose crisp looking endive without any signs of broken leaves or wilt and store in the crisper of the fridge.

Stir-fried baby endive

1 tbsp extra virgin olive oil

1 clove garlic, finely chopped

2 baby endive, trimmed

2 tbsp grated parmesan

1/2 tsp dried chilli flakes

salt

2 tsp lemon juice

Heat olive oil in a wok or large frying pan and add garlic and endive leaves. Toss over medium heat for about 1 minute, until the endive begins to wilt. Remove from heat, add parmesan, chilli flakes, salt to taste and lemon juice. Toss and serve immediately.

Great with barbecued T-bone steaks.

Serves 4

Curly endive, fennel, soft-boiled egg and bacon salad

6 eschalots, peeled

1 tbsp extra virgin olive oil

3 eggs

200g bacon rashers cut into 2 x 3cm pieces

2 cloves garlic, finely sliced

300g curly endive leaves, washed and torn

1 bulb fennel, trimmed and finely sliced

1/2 cup flat-leaf parsley, torn

salt and cracked black pepper

juice of 1/2 lemon

salt and cracked black pepper

toast fingers, to serve

Preheat oven to 180C.

Toss eschalots in olive oil and roast for 25 minutes or until tender. Boil eggs for 6 minutes, drain and refresh in cold water.

Heat a non-stick pan over medium heat and cook bacon pieces for about 6-8 minutes, until crisp. Add garlic, stir and remove from heat.

Spread endive, fennel and parsley on a serving platter. Add eschalots and cut tops from eggs and spoon onto salad. Pour bacon mixture (including fat) over salad. Add salt and pepper and lemon juice. Place toast on the side.

Serves 4-6

Cahors Market, France

Fennel

Originally from Italy, where it is known as finocchio, fennel has the bite of aniseed and the crunch of an apple. The crisp white bulb is often labelled Florence fennel and can be cooked or used raw in salads, where it refreshes the palate and aids digestion at the end of a meal.

The feathery leaves at the top of the bulb give a subtle aroma to soups, stuffings and sauces and can be used as a substitute for dill or as a fresh green garnish.

Tiny, sweet baby fennel is readily available and, when cooked whole, has a delicate perfume and texture similar to celery.

Choose crisp bulb fennel with the green, sweet-smelling foliage still attached to ensure freshness. It can be stored in a plastic bag in the fridge, but after a few days will lose its sheen and crispness so is best eaten as soon as possible. Trim the base before using and remove the outside leaves, which can be tough and stringy.

Quick creamy fennel soup

(pictured page 231)

50g butter

1 brown onion, finely chopped

2 large fennel bulbs, trimmed and sliced

1 small potato, peeled and chopped

3 sprigs flat-leaf parsley

6 cups chicken stock

1 tbsp pernod

$\frac{1}{2}$ cup light cream

salt and cracked black pepper

snipped chives

parmesan sticks, to serve

Melt butter in a large saucepan and add onion, fennel bulbs, potato and flat-leaf parsley. Cook for about 5 minutes, stirring occasionally. Add chicken stock and bring to the boil. Reduce heat and simmer for about 10 minutes or until vegetables are tender, then combine in a food processor until smooth. Return to the saucepan and stir in pernod, cream, salt and pepper.

Pour into large soup bowls and serve topped with snipped chives and parmesan sticks.

Serves 4

Sauteed fennel with butter and cheese

2 large fennel bulbs

2 tbsp butter, chopped

salt and cracked black pepper

3 tbsp freshly grated parmesan

Cut the tops off fennel and remove the core and any outside bruised or tough pieces. Cut the bulb into vertical slices 1cm thick, place in a large frying pan and add enough water barely to cover. Dot with butter and season with salt and pepper. Cook, uncovered, over medium heat for about 5-8 minutes or until fennel is just tender and the water is absorbed. Sprinkle grated cheese over fennel and serve while hot.

Serves 4

Crispy fennel coated with parmesan and garlic

2 fennel bulbs, trimmed and cut into 1/2cm-thick slices

1 egg

1/2 cup milk

50g dried breadcrumbs

1 clove garlic, very finely chopped

50g grated parmesan

1 tbsp flat-leaf parsley, chopped

1 cup extra virgin olive oil

grilled pork loin chops, to serve

Blanch fennel for 2 minutes in boiling water, refresh in cold water and dry on paper towel. Combine egg and milk and whisk until smooth. In a medium-sized bowl, mix breadcrumbs, garlic, parmesan cheese and flat-leaf parsley. Dip fennel into milk mixture and then into breadcrumb mixture.

Heat olive oil in a heavy-based frying pan and when hot, shallow-fry fennel until golden and crisp on both sides. Drain on paper towel and serve with grilled pork loin chops.

Serves 4

Warm winter salad of fennel and pumpkin

2 tbsp canola oil

750g butternut pumpkin, peeled and thinly sliced

1 bunch watercress sprigs

1 bulb fennel, trimmed and very thinly sliced

Dressing

2 tbsp sesame seeds

1 tbsp canola oil

1 tbsp red-wine vinegar

1 tbsp orange juice

1 tsp honey

salt

pinch of cayenne pepper

Heat canola oil in a large, heavy-based frying pan and cook pumpkin over high heat for about 3-5 minutes, turning once. Place watercress sprigs on a serving platter and top with pumpkin slices. Top pumpkin with fennel.

For the dressing, toast sesame seeds in a small dry frying pan over low heat until golden.

In a small saucepan, combine canola oil, red-wine vinegar, orange juice, honey, salt to taste and cayenne pepper and stir over low heat until smooth. Drizzle warm dressing over fennel and sprinkle with sesame seeds.

Serve with mash and roast chicken.

Serves 4

Garlic

Garlic has been associated with herbal medicine for more than 4000 years and is among the oldest of cultivated plants. There are many myths and beliefs concerning this member of the onion family. Garlic soup was extremely fashionable in France in the 12th century for its antiseptic qualities and the prevention of coughs and colds.

There are many varieties, including the new gourmet single clove, about the size of a golf ball and very easy to peel. It has a slightly sweeter flavour and smooth, creamy texture, making it perfect to bake whole; it can also be microwaved, boiled, fried or used raw.

Fresh garlic shoots are plentiful throughout spring and sold with their stalks attached to the petite white bulb. Sometimes labelled green garlic, they look similar to pencil leeks and have a fresh, mild taste. Of the two types of culinary chives, the garlic variety has distinctly flat leaves and grows much taller, displaying elegant white flowers. Some prefer these to garlic for their fresh, mellow taste, as they contain considerably less sulphur.

Buy garlic bulbs that hold firmly together without any soft spots. And, if given a choice, buy Australian grown. Keep it in a basket at room temperature in a cool, airy place, as it tends to sprout in damp conditions such as the fridge. Gourmet single cloves are best wrapped and stored in the fridge.

The most convenient way to peel garlic is to crush the clove with the flat side of a large knife, then the skin can easily be removed.

The longer garlic is cooked, the more mellow and sweet the flavour and the softer the flesh.

Place d'Aligre Market, Paris

Queen Victoria Market, Melbourne

Roasted pork loin with garlic and macadamia stuffing

1.25kg loin of pork

1 cup chicken stock

1 tbsp redcurrant jelly

Stuffing

1 tbsp olive oil

$^1/_2$ small onion, finely chopped

2 cloves garlic, finely chopped

$^1/_2$ tsp mixed dried herbs

1 rasher bacon, chopped

$^1/_4$ cup wild rice

1 cup chicken stock

100g ($^2/_3$) cup macadamias, chopped

For the stuffing, heat oil in a saucepan, add onion and garlic and stir over low heat for 5 minutes or until onion is soft. Add herbs, bacon and rice and mix well. Add stock and bring to the boil, then reduce heat and simmer, covered, for 12-15 minutes or until rice is tender and liquid absorbed. Stir in macadamias and season to taste. Cool.

Place pork, skin-side down, on the bench, spoon stuffing over, then roll pork up and secure with string at 4cm intervals. Place on a wire rack in a roasting pan and roast at 200C for 60-75 minutes or until cooked.

Remove from pan and rest in a warm place for 15 minutes. Remove excess fat from pan, add chicken stock and jelly to pan juices and stir over low heat until reduced and slightly thickened. Strain.

Slice pork thickly and serve with sauce, sweet potato mash and a green salad.

Serves 4

Warm eggplant, tomato and garlic salad

1 large eggplant, cut into 2cm pieces

vegetable oil, for shallow frying

2 tbsp extra virgin olive oil

2 sticks celery, thinly sliced

1 onion, chopped

3 cloves garlic, finely chopped

500g tomatoes, chopped

2 desiree potatoes, cut into 2-3cm pieces and boiled until tender

2 tbsp sultanas

12 kalamata olives,

1 tbsp red-wine vinegar

2 tsp caster sugar

2 tbsp pinenuts roasted

Shallow fry eggplant in batches in hot vegetable oil until golden and tender, then drain on absorbent paper.

Heat olive oil in a large frying pan, add celery, onion and garlic and stir over low heat for 5-8 minutes or until tender. Add tomatoes and potatoes and cook for 5 minutes. Stir in remaining ingredients and eggplant and mix until well combined. Remove from heat and season to taste.

Serve with grilled fish or chicken.

Serves 6

Kidney bean soup with silverbeet, garlic, tomato and bacon

1 tbsp extra virgin olive oil

2 rashers bacon, chopped

1 brown onion, chopped

2 sticks celery, chopped

3 cloves garlic, chopped

2 x 400g cans chopped tomatoes

800ml chicken stock

1 x 420g tin kidney beans, rinsed and drained

2 large leaves silverbeet, stems removed

4 tbsp basil, torn

cracked black pepper

crusty bread, to serve

Heat olive oil in a large pan over medium heat and cook bacon until crisp. Add onion, celery and garlic and cook over low heat for 6-8 minutes. Add tomatoes and chicken stock and bring to the boil, reduce heat and simmer for 5 minutes. Add kidney beans and simmer for 3-5 minutes. Shred silverbeet leaves finely and stir into soup and simmer until wilted.

Serve soup in 4 warm soup bowls and top each with 1 tablespoon torn basil leaves and pepper. Serve with crusty bread.

Serves 4

Steamed broccolini with garlic, sesame and soy sauce

2 bunches broccolini, trimmed and halved

2 green onions, finely sliced on the diagonal

1 tbsp fried eschalots (available at Asian food stores)

$\frac{1}{2}$ large red chilli, seeds removed and finely sliced

Sauce

2 cloves garlic, unpeeled, bruised

3 tbsp Chinese black vinegar

2 tbsp brown sugar

2 tbsp soy sauce

$\frac{1}{2}$ tsp sesame oil

1 tbsp shaoxing wine

Steam broccolini for 2-4 minutes until tender, but still crisp.

For the sauce, combine all the ingredients in a small saucepan, stir over low heat until sugar dissolves then simmer for about 3-4 minutes or until syrupy. Remove garlic.

To serve, place broccolini on a platter, pour warm sauce over and scatter with green onions, fried eschalots and red chilli.

Serves 4

Jerusalem artichokes

They are not really artichokes and have nothing to do with Jerusalem, but these small, knobbly tubers have an appealing taste.

Low in calories, with a nutty flavour, they can be eaten raw, steamed, roasted or fried. Jerusalem artichokes have a texture similar to water chestnuts when eaten raw – under the brown exterior, the crisp, white flesh is crunchy and slightly sweet. They can also be substituted for potatoes in many recipes.

Easy to spot in the shops because they are similar in appearance to fresh ginger, the tubers can be yellow, brown or cream and some types are tinged with pink. As most of the vitamins are under the skin, there's no need to peel them before cooking, unless you want a smooth, white puree.

Choose firm tubers with no signs of sprouting or softness and keep them in a plastic bag or airtight container in the fridge, as they will dehydrate when exposed to warm, dry conditions. Like most root vegetables, Jerusalem artichokes tend to sprout if exposed to light.

To cook, remove any brown stringy roots and then scrub or peel them and drop into cold, salted water with a little lemon juice added to prevent them from discolouring and add a teaspoon of vinegar or lemon juice to the water when boiling so they stay pearly white.

Jerusalem artichoke soup with goat's cheese toast

It's worth taking the time to peel the artichokes for a full-bodied but delicate flavour. The soup will also be rich, creamy and white if they are peeled.

750g Jerusalem artichokes

1 tbsp butter

1 onion, chopped

1 clove garlic, finely chopped

1.25 litres vegetable stock

1 sebago potato (about 200g), peeled and chopped

100ml pouring cream

salt and cracked black pepper

4 slices sourdough bread

100g goat's cheese

chervil sprigs, to serve

Peel artichokes and halve if large, then place in a bowl of acidulated water (with lemon). Melt butter in a large saucepan, add onion and garlic and cook over low heat for 5-8 minutes or until onion is soft. Add drained artichokes, vegetable stock and potato, bring to the boil and simmer, covered, over low heat for 25 minutes or until potato is tender. Cool, then process in batches in a food processor until smooth. Return mixture to same saucepan, stir in cream, season to taste with salt and pepper and cook over low-medium heat until heated through.

Grill bread until golden on both sides, then spread with goat's cheese and cut in half diagonally.

Ladle soup into warm bowls, top with chervil sprigs and serve with goat's cheese toasts.

Serves 4

Jerusalem artichoke, potato and cheese bake

600ml hot chicken stock

400ml light cream

1 bay leaf

6 large potatoes, peeled and very thinly sliced

10 large Jerusalem artichokes, peeled and thinly sliced

1 small brown onion, peeled and finely sliced

80g butter

salt and cracked black pepper

$1/4$ tsp ground nutmeg

150g grated gruyere cheese

Preheat oven to 200C.

Combine stock and cream in a saucepan with bay leaf and bring to the boil over medium heat. Remove and rest for 5 minutes. Discard bay leaf.

Place a layer of potato (overlapping slightly) in the base of a greased, large, shallow ovenproof dish and top with a layer of artichokes. Sprinkle with some of the onion slices. Repeat layers, adding a little onion and butter in between each layer. Finish with a layer of potato and remaining butter. Pour stock mixture over potatoes, season well with salt and pepper and nutmeg and bake (covered with foil) for 45 minutes.

Remove foil, top with gruyere and bake for a further 20-30 minutes or until potatoes are tender and cheese is golden.

Serves 8

Leeks

Leeks are the gentle members of the onion family. They blend discreetly with other vegetable flavours and give depth to braises, sauces and soups or melt delicately into egg and cream mixtures.

Leeks have been the national emblem of Wales for hundreds or years. During the 12th century, the Welsh wore them in their hats to distinguish them from their enemies, a tradition continued each year on St David's Day.

They are sold in a variety of thicknesses, from pencil-thin to 4-5cm thick. Large leeks are preferred for soups, such as vichyssoise, because of their stronger flavour while slim, fresh, young specimens are delicious served whole alongside roast meat. Tiny pencil leeks can be steamed, braised, grilled or sauteed.

The edible portion of the stem consists of the thick, white part and the pale-green section. Always look for crisp tops and firm, white bulbs. There should be no sign of damage or yellowing of leaves.

Leeks do not store as well as onions because they lack a tough outer skin, but can be kept in a plastic bag in the crisper of the fridge for up to a week. They are a good source of calcium, potassium, vitamins A and C.

To prepare them, cut off the dark-green leaves where they join the light-green area, then peel away a couple of outside layers. Cut the leek in half lengthwise and hold it under the tap, fanning the layers slightly to wash away any sand or grit.

Leek and vegetable tarts

225g plain flour

pinch of salt

150g butter, chopped

1 egg yolk

Filling

60g butter

$^1/_2$ tsp ground turmeric

$^1/_2$ tsp curry powder

1 leek, cut into 5cm lengths and julienned

2 carrots, cut into 5cm lengths and julienned

4 sticks celery, cut into 5cm lengths and julienned

1 zucchini, cut into 5cm lengths and julienned

1 tbsp ginger, grated

1 cup coconut milk

salt

6 coriander sprigs

Process flour, a pinch of salt and butter in a food processor until mixture resembles breadcrumbs. Add egg yolk and 2-3 tablespoons cold water and process until mixture forms a ball. Knead pastry gently on a lightly floured surface, then wrap in plastic and refrigerate for up to 1 hour.

Roll pastry out on a lightly floured surface to about 5mm thick and line six 10cm individual tart tins with removable bases. Lightly prick pastry with a fork and freeze for 20 minutes. Place on an oven tray and bake at 190C for about 15 minutes, or until pale-golden.

For the filling, heat butter in a large frying pan, add turmeric and curry powder and stir over medium heat for about 2 minutes or until aromatic. Add vegetables and cook, stirring occasionally, for about 5 minutes or until they are tender. Add ginger, coconut milk and salt to taste and stir over medium heat for 2 minutes.

Fill tart cases with warm vegetable mixture and top with coriander sprigs.

Serves 6

Braised baby leeks with a gremolata-style crust

3-4 bunches of baby leeks, trimmed and washed

1 tbsp unsalted butter

1 tbsp extra virgin olive oil

½ cup chicken stock

½ cup white wine

2 slices wholemeal bread, crumbed

½ cup flat-leaf parsley, chopped

zest of 1 lemon

2 cloves garlic, very finely chopped

2 tbsp freshly grated parmesan

salt and cracked black pepper

Preheat oven to 190C.

Melt butter and olive oil in a shallow ovenproof dish over low heat and add leeks. Turn leeks to coat with butter and oil. Pour stock and wine over leeks and bake uncovered for 15 minutes.

Combine breadcrumbs, parsley, lemon zest, garlic, parmesan and salt and pepper in a medium-sized bowl and stir well. Sprinkle breadcrumb mixture over leeks and bake for a further 10-15 minutes or until crust is golden and leeks are cooked.

Serves 4

Leek and mushrooms on toast

3 tbsp butter

1 leek, white part only, finely sliced

2 cloves garlic, finely chopped

300g swiss brown mushrooms, sliced

¼ cup verjuice or white wine

2 tbsp chives, snipped

2 tbsp flat-leaf parsley, chopped

¾ cup light sour cream

salt and cracked black pepper

wilted spinach, to serve (optional)

4 slices toasted sourdough bread

Melt butter in a large non-stick frying pan, add leek and cook over medium heat for 4-5 minutes or until soft. Add garlic and mushrooms and cook for about 5 minutes or until mushrooms are almost cooked. Add verjuice or white wine and bring to the boil. Stir in chives, flat-leaf parsley and light sour cream, season with salt and pepper and cook until warmed through.

Serve on a bed of wilted spinach with sourdough toast.

Serves 4

Leek and zucchini risotto with sun-dried tomato

2 small zucchini, sliced

2 tbsp extra virgin olive oil

1 leek, white part only, finely sliced

2 cups (400g) arborio rice

½ cup white wine

1.5 litres hot chicken stock

50g grated pecorino cheese

2 tbsp butter

salt and cracked black pepper

8 sun-dried tomatoes, chopped

Cook zucchini in boiling, salted water for 1 minute then drain. Heat olive oil in a large, heavy-based saucepan, add leek and cook over medium heat for 5 minutes or until soft. Add rice and stir over low heat until coated with oil. Add white wine and stir until liquid is absorbed. Gradually add chicken stock, a ladle or two at a time, stirring until stock is absorbed. When rice is al dente, stir in zucchini with pecorino cheese and butter, then season with salt and pepper.

Serve risotto scattered with sun-dried tomatoes.

Serves 4

Lettuce

There are thousands of varieties, but purchase lettuce with the darkest leaves, as they contain the most beta carotene. Iceberg lettuce, also known as crisphead, has more crunch but contains less vitamin C than other types.

Butter or boston lettuce has vivid lime-green leaves, a delicate buttery taste and soft texture, but needs to be carried on top of the shopping bag because it bruises very easily.

Often brownish red in colour, mignonette is a popular variety of butter lettuce. Bitter, crisp radicchio, a member of the chicory family, comes in variegated shades of green, red and cream. The long, crunchy spears of cos are essential in a Caesar salad. Sometimes called romaine, the dark-green leaves turn to pale-yellow at the centre. Also available are cute baby cos, often labelled little gem.

Buy red or green oakleaf lettuce when you want a sharper taste or frilly, frizzy coral lettuce that is slightly grassy in flavour.

Many lettuces are grown hydroponically, but varieties grown in the ground usually have a superior flavour. Hydroponics are easy to identify in the shops because they are usually sold with the root still attached.

Look for the freshest, crispest lettuce and check it has no brown or slimy leaves, which indicates it has had too much water or is old. Loose leaves are best kept in a paper-lined plastic bag or tea towel in the fridge crisper and washed just before using. Store whole lettuce in a plastic container with a snap-on lid and never store salad leaves next to apples, bananas, pears or melons, as they will cause the greens to deteriorate rapidly.

Wash and dry lettuce, preferably in a salad spinner. If the leaves are large, tear them gently. The leaves should be quite dry before being dressed, otherwise the dressing will roll off the leaves and into the base of the salad bowl.

Green oakleaf lettuce and herb frittata with parmesan

2 tbsp butter

1 small onion, finely chopped

1 small potato, peeled and finely chopped

1 small green oakleaf lettuce

6 eggs

$^1/_3$ cup finely grated parmesan

salt and cracked black pepper

1 tbsp extra virgin olive oil

2 tbsp flat-leaf parsley, chopped

3 tbsp basil, chopped

1 tbsp lemon rind, grated

Heat 1 tablespoon butter in a frying pan, add onion and potato and cook over medium heat until potato is soft. Remove core from lettuce and cut into strips. Add to frying pan and cook until wilted. Drain well and transfer to a bowl.

Break eggs into a medium-sized bowl and beat well with a fork. Add lettuce mixture and parmesan and season with salt and pepper. Stir well.

Place remaining butter in a medium-sized ovenproof, non-stick frying pan and swirl over medium heat to coat base of pan. Add egg mixture and cook frittata until top is just moist. Run a flexible spatula around sides to ensure it is not sticking. Slide pan under a preheated griller for a minute or two until top has set then loosen with spatula and invert onto a plate.

To serve, scatter with fresh herbs and grated lemon rind.

Serves 4

Mignonette, orange and fennel salad

Perfect with roast chicken and baked potatoes.

2 oranges, peeled and segmented

leaves from 1 mignonette lettuce, torn

1 small red onion, halved and finely sliced

1 bulb fennel, trimmed and very finely sliced

4 red radishes, trimmed and finely sliced

4 sprigs flat-leaf parsley, torn

Dressing

2 tbsp pomegranate molasses

3 tbsp extra virgin olive oil

salt and cracked black pepper

Combine orange segments, lettuce leaves, onion, fennel and radishes in a large bowl.

For the dressing, combine all the ingredients in a small bowl and whisk until smooth. Pour dressing over salad and toss to combine. Scatter with parsley.

Serves 4-6

Iceberg salad with seafood, cucumber, carrot and Asian dressing

100g snowpeas, trimmed

1 small carrot, peeled

1 Lebanese cucumber, unpeeled

1 cup shredded iceberg lettuce

1 stick celery, sliced diagonally

20 large cooked prawns, shelled and deveined

8 trimmed steamed scallops

2 green onions, finely sliced diagonally

leaves from 3 sprigs mint, torn

leaves from 3 sprigs coriander, torn

Dressing

2 tbsp extra virgin olive oil

$1^{1}/_{2}$ tbsp malt vinegar

2 tbsp soy sauce

1 tsp brown sugar

Blanch snowpeas in boiling water for 30 seconds. Drain and refresh under cold water and drain again. Slice carrot lengthways with a vegetable peeler. Cut cucumber in half lengthways, scoop out seeds with a teaspoon and slice diagonally.

Combine snowpeas, carrot and cucumber in a large bowl. Add lettuce, celery, prawns, scallops and green onions and toss gently.

For the dressing, mix all the ingredients in a small bowl until smooth. Drizzle over salad, toss gently and divide evenly between 4 bowls.

Serves 4

Cos, pear and parmesan salad

(pictured page 245)

1 large ripe pear, quartered, cored and sliced

juice of 2 limes

$^{1}/_{4}$ cup extra virgin olive oil

pinch of salt

1 cos lettuce, leaves separated and torn into bite-sized pieces

50g flaked almonds, toasted

50g pinenuts, toasted

100g shaved parmesan

cracked black pepper

Toss pear, juice, oil and salt in a bowl. Place cos in a large bowl, scatter with pear mixture, almonds, pinenuts and parmesan. Drizzle with a little extra virgin olive oil and season with pepper.

Serves 4

Bacon, lettuce, frozen peas and herbs with crumbed baby lamb cutlets

4 green onions, sliced

4 large iceberg lettuce leaves, sliced

2 tbsp butter

2 sprigs thyme

2 rashers bacon, chopped

2 cups (250g) peas

salt and cracked black pepper

1 tbsp chives, snipped

1 tbsp chervil, chopped

crumbed baby lamb cutlets, cooked medium-rare, to serve

Combine green onions, lettuce leaves, butter, thyme and bacon in a large saucepan and cook, covered, over low heat, stirring frequently, for about 5 minutes or until onion is soft. Add peas and cook, covered, for 2 minutes. Season with salt and pepper, remove thyme and add chives and chervil. Toss gently to combine and serve with crumbed baby lamb cutlets.

Serves 4

Spicy beef and water chestnuts in lettuce cups

1 tbsp vegetable oil

500g lean beef mince

2 tsp ginger, grated

1 tbsp lemongrass, very thinly sliced

$^1/_2$ cup coarsely water chestnuts, chopped

2 long red chillies, very thinly sliced

1 tbsp shaoxing wine

$^1/_2$ tsp caster sugar

1 tbsp oyster sauce

1 tbsp soy sauce

$^1/_3$ cup water

4 large crisp iceberg lettuce leaves

3 green onions, thinly sliced

sweet chilli sauce, to serve

Heat vegetable oil in a wok, add beef mince and stir-fry over medium heat for 4-5 minutes, breaking up any lumps with a wooden spoon. Add ginger, lemongrass, water chestnuts and red chillies and cook for 2-3 minutes, then add shaoxing wine, caster sugar, oyster sauce, soy sauce and $^1/_3$ cup water and simmer for 3-5 minutes.

Divide mince among lettuce leaves and top with green onions. Serve with sweet chilli sauce.

Serves 4

Chicken caesar salad

3-4 chicken breast fillets

1 small French bread stick, cut into croutons

$^1/_2$ cup olive oil

4 rashers bacon

1 cos lettuce, trimmed

$^1/_2$ cup flat-leaf parsley

100g parmesan, shaved

Dressing

1 cup peanut oil

2 tbsp lemon juice

1$^1/_2$ tsp Dijon mustard

2 egg yolks

salt and cracked black pepper

2-3 anchovies

1 clove garlic, chopped

salt flakes and cracked black pepper

Preheat oven to 180C.

For the dressing, combine all the ingredients in a food processor until smooth.

Cook chicken on a heated, oiled grill plate or barbecue until browned on both sides and cooked through. Remove and cool. Cut into bite-sized pieces.

Place croutons in a bowl and toss with olive oil to coat, then place in a single layer on an oven tray and cook in the oven until golden and crisp.

Cook bacon on grill plate until cooked and crisp. Drain on absorbent paper and cut into pieces.

Tear lettuce into bite-sized pieces and place in a large bowl. Add chicken, croutons, bacon, and parsley. Drizzle with dressing and toss to combine.

Place salad on 4 serving plates and top with parmesan.

Serves 4

Spring salad with pecans, pears and sultanas

This versatile recipe serves 4 as a light entree with the blue cheese and 6 as a side-dish with char-grilled lamb chops or barbecued rump steak (in which case omit the blue cheese in the salad and accompany the meat with baked jacket potatoes).

100g pecan nuts

3 corella pears, cored and thinly sliced

juice of ½ lemon

80ml extra virgin olive oil

80g (½ cup) sultanas

5½ tbsp cabernet sauvignon vinegar

2 baby cos lettuce, trimmed and cut into wedges

1 cup watercress sprigs

2 tbsp sour light cream

salt and cracked black pepper

1 cup lamb's lettuce (mache)

100g blue cheese (e.g., King Island Roaring Forties), crumbled (optional)

Preheat oven to 200C.

Place pecans in an ovenproof dish and roast for 5-8 minutes or until toasted and crisp.

Combine pears, lemon juice and 20ml of oil in a large bowl and toss gently. Combine sultanas and 4 tablespoons of the cabernet sauvignon vinegar in a small saucepan and bring to the boil. Remove from heat and rest for 1 minute. Drain.

Add sultanas, pecans, cos lettuce and watercress to pears.

Combine sour cream, remaining extra virgin olive oil, 2 tablespoons water and remaining vinegar and mix until smooth. Season with salt and pepper and pour dressing over salad and toss gently to combine. Scatter with lamb's lettuce and blue cheese, if using.

Serves 4-6

Place d'Aligre, Paris

Mushrooms

Fat free and full of goodness, mushrooms need little preparation.

Buttons or champignons, the small, tightly closed white mushrooms are perfect raw in salads or in dishes that require delicate seasoning. When the veil begins to open around the stem, revealing pale-brown gills, the mushroom is graded as a cup. This is the most sought-after size, deeper in flavour, with a firm texture. Mature flats are broad and fully open with a stronger flavour and liver pink gills.

Of the many varieties of exotic mushrooms, oyster or abalone are one of the prettiest. They are shaped like a fluted shell and the newer, stunning pink variety has a subtle delicate flavour that teams well with seafood. This type retains a firm texture when cooked and rapidly absorbs other flavours. Yellow and grey oyster mushrooms are tasty with chicken and veal, and are best cooked quickly over high heat.

Fresh shiitakes have a distinctive flavour and were first cultivated in Japan more than 2000 years ago. They have many tags including brown oak, Chinese black forest and shiang ku. These are best eaten cooked, as the flavour is rich and woody with a wonderful meaty texture.

Elegant chestnut mushrooms have a long slinky stem and are also known as cinnamon caps because of their colour. A few of these will add another dimension to stir-fries. Swiss browns have a deeper, more robust flavour than white mushrooms and have several names – cremini, honey brown and roman browns among them. The smallest, called buttons, are suitable for risotto or an antipasto platter. Larger swiss brown cups, the biggest of which are known as portobello, compliment pasta sauces and braises. These have a more intense flavour and a dense, meaty texture.

Enoki or snow puffs are delicate slender mushrooms with tiny button caps on long, thread-like stems. Creamy white, they are sold in clumps and need to be separated and trimmed before using. Shimeji are a Japanese variety whose colour ranges from tawny white to woody brown. They have a sweet, nutty flavour and are also sold in clumps so need to be separated from the base before using. Pine mushrooms, including slippery jacks, have a moist, slippery skin, spongy flesh and a nutty flavour.

Fresh common cultivated mushrooms should be white or creamy and feel firm. Use a paper or cloth bag to store them in the crisper of the fridge. As mushrooms are grown under quite hygienic conditions, they generally don't need washing; just wipe them with a clean, damp cloth. Many of the exotics are now packed on small plastic trays with plastic wrap that allows them to breathe, not spoil. Store these in the crisper and use as soon as possible.

Oven-baked penne with mixed mushrooms and fontina

2 tbsp extra virgin olive oil

1 tbsp butter

2 cloves garlic, finely chopped

500g mixed mushrooms, sliced

400g penne or macaroni pasta

300ml light cream

1 tsp fresh thyme leaves

1 tbsp flat-leaf parsley, chopped

2 tsp lemon zest

salt and cracked black pepper

175g fontina cheese, grated

$^1/_2$ cup grated parmesan

Preheat oven to 200C.

Heat olive oil and butter in a large frying pan over medium heat and cook garlic for 1 minute. Add mushrooms and cook, stirring occasionally, for 6-8 minutes or until mushrooms are almost tender. Meanwhile cook pasta in plenty of lightly salted, boiling water until al dente. Drain.

Add cream, thyme, parsley, lemon zest, salt and pepper to mushrooms and stir over low heat for 2-3 minutes. Combine mushrooms, pasta and fontina cheese and spoon mixture into a large, greased ovenproof dish; sprinkle with parmesan and bake, covered with foil, for 15 minutes. Remove foil and bake for 10 minutes then rest for 3-4 minutes.

Serve with a green salad.

Serves 4

Beef bourguignon (beef in red-wine sauce)

1.5kg topside, blade or chuck steak

plain flour

1 tbsp butter

1 tbsp olive oil

2 rashers bacon, sliced

1 cup red wine

1 cup water

1 large sprig thyme

1 bay leaf

2 cloves garlic, finely chopped

sea salt and cracked black pepper

12 small white onions (spring or pearl), peeled

250g mushrooms, trimmed

2 tbsp flat-leaf parsley, chopped

Preheat oven to 150C.

Cut steak into 5cm pieces, dust with flour and shake off excess. Melt butter and oil in a heavy casserole and brown steak pieces on all sides. Remove. Add bacon and stir over low heat for 2-3 minutes. Add red wine and water and bring to a simmer, stirring well. Return meat to pan, add thyme, bay leaf, garlic, salt and pepper. Cover and cook for 2 hours. Add onions and a little more water if necessary and cook for a further 20 minutes or until meat is very tender. Add mushrooms and cook for a further 10 minutes or until mushrooms are cooked.

Serve sprinkled with parsley and accompanied by creamy mashed potato.

Serves 4

Wok-fried mushrooms with honey and soy

1 tbsp soy sauce

1 tbsp oyster sauce

1 tbsp honey

1 tbsp sesame seeds

2 tbsp peanut oil

400g button mushrooms, trimmed

200g swiss brown mushrooms, trimmed

6 green onions, thinly sliced

1 small red chilli, deseeded and finely chopped

1/2 cup coriander leaves

2 tsp lime zest

Combine soy sauce, oyster sauce and honey in a small jug. Set aside.

Heat a wok over high heat. Add sesame seeds and cook, stirring constantly, for 2-3 minutes or until golden. Remove to a plate and set aside. Add the oil to the wok and heat over high heat until hot. Add the mushrooms and stir-fry for 1 minute or until well coated with oil.

Add soy sauce mixture and stir-fry for 2 minutes or until mushrooms are just tender. Add green onions, chilli and sesame seeds and stir-fry for 1 minute.

Serve scattered with coriander leaves and lime zest.

Serves 4

Pan-fried exotic mushrooms with grilled polenta wedges

olive oil

50g unsalted butter

4 green onions, finely sliced

1kg mixed exotic mushrooms, sliced

1 clove garlic, finely chopped

1 tbsp lemon juice

2 tbsp flat-leaf parsley, chopped

100ml dry white wine

300ml pouring cream

polenta

1 cup polenta

1/2 cup semolina

1/2 tsp salt

40g unsalted butter

60g finely grated parmesan

For the polenta, bring 1.5 litres of water to the boil in a large saucepan, gradually pour in polenta and semolina in a steady stream, whisking constantly. Add salt and cook, stirring occasionally, over low heat for 25-30 minutes until thick. Stir in butter and parmesan, then pour mixture into a greased 18 x 28cm tray and cool.

Heat 1 tablespoon of olive oil and half the butter in a large frying pan, add the green onion and cook for 1 minute, then add half the mushrooms and garlic and cook until mushrooms are soft. Remove from pan. Heat a further tablespoon of oil and remaining butter in same pan, add remaining mushrooms and cook until soft. Return first batch to pan and stir in lemon juice and parsley and cook for 1-2 minutes. Add wine and cream and cook until slightly thickened and reduced.

Cut cold polenta into wedges, brush both sides with olive oil. Cook under a hot grill until crisp and browned. Serve topped with mushrooms.

Serves 6

Roasted mushrooms with herbs and hazelnuts

400g swiss brown mushrooms, trimmed

2 tbsp grated parmesan

1 clove garlic, finely chopped

2 eschalots, peeled and finely sliced

2 tbsp hazelnuts, toasted and chopped

2 sprigs flat-leaf parsley

3 sprigs fresh thyme

2 tbsp hazelnut oil

2 tbsp butter

salt and cracked black pepper

4 slices thick sourdough toast, to serve

extra butter

Preheat oven to 200C.

Place a large sheet of foil on a baking tray and lightly grease. Place mushrooms on foil and top with parmesan, garlic, eschalots, hazelnuts, parsley and thyme. Drizzle with oil, dot with butter and season with salt and pepper. Cover with another sheet of foil and fold edges to seal. Bake for 15-18 minutes or until mushrooms are cooked.

Smear hot toast with extra butter and pile mushrooms on top.

Serves 4

Oxtail and mushrooms in red-wine sauce

$1/4$ cup extra virgin olive oil

1 clove garlic, finely chopped

1 carrot, sliced

2 sticks celery, sliced

125g bacon, chopped

2kg oxtail, cut into 4cm pieces

35g plain flour, seasoned with salt and pepper

2 large tomatoes, chopped

2 sprigs thyme

2 x 1cm-wide strips orange peel

1 tsp sweet paprika

1 cup dry white wine

$1^1/2$ cups beef stock

8 small spring onions, trimmed

150g button mushrooms

Preheat oven to 150C.

Heat 1 tablespoon olive oil in a large frying pan, add garlic, carrot, celery and bacon and cook over medium heat for 2-3 minutes, then transfer to a large ovenproof dish.

Dust oxtail with seasoned flour and shake off excess. Heat remaining oil in the same frying pan and cook oxtail in batches over medium-high heat until browned, adding more oil if necessary.

Add oxtail, tomatoes, thyme, orange peel and paprika to vegetables. Pour wine and stock over oxtail, then cover and cook for 2 hours.

Remove $1/4$ cup of vegetables and process with a little of the cooking juices in a food processor until smooth, then return to oxtail and vegetables. Add spring onions and mushrooms and cook for a further 30 minutes or until oxtail is very tender.

Skim fat from surface and serve with creamy mashed potato.

Serves 6

Mushroom and steak sandwiches with rocket

4 rump steaks (about 100g each)

salt and cracked black pepper

vegetable oil, for greasing

300g button mushrooms, thinly sliced

2 large onions, halved and thinly sliced

1 loaf turkish bread, cut into 4 and halved

2 cups baby rocket leaves, trimmed

Place the steaks between 2 sheets of baking paper and flatten with a meat mallet. Season with salt and pepper.

Lightly grease a barbecue plate and cook mushrooms over medium heat for 3-5 minutes turning occasionally until tender. Remove. Cook onions on barbecue for about 5-6 minutes or until tender and then combine with mushrooms. Place steaks on the barbecue and cook for about 1 minute each side or until cooked as desired.

Toast bread until golden and place one piece on serving plates. Top with rocket leaves, steak and mushroom mixture. Top with remaining bread and serve immediately.

Serves 4

Richard Lenoir Market, Paris

Asparagus, carrot, pancetta and mushroom linguine

400g linguine

2 tbsp extra virgin olive oil

2 cloves garlic, finely chopped

1 medium-sized brown onion, peeled
   and cut into wedges

8 thin slices spicy pancetta, coarsely chopped

300g swiss brown mushrooms, sliced

1 bunch asparagus, cut into 1-2cm pieces

1 carrot, thinly sliced

1 cup frozen peas

$^2/_3$ cup chicken stock

$^1/_2$ cup light cream

salt and cracked black pepper

shaved parmesan, to serve

Cook linguine in a large saucepan of lightly salted, boiling water for 8-10 minutes or until al dente. Meanwhile, heat a large frying pan and add extra virgin olive oil and, when hot, add garlic and onion and pancetta. Cook, stirring occasionally, for 2-3 minutes or until onion is soft. Add mushrooms, asparagus, carrot, peas and chicken stock. Cook for 3 minutes, until mushrooms are just tender.

Drain pasta and return to pan. Stir in cream and onion mixture and toss gently to combine. Season with salt and pepper and serve immediately with shaved parmesan.

Serves 4

Mushrooms, grilled tomato and crispy bacon on toast

8 rashers bacon

2 ripe roma tomatoes, halved

50g butter

400g swiss brown mushrooms, sliced

2 tbsp flat-leaf parsley, chopped

dash of Tabasco sauce

4 thick slices hot sourdough toast, buttered

Cook bacon rashers in a large non-stick pan over medium heat for 3-5 minutes each side or until crisp and cooked. Drain on paper towel and keep warm.

Place tomatoes under a hot grill and cook for 5-8 minutes or until soft. Remove and keep warm.

Heat butter in a large frying pan and, when hot, add mushrooms and cook over medium heat for 4-5 minutes, stirring occasionally until tender. Add flat-leaf parsley and a dash of Tabasco and stir.

Pile mushrooms onto hot toast. Serve with bacon and tomatoes.

Serves 4

Mushroom, snowpea and beef salad with ginger and coriander

500g beef eye-fillet, thinly sliced and cooked
    medium rare

150g oyster mushrooms, thinly sliced

200g snowpeas, trimmed and blanched

100g snowpea shoots

1 red capsicum, thinly sliced

150g beansprouts

4 green onions, thinly sliced

1 large red chilli, very finely sliced

3 tsp white-wine vinegar

2$^1/_2$ tbsp peanut oil

2 tbsp soy sauce

2 tsp ginger, grated

$^1/_2$ cup coriander leaves

Combine eye-fillet in a large bowl with oyster mushrooms, snowpeas, snowpea shoots, red capsicum, beansprouts, green onions and red chilli.

Combine vinegar, peanut oil, soy sauce and fresh ginger in a small bowl and whisk well.

Pour dressing over salad and toss gently to combine. Divide among 4 plates and top with coriander leaves.

Serves 4

Mushroom, tomato, beef and zucchini tacos with avocado

1 tbsp vegetable oil

1 brown onion, chopped

400g lean beef mince

12 taco shells

1 medium-sized zucchini, grated

250g button mushrooms, thinly sliced

1 ripe tomato, thinly sliced

taco seasoning

4 iceberg lettuce leaves, shredded

1 medium-sized ripe avocado, mashed

Preheat oven to 180C.

Heat vegetable oil in a large, non-stick frying pan over medium heat, add onion and cook for about 3-4 minutes or until soft. Add mince and cook, stirring often, for 6-8 minutes or until browned.

Place taco shells on a baking tray and heat in the oven for 8-10 minutes.

Add zucchini, mushrooms, tomato and taco seasoning mix to mince with $^1/_4$ cup water and cook, stirring occasionally, for 6-8 minutes.

Place lettuce leaves in hot taco shells then top with mushroom mixture. Serve a dollop of avocado on top of each taco.

Serves 4

Warm mushroom, chicken and rocket salad

4 tbsp olive oil

500g chicken breast fillets

juice of 1 lemon

1 tbsp soy sauce

1 clove garlic, finely chopped

400g button mushrooms, sliced

1 bunch rocket leaves, trimmed

250g cherry tomatoes, halved

1 large red chilli, very finely sliced

$^1/_2$ cup (60g) pecan nuts, toasted and chopped

$^1/_4$ cup chives, snipped

crusty bread, to serve

Heat 1 tablespoon olive oil in a large frying pan over medium heat and add 500g chicken breast fillets and cook for 4-5 minutes each side or until cooked, then remove. Add remaining olive oil, lemon juice, soy sauce and garlic to the pan and stir to combine. Add mushrooms and cook over medium-high heat for 3-4 minutes or until mushrooms are just tender.

Place rocket leaves in a large serving bowl, add cherry tomatoes and red chilli. Slice chicken into 1cm pieces and arrange on tomatoes. Add mushrooms and pan juices and toss gently to combine. Scatter with pecan nuts and chopped chives.

Serve with crusty bread.

Serves 4

Okra

Some people love okra for its crispness when fried. Others hate the slippery juices it exudes when cooked slowly.

Also known as lady's fingers, okra is a small, tapering, green pod with many tiny white seeds The furry pods have five sides, which can be ridged or smooth depending on type, and the colour varies from pale-green to dark-purple.

Generally regarded as native to Africa, okra has found its way into many of the world's cuisines. It has become a staple in creole and cajun cooking, where it is called gumbo, the name given to the New Orleans stew of chilli, okra, tomatoes and seafood, pork or chicken.

Okra contains mucilaginous gums, which make it a useful thickening agent in slow-simmered dishes such as curries, and the juice is a valuable form of dietary fibre.

When buying okra, avoid large thick specimens, as they are often fibrous, stringy and not particularly digestible. Choose young pods that are less than 6cm long and no thicker at the middle than the stem end. Fresh okra is quite firm and the end should snap easily, like a green bean. Often a mixture of old and young pods are sold together, so make sure you avoid any with damaged ridges or discoloured skin.

Okra keeps well for a few days stored in a plastic bag in the fridge. Don't wash before storing or it will quickly become sticky.

Okra with lamb, tomato and goat's cheese

2 tbsp olive oil

800g lamb, leg cut into bite size pieces

1 onion, finely chopped

4 cloves garlic, finely chopped

1 x 400ml tin crushed tomatoes

1 tbsp tomato paste

2 tsp ground cumin

1 tsp ground allspice

sea salt and cracked black pepper

300g okra, stalks trimmed

2 tbsp lemon juice

1 tbsp flat-leaf parsley, chopped

200g goat's cheese, broken into small pieces

Heat olive oil in a large, heavy-based saucepan, add lamb and onion and cook over medium heat, until onion is soft and meat is browned. Add garlic and stir. Add crushed tomatoes, tomato paste, 1/2 cup water, cumin and allspice. Season to taste and simmer, covered, for 45 minutes or until lamb is tender.

Add okra and simmer for a further 15 minutes or until okra is cooked. Add lemon juice and parsley and stir. Remove from heat and add goat's cheese.

Serve with boiled rice and Turkish bread.

Serves 4-6

Okra and chicken curry

2 onions, chopped

2 cloves garlic

3 sprigs coriander

2cm piece fresh ginger

2 small red chillies, or to taste

2 tbsp vegetable oil

500g chicken thigh fillets, quartered

1 tsp ground coriander

1 tsp ground cardamom

1 1/2 tsp ground cumin

1/2 tsp garam masala

200ml chicken stock

salt

200g small okra, tops trimmed

270ml light coconut milk

1 tbsp lemon juice

leaves from 4 sprigs coriander

Combine onions, garlic, coriander sprigs, ginger and chillies in a food processor and process briefly.

Heat vegetable oil in a heavy-based pan over medium heat, add chicken and cook until browned. Remove chicken and add onion mixture and spices and stir over medium heat for 2-3 minutes, until aromatic. Return chicken to pan with chicken stock and salt and cook covered, over low heat for 8-10 minutes. Add okra and coconut milk and cook for a further 12-15 minutes or until okra is tender. Add lemon juice and stir.

Serve sprinkled with coriander leaves and steamed rice.

Serves 4

Onions

There are hundreds of varieties of onion, but two types: those left in the ground to mature when their tops die off and those harvested while still young and green. Brown, white, red and yellow onions are the main dry types. The warmer the conditions in which they are grown, the milder their flavour.

Green onions, sold in bunches, do not have a bulb above the root and are best eaten raw or lightly cooked. Spring onions (with bulb on the end) are available all year, but are at their best during spring and summer.

Eschalots, also labelled shallots or red shallots, are small, golden-brown or maroon bulbs that grow in clusters and have a mild flavour. They are popular in French and Asian dishes.

Chives contain less sulphur than onions and add a more subtle taste to recipes. Garlic chives, popular in Asian dishes, are easily identified by their thin, flat leaves.

Select dry onions that are crisp and unblemished, with firm, brittle skin and no soft spots. Store them in a cool dark place. Keep green onions and chives in a plastic bag in the crisper of the fridge and don't wash them until ready to use as moisture causes them to go slimy.

Mussels poached in white wine and creamy tomato sauce

(pictured left)

1 tbsp extra virgin olive oil

1 large brown onion, sliced

2 cloves garlic, finely chopped

1 cup dry white wine

2 x 400g cans chopped tomatoes

3 sprigs oregano

2 sprigs thyme

1 tsp dried chilli flakes

1 tsp sugar

2 tbsp tomato paste

2kg scrubbed, de-bearded mussels

$^1/_2$ cup flat-leaf parsley, chopped

$^1/_2$ cup light cream

crusty bread, to serve

Heat olive oil in a very large, deep pan and cook onion and garlic over low heat for 2-3 minutes. Add white wine and bring to the boil. Simmer for 3 minutes then add tomatoes, oregano, thyme, dried chilli flakes, sugar and tomato paste. Stir well and bring to the boil. Add mussels, cover and cook over high heat for 2-3 minutes, shaking pan occasionally. Using a slotted spoon, remove mussels as soon as they open and place in a large serving dish. Remove pan from heat and add flat-leaf parsley and light cream, stir well.

Pour sauce over mussels and serve immediately with crusty bread.

Serves 4

Pan-seared balmain bugs with chickpeas, chilli and herbs

5 tbsp extra virgin olive oil

8 large green (raw) balmain bugs, halved

salt and cracked black pepper

2 eschalots, finely sliced

2 x 400g cans chickpeas, drained and rinsed

2 witlof, sliced

2 long red chillies, very finely sliced

1 bulb fennel, trimmed and finely sliced

$1^1/_2$ tbsp fresh lime juice

salt and cracked black pepper

$^1/_2$ cup coriander leaves

3 tbsp chives, snipped

Heat 2 tablespoons extra virgin olive oil in a large pan over high heat and sear bugs for 2-4 minutes each side. Season with salt and pepper. (This may need to be done in batches). Remove bugs, add eschalots and cook for 2-3 minutes. Add chickpeas and cook until just heated through. Remove from heat, return bugs to pan and stir to combine.

To serve, spoon bug mixture onto a large, shallow serving platter. Scatter with witlof, red chillies and fennel bulb.

Combine lime juice and remaining oil in a small bowl. Add salt and pepper and whisk well. Pour over salad and top with coriander leaves and chives.

Serves 4

Baby snapper with pistachio stuffing

4 baby snapper, cleaned and scaled

4 tbsp melted butter

lime wedges, to serve

Stuffing

1 tbsp extra virgin olive oil

4 green onions, finely sliced

200g fresh pistachio nuts (shelled to produce about $^2/_3$ cup), chopped

$^1/_2$ cup fresh breadcrumbs

$^1/_4$ cup flat-leaf parsley, chopped

2 tsp oregano, chopped

$^1/_4$ cup freshly grated parmesan

salt and cracked black pepper

Preheat oven to 180C.

For the stuffing, heat olive oil in a pan and cook green onion over medium heat for 2-3 minutes. Add pistachio nuts and breadcrumbs and cook for 2-3 minutes. Remove from heat and stir in parsley, oregano and parmesan. Season to taste with salt and pepper, then cool.

Fill snapper cavities with stuffing and secure with toothpicks or cake skewers to close. Cut two slits on each side of snapper and brush both sides with melted butter. Cook quickly in a preheated grill pan over medium-to-high heat for 1-2 minutes each side. Transfer to a lightly greased baking dish and bake for 10 -12 minutes or until fish is just cooked.

Serve with lime wedges.

Serves 4

Fried rice with beansprouts, prawns and green onions

This goes wonderfully with barbecued duck, which can be bought from a Chinese foodstore.

$1^1/_2$ cups long-grain rice (300g)

2 tbsp vegetable oil

2 rashers lean bacon, chopped

2 eggs, lightly beaten with 1 tbsp cold water

$1^1/_2$ tbsp soy sauce

100g tin baby prawns, drained

100g beansprouts

6 green onions, sliced diagonally

Combine rice with 3 cups cold water and cook, covered, over low heat for 10-12 minutes or until tender. Spread on a tray and refrigerate until cold.

Heat 1 tablespoon vegetable oil in a large wok or fry-pan, add bacon and cook over medium heat, stirring occasionally, for 4-5 minutes or until crisp. Remove bacon with a slotted spoon and drain on paper towel.

Discard excess fat from wok, add eggs and cook until just set. Remove and coarsely chop. Add remaining vegetable oil to wok along with rice, bacon and egg and stir over medium heat with a wooden spoon. Add soy sauce, prawns, beansprouts and green onions. Toss until hot and serve straight away.

Serves 4

French onion soup with cheesy croutons

(pictured page 261)

6 medium-sized brown onions, peeled and sliced

1 tbsp olive oil

1 tbsp butter

2 tbsp plain flour

1 tsp brown sugar

1 bay leaf

1 sprig thyme

2 sprigs flat-leaf parsley

$^1/_2$ cup dry white wine

6 cups stock

sea salt and cracked black pepper

6 slices baguette

1 cup grated Swiss cheese

snipped chives (optional)

Preheat oven to 180C.

Combine onions, olive oil and butter in a large, heavy-based saucepan. Cook over very low heat, stirring frequently, for 30-40 minutes or until onions are soft, shiny and golden brown (add a little water if they stick to base of the pan). Add flour and brown sugar and cook, stirring, for 3-4 minutes. Add bay leaf, thyme, parsley and white wine and stir. Add stock, bring to the boil and then simmer for 30 minutes. Season to taste.

Bake bread slices in the oven for 15-20 minutes or until crisp and golden. Sprinkle with grated cheese and bake for a further 8-10 minutes or until cheese is melted. Remove herbs from soup and serve in warmed bowls, topped with a crouton and sprinkled with snipped chives.

Serves 6

Herb, chilli and green onion couscous with char-grilled calamari

300g couscous

1 tbsp butter

4 tbsp extra virgin olive oil

2 cloves garlic, finely chopped

2 small chillies, finely chopped

1/2 cup torn mint leaves

1/2 cup torn flat-leaf parsley

1/3 cup coriander, coarsely chopped

1/2 cup currants plumped in hot water for
    5 minutes then drained

4 green onions, thinly sliced

salt and cracked black pepper

500g cleaned calamari tubes

juice and zest of 1 lime

lime cheeks, to serve

Place couscous in a heatproof dish with butter and 2²/₃ cups boiling water. Stir, cover and let stand for 5 minutes or until water is absorbed.

Heat 1 tablespoon extra virgin olive oil in a small pan and cook garlic and chillies over medium heat for 1-2 minutes or until aromatic.

Stir couscous to break up any lumps and add garlic mixture, mint, flat-leaf parsley, coriander, currants and green onions. Season and mix well.

Slice into 4-5cm pieces and toss in remaining extra virgin olive oil and char-grill over high heat for 3-5 minutes or until opaque. Place in a bowl and toss with lime zest and juice. Place couscous on serving plates and top with calamari. Serve with lime cheeks.

Serves 4

Sun-dried tomato and parmesan tart

Pastry

225g (1¹/₂ cups) plain flour

100g butter, cubed

1 tsp salt

2-3 tbsp iced water

Filling

1 tbsp extra virgin olive oil

1 bunch green onions, cut into 5cm lengths

salt and pepper

³/₄ cup pouring cream

4 large eggs

150g grated parmesan

4 tbsp light sour cream

4 tbsp skim milk

8 sun-dried tomatoes, finely sliced

For the pastry, place flour, butter and salt in a food processor and blend until it resembles coarse breadcrumbs. Add water and process until the mixture forms a ball. Remove, knead lightly and roll out on a lightly floured surface. Line a 23cm flan tin or pie dish with the pastry and rest, covered, in the refrigerator for 30 minutes.

Preheat oven to 180C.

Line the pastry shell with baking paper and then fill with dried beans, rice or pastry weights and bake for 10-12 minutes or until pastry is golden and dry. Remove weights and bake for 5 minutes or until pastry is golden and dry.

For the filling, heat olive oil in a pan over medium heat and saute onions until wilted. Season with salt and pepper. Set aside to cool.

Add cream to a large bowl and mix in eggs, one at a time, beating well after each addition. Add parmesan, sour cream, milk and sun-dried tomatoes. Add salt and pepper to taste. Pour cream mixture into pastry shell and arrange green onions on top. Bake for 30-40 minutes or until cooked and golden.

Serve with a green salad.

Serves 6-8

Barbecued T-bone with caramelised onions and sweet potato mash

1tbsp extra virgin olive oil

2 tbsp butter

2 large red onions, thinly sliced

2 tbsp brown sugar

2 tbsp balsamic vinegar

salt and cracked black pepper

750g sweet potato, peeled and thinly sliced

4-5 tbsp skim milk

4 T-bone steaks (about 400g each)

Heat olive oil and half the butter in a frying pan, add red onions and cook over medium heat, stirring often, for 4-5 minutes, until onion is soft. Add brown sugar, balsamic vinegar, salt and pepper and cook over low heat. Stir occasionally for about 10-15 minutes or until onion is caramelised. Keep warm.

Cook sweet potato in lightly salted, boiling water over medium heat for about 10 minutes, until cooked and tender. Drain and mash with skim milk and remaining butter.

Cook the T-bone steaks on a hot barbecue for 3-4 minutes each side or until cooked as desired. Rest in a warm place for 5 minutes.

Serve T-bones topped with onion and accompanied by sweet potato mash and salad leaves.

Serves 4

Richard Lenoir Market, Paris

Parsnips

Nutty, earthy parsnips are available all year, but at their sweetest during the colder months when some of their starch is converted to sugar. They can be steamed, baked or fried and make great chunky chips sprinkled with salt flakes, but they become soggy when boiled.

Sometimes called white carrots, parsnips belong to the same family as parsley, fennel, carrots, celeriac and celery.

Buy crisp, fresh, even-shaped parsnips with no soft spots. Choose small- to medium-sized specimens, as large parsnips can be woody and tough inside. If they have a tough core, remove before cooking. Keep them in the crisper but not in a plastic bag, as they will sweat.

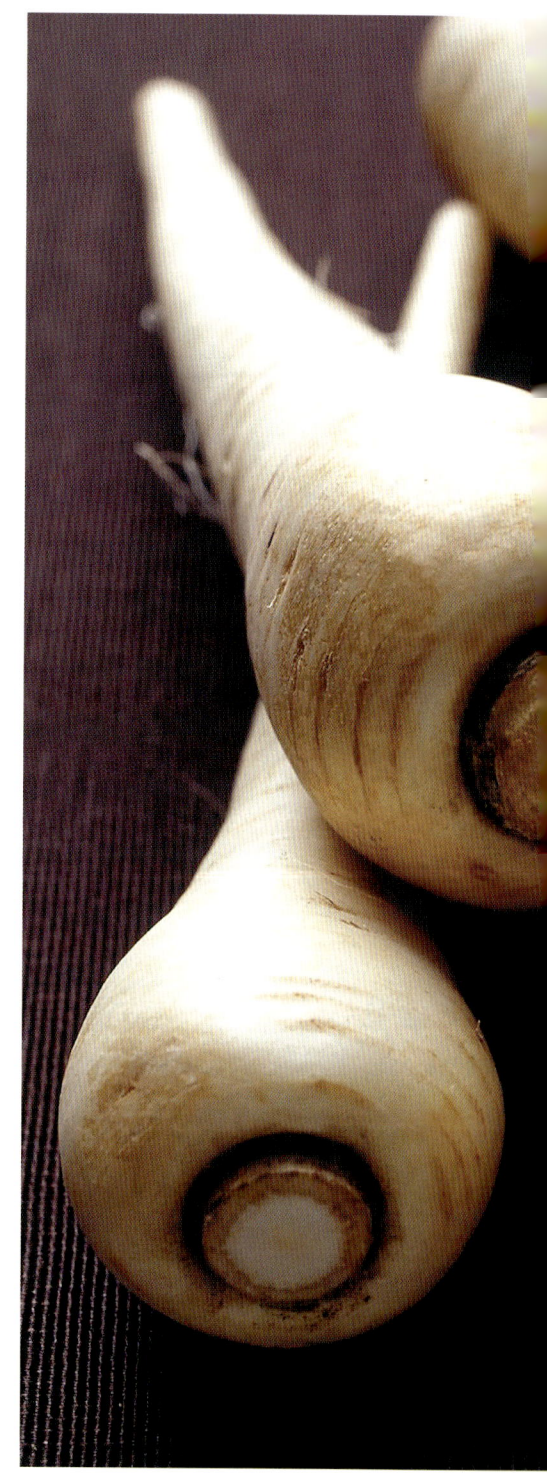

Roasted parsnips with parsley, thyme, oregano and breadcrumbs

4 medium-sized parsnips, peeled and halved

3 tbsp extra virgin olive oil

salt and cracked black pepper

2 tsp thyme leaves

1/4 cup fresh breadcrumbs

1 tbsp oregano, chopped

1 tbsp flat-leaf parsley, chopped

barbecued lamb and rosemary sausages, to serve

Preheat oven to 200C.

Cook parsnips in lightly salted, boiling water for 5 minutes then drain. Place in an ovenproof dish and add olive oil, salt and pepper, thyme leaves and breadcrumbs. Toss to combine then roast for 20-25 minutes or until caramelised and golden. Remove and sprinkle with oregano leaves and flat-leaf parsley.

Serves 4

Marsala and orange sauteed parsnips

4 medium-sized parsnips, peeled and cut into thick slices

chicken stock, to cover

1 tbsp butter

salt and cracked black pepper

2 tbsp fresh orange juice

2 tbsp sweet marsala

1 tbsp flat-leaf parsley, chopped

Place parsnips in a medium-sized saucepan and add chicken stock or water to just cover. Bring to the boil over medium heat and simmer for 8-10 minutes, until just tender. Drain.

Melt butter in a heavy-based frying pan over high heat and add parsnips. Season with salt and pepper. Add orange juice and marsala and toss to combine then cook, stirring often, for 2-3 minutes until parsnips are caramelised and juices have almost evaporated.

Serve topped with parsley.

Serves 4

Peas

Freshly harvested garden peas are at their best during spring and, after shelling, only need to be cooked briefly in lightly salted, boiling water. These days, however, they have largely been replaced by frozen peas, but modern freezing techniques preserve peas in a fresher state than those found in some produce markets. Peas lose their freshness rapidly after shelling, when their natural sweetness turns to starch. It is preferable to eat young snap-frozen peas rather than ones that have been podded for some time. They are very nutritious and an excellent source of vitamin C, dietary fibre, iron and folate.

Snowpeas are a distinct variety of pea, originally adapted in China from European varieties and eaten before the string develops and the peas start to swell. Also known as sugar peas or mange tout, these flat-podded, immature peas have a sweet flavour and crunchy texture. They are a favourite in stir-fries and salads because of their attractive colour and the fact that they need little preparation.

Sugar snap peas are a snowpea hybrid, available in climbing, dwarf and bush varieties. This unusual pea has thick walls, snaps like a green bean and is completely edible except for the small husk and strings. Unlike snowpeas, sugar snaps are allowed to mature and become fully rounded. The pods are delicious raw or cooked.

Choose small sugar snaps and snowpeas as they will be younger and more succulent. Remove the thread-like strings on both sides of the crisp pod before using. Sugar snaps and common peas should be shiny while snowpeas should be dull if fresh.

Pea shoots, the growing tip of the plant, are popular in Cantonese dishes and considered a great delicacy. They are available during the early part of the growing season, but wilt quickly after picking so use them on the day of purchase.

Buy peas that feel waxy, avoiding any yellow or dry ones. Store them in the crisper of the fridge, as peas left at room temperature quickly lose their sweetness.

Barbecued chicken with snowpeas, roasted tomato and rocket

Marinade

1 clove garlic, crushed

juice of 1 lemon

2 tbsp Dijon mustard

2 tbsp sweet chilli sauce

good pinch of dried chilli flakes

2 tbsp extra virgin olive oil

4 chicken marylands, deboned, skin on

sea salt and cracked black pepper

4 roma tomatoes

2 tbsp olive oil

120g snowpeas, trimmed, halved and blanched

1 small bunch rocket leaves

1 tbsp extra virgin olive oil

Combine garlic, lemon juice, mustard, sweet chilli sauce and chilli flakes in a bowl with the extra virgin olive oil and stir well.

Place chicken pieces in a large shallow dish and pour marinade over. Turn to coat then rest, covered in the fridge, for at least 2 hours or overnight.

Heat barbecue to medium-high, season chicken and cook, turning occasionally, until skin is crisp and chicken is cooked through. Set aside in a warm place.

Halve tomatoes and brush with olive oil. Season and cook on the barbecue, cut-side down, until tender.

Combine snowpeas and rocket in a bowl. Season and drizzle with extra virgin olive oil. Toss gently.

Place chicken on serving plates, top with snowpea salad and serve tomatoes on the side.

Serves 4

Pea and herb salad with mustard vinaigrette

300g (2¹/₂ cups) peas (fresh or frozen)

50g trimmed halved snowpeas

¹/₂ red onion, very finely sliced

¹/₄ cup torn mint leaves

¹/₄ cup basil, torn

1 tbsp flat-leaf parsley, chopped

1 tbsp chives, snipped

100g feta

Dressing

1 tsp Dijon mustard

salt and cracked black pepper

2 tbsp extra virgin olive oil

2 tsp red-wine vinegar

pinch of sugar

Cook fresh peas in lightly salted, boiling water for 3-4 minutes (or frozen peas in lightly salted, boiling water for 1 minute) then drain.

Combine peas, onion and herbs in a bowl.

For the dressing, combine all the ingredients in a small bowl and whisk until smooth.

Drizzle dressing over peas and herbs and crumble feta over salad.

Serve with pan-fried lamb cutlets and mash.

Serves 6

Pea and pumpkin risotto

2 tbsp extra virgin olive oil

1 onion, finely chopped

400g (2 cups) arborio rice

125ml dry white wine

1.5 litres vegetable or chicken stock

2 cups peeled, seeded and
    coarsely chopped pumpkin

1 cup fresh or frozen peas

60g parmesan, grated

60g butter, chopped

shaved parmesan, to serve

Heat olive oil in a large, heavy-based saucepan, add onion and cook over low heat for 5 minutes or until soft. Add rice and stir over low heat until coated with oil and lightly toasted. Add wine and stir over medium heat until liquid is absorbed.

Have stock simmering in another saucepan, then add 1 cup to rice and stir over medium heat for 5 minutes or until stock is absorbed. Add pumpkin and peas and stir. Add remaining stock, ¹/₂ cup at a time, stirring continuously, allowing each addition to be absorbed before adding the next. When rice is al dente, stir in grated parmesan and butter, then season to taste with salt and pepper.

Serve risotto scattered with shaved parmesan.

Serves 4

Warm salad of poached salmon with fennel, sugar snap peas and citrus dressing

4 x 180g salmon portions, skinned and pin boned

2 cups fish stock

2 x 400g cans cannellini beans, rinsed and drained

100g sugar snap peas, trimmed

1 baby fennel, trimmed and very finely sliced

¹/₄ cup orange zest

¹/₄ cup lime zest

Dressing

1¹/₂ cups extra virgin olive oil

¹/₄ cup orange juice

¹/₄ cup lemon juice

50ml verjuice

salt and cracked black pepper

For the dressing, combine all the ingredients in a small bowl and whisk well.

Place stock in a large saucepan and bring to the boil over medium heat, add salmon, reduce heat and simmer gently for 2-4 minutes or until cooked as desired. Remove salmon with a slotted spoon. Blanch sugar snap peas in lightly salted, boiling water for 1 minute then drain. Combine cannellini beans, sugar snaps, baby fennel and half the zest in a bowl. Pour dressing over and toss gently. Divide cannellini bean mixture evenly between 4 shallow bowls and top each with a portion of salmon. Scatter with remaining citrus zest and serve warm.

Serves 4

Greek lamb salad with peas, mint and oregano

2 lamb backstraps

5 tbsp extra virgin olive oil

salt and cracked black pepper

1 cup (125g) frozen peas

1 clove garlic, finely chopped

1/3 cup torn mint leaves

1/3 cup oregano leaves

300g feta, cubed

2 cups baby cos leaves, torn

1/2 red onion, finely sliced

2 tbsp lemon juice

Brush lamb backstraps with 1 tablespoon extra virgin olive oil, season with salt and black pepper and cook in a non-stick fry pan over high heat for 3- 4 minutes each side. Remove and rest in a warm place for 5 minutes.

Blanch frozen peas in lightly salted, boiling water for 30 seconds, drain. Combine peas with garlic, mint leaves, oregano, feta, cos leaves and red onion in a large bowl.

Whisk remaining extra virgin olive oil, lemon juice, pinch sugar, salt and pepper in a small bowl until thick. Drizzle dressing over herb mixture and toss gently to combine.

Slice lamb thinly on the diagonal and place on 4 serving plates. Top with pea and herb salad.

Serves 4

Pea and lettuce soup with fresh herbs

1 tbsp extra virgin olive oil

1 clove garlic, finely chopped

1 small onion, chopped

4 cups chicken stock

2 cups lettuce, shredded

3 sprigs mint

1/2 tsp salt

1 tsp caster sugar

500g frozen peas

3 tbsp light cream

2 tbsp mint, chopped

2 tbsp chervil, chopped

cracked black pepper

Heat olive oil in a saucepan over medium heat, add garlic and onion and saute for 2-3 minutes. Add chicken stock and bring to the boil. Add shredded lettuce, mint sprigs, salt, caster sugar and simmer, covered, for 8 minutes. Add frozen peas and bring to the boil and simmer for 1-2 minutes.

Remove mint sprigs and puree the mixture in a blender or food processor. Return to saucepan and stir in light cream over low heat until hot.

Serve soup sprinkled with chopped mint, chervil and pepper.

Serves 4

Chicken, sesame and pea salad

2 chicken breast fillets

500g baby spinach leaves

200g frozen peas

4 tbsp lemon juice

1/4 cup sesame seeds, toasted

1 tbsp sugar

1/4 cup soy sauce

1 tbsp mirin

1/4 cup dashi

Place chicken breast fillets in a deep frying pan, cover with water and bring to a gentle simmer. Poach for about 10 minutes or until cooked. Drain, cool slightly then slice very finely.

Steam baby spinach leaves and frozen peas until just tender then divide between 4 serving plates. Drizzle 1 teaspoon of lemon juice over each and top with the chicken.

For the dressing, crush sesame seeds in a mortar and pestle then add sugar, soy sauce, mirin and dashi and stir well. Pour over salads.

Serves 4

Stir-fried Chinese roasted duck with snowpeas and noodles

2 tbsp vegetable oil

1 tbsp ginger, grated

1 clove garlic, finely chopped

4 green onions, finely sliced on the diagonal

2 cups trimmed halved snowpeas

1 de-boned sliced Chinese roast duck
   (available from Chinese barbecue shops)

2 tbsp soy sauce

2 tbsp oyster sauce

1 lebanese cucumber, sliced on the diagonal

steamed rice or hot noodles, to serve

Heat vegetable oil in a wok over high heat, add ginger and garlic and stir-fry for 30 seconds. Add green onions and snowpeas and stir-fry for 1 minute. Add duck and stir-fry for another minute, then add $\frac{1}{4}$ cup water, soy sauce, oyster sauce and bring to the boil and stir-fry for a further minute or until duck is heated through.

Transfer to 4 serving bowls and top with Lebanese cucumber. Serve with steamed rice or noodles.

Serves 4

Potatoes

There are hundreds of varieties of potatoes and two main types. Waxy potatoes, high in moisture and lower in starch, are suitable for salads as they stay firmer when boiled; floury potatoes are lower in moisture and higher in starch, making them ideal for chips and baking.

Usually sold as washed potatoes, sebagoes account for more than 60 per cent of the Australian crop and are a good all round variety. Desirees, with yellow flesh and pink skin, make good gnocchi, especially when roasted first; they are also tasty microwaved. The main red variety, pontiac, is recognisable by its bright, rose-coloured skin and is good mashed or roasted, but not for chipping. Kipflers, also called finger or peanut potatoes because of their shape, are excellent in soups and potato salads, but not mashed, and have a creamy texture and slightly nutty flavour. White with pink blushes, king edwards, make particularly good chips. Spuntas, originally from Holland, have a subtle, yellow skin and flesh – use them in gratins.

Elongated purple congoes tend to leach their colour when boiled. Slice thinly, cook briefly and use in salads or as a garnish. Pink-eye potatoes have firm, waxy flesh and are often sold as new potatoes – boil or roast them. Pink fir apple, the old English variety, is tubular with creamy flesh and pale-pink skin. It is good as a salad potato and also tasty boiled and mashed.

New potatoes have thin, fragile skin, as they have been harvested when a little immature while old potatoes have drier flesh and thicker skins and are good for mashing. Gourmet varieties, such as bintje, kennebec, nicola, patrone and toolangi delight are available in specialist fruit and vegetable shops and growers' markets.

Buy unwashed potatoes and look for smooth, firm specimens with no sprouts, bruises or cracks. Ideally, buy them loose. Exposed to light, potatoes go green and develop a bitter taste – to avoid this keep them in a cool, dark, dry place. Remove from plastic bags, as sweating or dampness will cause them to rot.

Olive oil mashed potatoes

1.5kg desiree potatoes, unpeeled and quartered

100ml warm pouring cream

3-4 tbsp extra virgin olive oil

1 tbsp oregano, chopped

1 tbsp flat-leaf parsley, chopped

2 tbsp soft butter

1 tbsp white-wine vinegar

salt and cracked black pepper

Cook potatoes in lightly salted, boiling water over medium heat 8-12 minutes or until tender. Drain and return to saucepan. Add cream and stir.

Over low heat, add olive oil, oregano, parsley, butter and vinegar and smash potatoes with a masher. Season with salt and pepper.

Serves 6

Tuna salad with baby potatoes, beans and tomatoes

300g baby potatoes, cooked with skin on, halved

100g baby beans, trimmed and cooked

125g ($^1/_2$ punnet) grape tomatoes

2 x 125g cans tuna slices in vegetable oil
    or spring water, drained

12 black olives

$^1/_2$ red capsicum, finely sliced

8 quail eggs, hard boiled, peeled and halved
    or 2 eggs hard boiled, peeled and quartered

Dressing

1 tbsp red-wine vinegar

2 tbsp extra virgin olive oil

$^1/_2$ tsp Dijon mustard

pinch of sugar

salt and cracked black pepper, to taste

For the salad, combine all the ingredients except quail eggs in a large bowl.

For the dressing, combine all the ingredients in a small bowl and whisk until well combined. Pour over salad and toss gently.

Divide salad evenly between two serving dishes and top with quail eggs.

Serves 2

Left: Salamanca Market, Hobart.

Grated potato, thyme and gruyere gratin

This is one of my favourite potato recipes because it is so versatile. Serve it with barbecued sausages, pan-fried steaks or teamed with grilled fish fillets

150ml light cream

125g light sour cream

3 eggs

6 sprigs thyme

125g gruyere cheese, grated

1/4 tsp cayenne pepper

sea salt

750g sebago potatoes, peeled

Preheat oven to 200C.

Combine cream and sour cream in a large bowl and mix until smooth. Add eggs and stir until well combined. Pull leaves from thyme and add to cream mixture. Add gruyere cheese and cayenne and season with salt.

Grate potatoes in a food processor or on a grater then stir into the cream mixture until well combined.

Spoon mixture into a medium-sized greased ovenproof dish and bake for 50-60 minutes or until potatoes are cooked and top is crisp and golden.

Serves 4

Potato and leek soup

40g butter

2 leeks, white part only, sliced

1 stick celery, sliced

1 small carrot, peeled and chopped

700g potatoes, peeled and chopped

1 litre (4 cups) chicken stock

300ml light cream

sea salt and cracked black pepper

fresh chives or parsley

Melt butter in a large saucepan, add leeks, celery and carrot and cook over low heat for about 5 minutes until vegetables are soft but not browned. Add potatoes and chicken stock and bring to the boil. Cover and simmer for about 25-30 minutes or until potatoes are tender.

Set aside to cool a little. Blend soup in a food processor or blender until smooth. Reserve 1/2 cup of the cream and pour remainder into the soup. Stir and season well with salt and pepper.

To serve, pour hot soup into warm soup bowls, add a swirl of cream and top with chopped herbs.

Serves 4

Quick creamy frittatas

A great alternative to sandwiches for the kids' lunch boxes, these tasty little vegetable cakes take only a few minutes to prepare and 20 minutes to cook in a muffin tin.

1 large potato (about 250g), peeled

1 small onion, peeled

1 medium-sized zucchini,

4 fresh baby corn, finely sliced

4 eggs, lightly beaten

1/2 cup pouring cream

100g swiss cheese, grated

cayenne pepper and salt

Preheat oven to 200C.

Grate potato, onion and zucchini. Place in a tea towel, roll up and squeeze out excess moisture. Place vegetables in a medium-sized bowl and add corn. Add eggs and stir to combine. Add cream and cheese and season with cayenne and salt, then stir. Spoon mixture into 6 x 1/2-cup capacity muffin tins and bake for 20-25 minutes or until golden and cooked. Serve warm or at room temperature.

Makes 6

Garlic mashed potatoes with parmesan-coated lamb cutlets

The secret to perfect lamb cutlets is to prepare them in advance and let them rest in the refrigerator before cooking, so they don't stick to the pan.

18 lamb cutlets, trimmed
150g rice flour
1½ cups milk
150g grated parmesan
1 tsp chilli powder
3 eggs, lightly beaten with 2 tbsp water
6 slices day old white bread, processed until fine
olive oil, for frying

1kg floury potatoes (e.g. king edward)
salt and cracked black pepper
2 cloves garlic, finely chopped
150ml milk
120g butter, chopped

Dust lamb cutlets with rice flour and dip in milk. Coat with combined parmesan and chilli powder then dip in egg mixture and coat with breadcrumbs. Cover and refrigerate until ready to use.

Heat 2 tablespoons of olive oil in a large frying pan and cook cutlets in batches over medium heat for 3-4 minutes each side or until cooked as desired, adding more oil if necessary.

Drain on absorbent paper.

For the potatoes, cover whole, unpeeled potatoes with cold water and 1 teaspoon salt and bring to the boil over high heat. Cook over medium heat for about 30 minutes or until tender. Drain and cool slightly.

Combine garlic and milk in a small saucepan and bring to a simmer then remove from heat.

Peel skins from potatoes and return to saucepan. Gently shake pan over low heat for 1 minute to remove any excess moisture. Gradually add butter and mash until smooth. Remove garlic from milk (and discard) and gradually add to potatoes and beat vigorously until smooth and creamy. Season with salt and pepper.

Serve cutlets with creamy mash and oven roasted tomatoes or green peas.

Serves 6

Warm potato salad with sage and mustard

750g sebago potatoes, unpeeled and cut into 2cm pieces
50ml extra virgin olive oil
2 tsp seeded mustard
1 tsp Dijon mustard
2 tsp lemon juice
salt and cracked black pepper
2 brown eschalots, finely sliced
1 tbsp sage, chopped
leaves from 2 sprigs flat-leaf parsley, torn
1 tbsp salted baby capers, rinsed

Cook potatoes in lightly salted, boiling water for 6-8 minutes or until tender. Drain and place in a large bowl.

Combine olive oil, mustards, lemon juice and salt and pepper in a small bowl and whisk until smooth.

Add eschalots to potatoes, pour dressing over and toss gently. Add sage and parsley and toss to combine. Scatter with capers and serve warm.

Serves 4

Potato wedges with chilli mayo

2 tbsp plain flour

2 tbsp breadcrumbs

2 tsp dried oregano

$^1\!/_2$ tsp salt

$^1\!/_2$ tsp cracked black pepper

$^1\!/_2$ tsp paprika

1kg scrubbed floury potatoes

2-3 tbsp extra virgin olive oil

1$^1\!/_2$ cups good mayonnaise

chilli powder, to taste

Combine flour, breadcrumbs, dried oregano, salt,
pepper and paprika in a large plastic bag and
shake well. Cut potatoes into about 2.5cm wedges
and toss half in the plastic bag, shaking to coat.
Repeat with remaining potatoes.

Drizzle a large baking tray with olive oil and
place wedges on tray. Bake at 220C for about
25-30 minutes, turning once until crisp, golden
and cooked.

Serve with mayo spiced with mild chilli powder
to taste.

Serves 4

Toscanos, Kew, Melbourne

Veal schnitzels with steamed baby potatoes and cos leaves

(pictured page 275)

12 baby potatoes, unpeeled

600g veal schnitzels

plain flour, seasoned

1 cup milk

1 egg, lightly beaten

2 cups day-old breadcrumbs

2-3 tbsp extra virgin olive oil

1 tbsp butter

1/2 cup white wine

1 clove garlic, finely chopped

2 tbsp salted baby capers, rinsed

1 tbsp lemon zest

1 tbsp flat-leaf parsley, coarsely chopped

salt and cracked black pepper

8 baby cos leaves

4 tbsp vinaigrette dressing

Cook baby potatoes in lightly salted, boiling water for 8-12 minutes or until tender. Drain.

Dust veal schnitzels in seasoned flour and shake off excess. Combine milk and egg in a shallow bowl and dip in schnitzels. Coat with breadcrumbs. Heat olive oil and butter in a large frying pan and cook veal, in batches, over high heat for 2-3 minutes each side. Remove and keep warm.

Add wine and garlic to pan, stir well, scraping the sediment from the base. Add capers, lemon zest and parsley, season with salt and pepper and stir for 1-2 minutes.

Place veal on serving plates and top with sauce. Serve potatoes and cos leaves on the side, drizzled with vinaigrette dressing.

Serves 4

Pan-fried chorizo with herbs, potatoes and verjuice

1 chorizo sausage (350g) chopped

4 green onions, sliced

2 sprigs oregano

2 sprigs thyme

750g small potatoes, peeled and sliced 5mm thick

salt and cracked black pepper

$^1/_2$ cup verjuice

2 tbsp flat-leaf parsley, chopped

Stir chorizo sausage in a non-stick pan over medium heat for 2-3 minutes. Add green onions, oregano, thyme and stir for 1 minute. Drain off excess fat and add potatoes; stir and season with salt and pepper. Add verjuice, bring to the boil and add 1$^1/_2$ cups water then simmer over low heat for 15-20 minutes or until potatoes are cooked and most of the liquid has evaporated. Top with flat-leaf parsley and serve.

Serves 4

Potato and onion bake

1kg desiree potatoes, peeled

1$^3/_4$ cups milk

$^1/_4$ cup light cream

1 large clove garlic, bruised

1 small onion, finely sliced

salt and cracked black pepper

ground nutmeg

1 tbsp butter, chopped

2 tbsp grated parmesan

Preheat oven to 200C.

Cut potatoes into 3mm-thick slices. Place in a large saucepan with milk, cream and garlic. Bring to the boil over medium-heat then reduce heat and simmer for 5 minutes, stirring often. Transfer half the mixture to a greased, medium-sized ovenproof dish and spread out evenly. Scatter onion over the potatoes. Season with salt, pepper and ground nutmeg. Spread remaining potatoes over onion, dot with butter and sprinkle with parmesan cheese.

Bake, covered with foil, for 20 minutes then remove foil and bake for a further 20-30 minutes or until golden and cooked.

Serve with roast chicken.

Serves 4

Salmon and potato fritters with tartare sauce

4 medium-sized potatoes, peeled

1 x 210g tin salmon, drained

1 x 105g tin salmon, drained

1 small white onion, finely chopped

2 tbsp flat-leaf parsley, chopped

1 egg

salt and cracked black pepper

Tabasco sauce, to taste

dry breadcrumbs

vegetable oil, for frying

tartare sauce and lime cheeks, to serve

Cut potatoes into chunks and boil in lightly salted water until tender. Drain and mash well. Place in a large bowl and add salmon, onion, flat-leaf parsley, egg, salt and pepper. Add Tabasco sauce to taste and mix well.

Chill for 15 minutes then shape mixture into flat cakes about 2cm thick. Coat with breadcrumbs and shallow-fry in hot vegetable oil, until golden on both sides. Drain on paper towel and serve hot with tartare sauce and lime cheeks.

Serves 4

Pumpkin

The word pumpkin is derived from the Greek *pepon*, which means a large, melon-like fruit. They are native to central and southern America, and in Europe were initially regarded as food for animals or the poor.

Along with marrows, squash, zucchini and chokoes, pumpkins are members of the cucurbita family and there are hundreds of varieties in a range of sizes and shapes.

Queensland blue is one of the most common in Australia. It has a tough, green-grey skin and a fluted shell and is difficult to peel, but it's worth the trouble for the bright-orange flesh that has a rich flavour and lower water content than many other varieties. The smaller, pear-shaped butternut was one of the earliest varieties grown in Mexico, with pale golden-brown skin and sweet flesh that is usually bright-orange and dry. They are excellent for making scones or soup.

Kent is one of the newer varieties, with intense golden flesh and dark-green, glossy skin with patches of yellow and greenish-brown stripes. Golden nugget grows on a bush instead of a vine and is one of the most sought-after miniature varieties. Good for stuffing, it has deep-yellow flesh and more seeds than most. Jarrahdale is a more recently developed variety from Western Australia. Easily identified by its blue-grey skin, the deep-orange flesh is more suitable for baking than boiling.

Select whole pumpkins that feel heavy for their size, with some stalk attached (to protect the flesh from damp). Avoid any with damaged skin. If cut, check that the edges look fresh and the seeds are not slimy. Whole pumpkins will keep for many months in a cool, dark place. Cut pumpkins should be cooked within a few days, as they can go mouldy fast if left in the fridge.

Angouleme markets, France

Pumpkin and prawn soup

(pictured page 283)

30g butter

1 tbsp olive oil

1 onion, peeled and chopped

1kg pumpkin, peeled and chopped

1 carrot, peeled and chopped

1 stick celery, chopped

6 cups chicken stock

salt flakes and cracked black pepper

$\frac{1}{2}$ tsp ground nutmeg

thick cream (optional)

12-16 peeled cooked prawns

Combine butter and oil in a large saucepan. Add onion and cook over low heat until soft. Add pumpkin, carrot and celery and stir to coat. Add chicken stock, salt, pepper and nutmeg and bring to the boil. Cover and simmer for 25-30 minutes or until pumpkin is very tender. Mix in a food processor and check seasoning.

Reheat soup and serve with a splash of thick cream and topped with prawns.

Serves 6-8

Spicy roasted pumpkin with pinenuts, creme fraiche and oregano

800g pumpkin, unpeeled, seeds removed
   and cut into 8 wedges

2-3 tbsp extra virgin olive oil

$1/4$ tsp ground cardamom

$1/2$ tsp ground cinnamon

$1/4$ tsp ground ginger

salt and cracked black pepper

$1/2$ cup creme fraiche

3 tbsp toasted pinenuts

1 small red chilli, very finely chopped

$1/4$ cup flat-leaf parsley, torn

$1/4$ cup oregano leaves, coarsely chopped

Preheat oven to 200C.

Combine pumpkin, olive oil and spices in a bowl with salt and pepper and toss gently to coat. Place pumpkin pieces on an oven tray and roast for 35-40 minutes or until golden and cooked.

Transfer to a serving platter and spoon over dollops of creme fraiche. Scatter with pinenuts, chilli and herbs.

Serves 4

Bruschetta with pumpkin, feta and sage

1.2kg pumpkin, peeled seeded
   and cut into 1cm pieces

2 sprigs torn sage leaves

7 tbsp extra virgin olive oil

salt and cracked black pepper

8 slices thick sourdough bread

2 cut cloves garlic

120g feta, crumbled

extra olive oil, to drizzle

Place pumpkin in a large roasting tray with sage leaves and drizzle with 3 tablespoons of olive oil. Season with salt and pepper and toss to coat in oil. Roast at 220C for 15-20 minutes or until pumpkin is tender.

Toast sourdough bread and rub with garlic. Brush with remaining olive oil and divide pumpkin and sage among slices.

Crumble feta over pumpkin, place on an oven tray and bake at 180C for about 5-6 minutes, until cheese is soft and pumpkin is hot. Drizzle with olive oil.

Serves 4

Warm pumpkin, bacon and feta salad

700g butternut pumpkin, peeled and cut
   into 2cm pieces

4 rashers bacon, chopped

1-2 tbsp extra virgin olive oil

1 red onion, thinly sliced

1 clove garlic, finely chopped

1 bunch English spinach, trimmed

$1/4$ tsp ground nutmeg

$1/4$ tsp cayenne pepper

juice of 1 orange

120g feta cheese, crumbled

55g toasted almonds

Cook pumpkin in lightly salted, boiling water for about 5 minutes or until just tender. Drain.

Cook bacon in a non-stick pan over medium heat for about 5-7 minutes or until crisp. Remove and drain on paper towel.

Heat extra virgin olive oil in a large frying pan over medium heat and add red onion and garlic and cook for about 5 minutes or until onion is soft. Add spinach, nutmeg, cayenne pepper and stir gently for 1 minute. Add pumpkin and orange juice and cook, stirring occasionally, for 2-3 minutes. Stir in crumbled feta cheese and almonds.

Serve warm topped with bacon pieces.

Serves 4 as a side dish

pumpkin

Linguine with pumpkin, mushrooms and peas

350g linguine or spaghetti

1 cup peeled pumpkin, cut into chunks

1 small zucchini, sliced

1 cup fresh peas

1 bunch asparagus, sliced into 3-4cm lengths

1 tbsp butter

100g swiss mushrooms, sliced

salt and cracked black pepper

1 cup pouring cream

40g grated parmesan

12 torn basil leaves

Cook linguine or spaghetti in a large pan of lightly salted, boiling water over medium heat until al dente. Drain.

Cook pumpkin, zucchini, peas and asparagus in a saucepan of lightly salted, boiling water over medium heat until tender but crisp (pumpkin should go in first as it takes longer to cook). Drain. Melt butter in a large pan and cook mushrooms until soft. Add drained vegetables to mushrooms, season with salt and pepper, add pouring cream and stir over low heat for 2 minutes. Toss pasta with vegetables and parmesan and serve topped with 12 torn basil leaves.

Serves 4

Roasted pumpkin, sage and couscous salad

500g pumpkin, peeled and sliced

3 tbsp extra virgin olive oil

1 cup couscous

1 tbsp butter

1 cup sugar snap peas

$^1/_4$ cup sage, chopped

$^1/_4$ cup vinaigrette dressing

$^1/_2$ cup yoghurt

1 tsp honey

1 tsp ground cumin

4 barbecued sirloin steaks, to serve

Place pumpkin in a baking dish and toss with olive oil. Bake at 200C for about 30 minutes or until cooked.

Place couscous in a medium-sized bowl and pour over 1$^1/_4$ cups boiling water. Add butter, stir, cover and rest for 5 minutes or until water is absorbed.

Blanch sugar snap peas in boiling water then refresh under cold water and drain. Combine couscous, pumpkin, peas and sage leaves in a large bowl.

Combine vinaigrette dressing with yoghurt, honey and ground cumin in a small bowl and mix well. Pour over pumpkin salad and serve. Great with barbecued sirloin steaks.

Serves 4

Pumpkin and leek risotto

4 tbsp butter

1 leek (white part only), finely sliced

2 cups(400g) arborio rice

$^1/_2$ cup dry white wine

1$^1/_2$ litres hot chicken stock

1$^1/_2$ cups pumpkin, chopped

salt and cracked black pepper

60g grated parmesan

shaved parmesan, extra

Melt 2 tablespoons butter in a large saucepan and add leek. Stir over medium heat for 4-5 minutes or until soft. Add rice and stir over low heat until coated with butter. Add white wine and stir until liquid is absorbed. Gradually add 1$^1/_2$ litres simmering chicken stock, ladle by ladle, stirring after each addition until stock is absorbed. When rice is half cooked, add pumpkin. Continue cooking, stirring and adding remaining stock, until rice is cooked but firm to the bite (about 15 minutes).

Season with salt and pepper, stir in grated parmesan and remaining butter and serve with extra shaved parmesan.

Serves 4

Macaroni with pesto, pumpkin and ricotta

$^1/_2$ tbsp extra virgin olive oil

600g pumpkin, peeled and cut into 2cm pieces

400g macaroni

Pesto

leaves from 2 bunches basil

2 tbsp toasted pinenuts

2 cloves garlic

60g grated parmesan

200ml extra virgin olive oil

salt and cracked black pepper

250g crumbled ricotta cheese

shaved parmesan, to serve

Preheat oven to 210C.

Combine 1$^1/_2$ tablespoons extra virgin olive oil in a roasting pan with pumpkin, toss to coat and roast for 20-25 minutes or until lightly browned and tender.

Cook macaroni in plenty of lightly salted, boiling water until al dente. Drain, reserving 3 tablespoons of the pasta water.

For the pesto, combine basil, pinenuts and garlic in a food processor and process briefly. Add parmesan and process until combined. Add extra virgin olive oil in a steady stream with motor running and process until smooth. Season with salt and pepper and remove to a bowl.

Stir reserved pasta water into pesto and toss with pasta and pumpkin. Serve in 4 warm bowls and top with ricotta and extra shaved parmesan.

Serves 4

Radicchio

Some salad leaves work as a background but not radicchio. It is a star in its own right, a very popular salad leaf. Its bold, bitter flavour mellows when cooked so add it to soup or risotto at the end of cooking – or try it grilled and drizzled with a little olive oil.

Radicchio is usually a mottled magenta colour, but depending on the climate it can grow with green patches and streaks of cream.

The four main varieties are radicchio di treviso, which is elongated and the best for cooking; soft, speckle-leaved castelfranco; the round-headed milder flavoured radicchio di chioggia; and the brilliant red radicchio di Verona.

Look for bright, crisp, tender leaves without any blemishes and no signs of browning. Like lettuce, they should be stored in a covered container or perforated plastic bag in the crisper of the fridge and used within a day or two.

Pan-fried snapper fillets with balsamic braised radicchio

2 tbsp extra virgin olive oil

1 bulb fennel, finely sliced

3 eschalots, finely sliced

1 heart radicchio, coarsely chopped

1 tbsp baby salted capers, rinsed and drained

2 tbsp aged balsamic vinegar

salt and cracked black pepper

4 snapper fillets (180-200g each)

Heat 1 tablespoon olive oil in a large pan over medium heat and add fennel and eschalots. Cook for about 2 minutes then add radicchio leaves and capers and cook a further 2 minutes or until half cooked. Add balsamic vinegar, salt and pepper and remove from heat.

Meanwhile, brush snapper fillets with remaining oil, season and cook in a large, non-stick pan over medium-high heat for 2-3 minutes each side or until just cooked.

To serve, place snapper fillets in the centre of serving plates and top with braised radicchio. Serve mash on the side.

Serves 4

Radicchio, celery and pancetta risotto

1.5-1.75 litres chicken stock

5 tbsp butter

1 medium-sized onion, chopped

1 stick celery, sliced

100g spicy pancetta, cut into matchsticks

2 cups (400g) arborio rice

$^1/_2$ cup dry white wine

1 heart of radicchio, shredded

$^1/_2$ carrot, grated

60g grated parmesan

salt and cracked black pepper

shaved parmesan, to serve

Heat chicken stock in a large saucepan over medium heat until almost boiling. Keep hot.

Melt 3 tablespoons of butter in a large saucepan and add onion, celery and pancetta and stir over medium heat until onion is soft. Add rice and stir until coated with butter. Add wine and stir. Cook, stirring constantly, until wine has evaporated. Stir in 2 ladles of chicken stock or enough to just cover rice. Stir over medium heat until stock has been absorbed. Continue cooking and stirring rice, adding stock a ladle at a time until absorbed. When rice is three-quarters cooked, add radicchio and carrot. Continue cooking, stirring and adding stock, until rice is cooked but firm to the bite, about 5 minutes. Stir in parmesan, remaining butter, salt and pepper. Serve with extra shaved parmesan

Serves 4

Radish

There are many varieties, but two main types of radish are sold at the markets. The small, fiery little red balls add texture, colour and spice to salads, especially when finely sliced and scattered over mesclun. Large, white daikon radish can be more than 50 centimentres long and are often labelled white carrot, Chinese or Japanese radish. It is crunchy, both raw and pickled, and particularly sought-after in Japan, where it is believed to aid the digestion of fatty foods.

Radishes belong to the mustard family and come in a range of colours and shapes. Their skin can be purple, black, yellow or green but the majority are radiantly red.

Daikon can be eaten raw, but need to be peeled first and can also be stir-fried, baked or added to braises and stews in place of turnips.

Red radishes have a reputation for stimulating the appetite and one of the best ways to enjoy their sharp, aromatic flavour is with brown bread and butter and a sprinkling of sea salt. The very young leaves are also edible and can be cooked like silverbeet or added to soups or salads.

An excellent source of vitamin C, radishes are a great convenience food because they need almost no preparation, just a quick rinse.

Choose bunches with fresh, bright crisp tops and no cracks. The thin roots at the base should look healthy and not withered. Radishes will feel firm and have smooth skin if fresh – avoid any that are spongy.

When buying daikon, look for fresh, white samples with no blemishes, browning or wrinkling and store in a plastic bag in the crisper of the fridge.

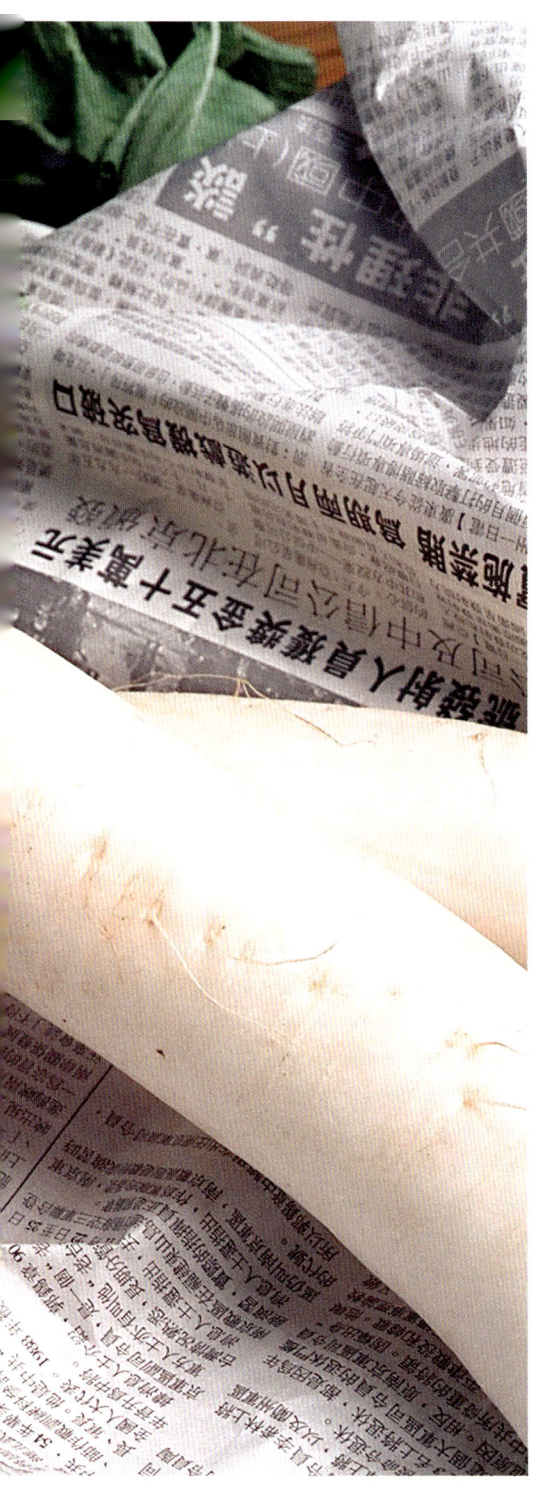

Red and white (daikon) radish salad with chives, mint and coriander

$^1/_4$ white radish, peeled and shaved into ribbons (with a vegetable peeler)

4 red radishes, finely sliced

1 carrot, peeled and shaved into ribbons

2 purple eschalots, finely sliced

$^1/_4$ wombok (Chinese cabbage), shredded

$1^1/_2$ tbsp lemon juice

$1^1/_2$ tbsp extra virgin olive oil

$1^1/_2$ tbsp peanut oil

$1^1/_2$ tbsp sour light cream

salt and cracked black pepper

$^1/_4$ cup chives, snipped

4 sprigs mint, torn

6 sprigs coriander, torn

Combine white and red radishes, carrots, eschalots and cabbage in a large bowl.

Combine lemon juice, olive oil, peanut oil, sour cream, salt and pepper in a small bowl and whisk until smooth.

Pour dressing over salad, add herbs and toss well.

Tasty with barbecued T-bone steaks.

Serves 4

Radish, mozzarella and chervil salad

This fresh, crisp salad is ideal as a light starter and also teams well with char-grilled lamb backstraps.

250g fresh mozzarella

1 bunch radishes, trimmed

1 bulb fennel, trimmed

3 small carrots, peeled

3 tbsp extra virgin olive oil

$1^1/_2$ tbsp fresh lime juice

salt and cracked black pepper

2 tbsp chervil, chopped

Slice mozzarella thinly and place on paper towel to absorb excess moisture. Thinly slice radishes and place in a large bowl. Cut fennel into fine slivers and add to radishes. Cut carrots into very thin diagonal slices and combine with radishes and fennel. Add mozzarella.

Combine olive oil, lime juice, salt and pepper in a small bowl and whisk well. Drizzle over salad and toss gently to combine.

Scatter chervil over salad and serve immediately.

Serves 4

Rocket

Taste-tingling, peppery rocket leaves are not only for the salad bowl. Try them scattered over hot pizza, tossed through pasta until just wilted or added to soup at the last minute. It has many names, including rucola, roquette and arugula, and still grows wild in the Mediterranean where for many years it was gathered by families who harvested edible wild plants to augment their diet.

A member of the mustard family, cultivated rocket has broad, bright-green leaves and is sold as baby rocket in its immature state. Wild rocket is usually sold loose and easily identified by its thin, small serrated leaves, similar in shape to mizuna.

Choose the brightest rocket leaves with no signs of wilt or brown patches. Fresh, springy leaves will stay crisp for 2-3 days if stored in a plastic bag in the crisper of the fridge. Wash just before using and eat as soon as possible.

Fettuccine with spicy pancetta, goat's cheese and wild rocket

(pictured page 293)

350g fettuccine

150g spicy pancetta, chopped

1 clove garlic, chopped

$^1/_2$ cup light pouring cream

240g fresh goat's cheese

$^1/_4$ cup chives, snipped

$^1/_4$ cup flat-leaf parsley, chopped

$^1/_4$-$^1/_2$ tsp dried chilli flakes

salt

80g grated parmesan

300g wild rocket leaves

50g shaved parmesan

Bring a large saucepan of lightly salted water to the boil and cook fettuccine over medium-high heat for 8-10 minutes or until al dente. Drain, reserving 2-3 tablespoons of cooking water.

Meanwhile, cook pancetta in a non-stick frying pan over medium heat for 3-4 minutes or until crisp. Place in a medium-sized bowl with garlic, pouring cream, goat's cheese, chives, parsley, dried chilli flakes, salt and parmesan. Stir well.

Toss hot pasta with cheese mixture and pasta cooking water. Add rocket leaves and toss together. Serve pasta in 4 warm bowls and top with shaved parmesan.

Serves 4

Salt-and-pepper squid with rocket salad and mayo

750g cleaned squid or calamari with tentacles

75g ($^1/_2$ cup) plain flour

35g ($^1/_4$ cup) rice flour

$1^1/_2$ tbsp salt

1 tbsp ground black pepper

1 tbsp Sichuan peppercorns, crushed

2 egg whites, lightly beaten

peanut oil, for deep-frying

2 bunches rocket leaves, trimmed

200ml good mayonnaise

lemon wedges, to serve

Score inside surface of squid or calamari and then cut into 3-4cm pieces. Halve tentacles.

Combine flours, salt and peppers in a large bowl. Coat squid in egg white and then in flour mixture. Shake off excess.

Heat oil in a large saucepan, wok or deep-fryer and, when hot, cook squid briefly until tender and golden. Drain on absorbent paper.

Spread rocket leaves on serving platter and top with squid. Serve with mayo and lemon wedges.

Serves 4

Rocket, macadamia and prawn salad with preserved lemon

2 bunches rocket, trimmed

1 large ripe avocado, sliced

$3^1/_2$ tbsp macadamia oil

$1^1/_2$ tbsp white-wine vinegar

$^1/_4$ tsp sugar

$^1/_2$ tsp Dijon mustard

salt and cracked black pepper

$^3/_4$ cup toasted macadamia nuts, coarsely chopped

$^1/_4$ preserved lemon rind, rinsed and finely chopped

20 large cooked king prawns, shelled and deveined

Combine rocket leaves and avocado in a large bowl.

Combine macadamia oil, vinegar, sugar, mustard and salt and pepper in a small bowl and whisk until smooth. Drizzle half the dressing over the rocket and avocado and toss gently.

Spread rocket and avocado on 4 large serving plates, sprinkle with macadamia nuts and preserved lemon and top with king prawns.

Drizzle remaining dressing over prawns and serve with crusty bread.

Serves 4

Char-grilled chorizo and calamari salad with rocket and capsicum

1 chorizo sausage (350g) thinly sliced

4 calamari (about 250g each), cleaned, cut into 4cm pieces and scored

$^1/_2$ cup extra virgin olive oil

$^1/_2$ tsp paprika

salt and cracked black pepper

2 bunches rocket, trimmed

1 roasted, peeled red capsicum, cut into strips

1 x 425g tin rinsed, drained cannellini beans

1 tbsp lemon juice

salt and cracked black pepper

pinch of sugar

crusty bread, to serve

Cook chorizo in a non-stick fry pan over medium heat for 3-4minutes until crisp. Drain on absorbent paper.

Combine calamari with $^1/_4$ cup extra virgin olive oil, paprika, salt and pepper in a bowl and toss well. Char-grill calamari over high heat for 1-2 minutes each side until just cooked. Combine calamari with rocket, red capsicum, cannellini beans and chorizo in a large bowl.

Whisk 1 tablespoon lemon juice with remaining olive oil, salt, pepper and sugar in a small bowl until smooth, pour over salad and toss gently to combine. Serve with crusty bread.

Serves 4

Silverbeet

Silverbeet (swiss chard) and spinach are not really similar in appearance, but often spinach is labelled as English spinach, so there is no confusion. The chunky white stalks on silverbeet are considered the prize part in many European countries, so don't discard them, just cook them for a little longer than the dark-green crinkly leaves. The stems are delicious tossed with a little light cream, parsley and blue cheese and baked until tender.

Five-coloured silverbeet (rainbow chard) is very decorative in the vegetable garden and colourful in many dishes. It can be bought at growers' markets and specialty greengrocers.

Many people prefer to cook silverbeet in just the water clinging to the leaves after washing, turning it as the leaves on the base of the saucepan wilt. This takes only a few minutes, so remove it while it's still bright-green and refresh under cold, running water then drain.

Before buying, check that the leaves are shiny and crisp-looking, not limp. Wash them just before using or they may go slimy and soft. To store, place in a large plastic bag in the crisper of the fridge, but cook within a few days for best results.

Wilted silverbeet with pinenuts, sultanas and crisp croutons

50g (¹/₃ cup) pinenuts

1 bunch silverbeet, stems removed

salt and cracked black pepper

80g (¹/₂ cup) sultanas

4 tbsp red-wine vinegar

3 slices day-old bread

5 tbsp extra virgin olive oil

3 cloves garlic, peeled

1 clove garlic, finely chopped

2 anchovy fillets, soaked in 2 tbsp milk for
    5 minutes, then drained and chopped

Preheat oven to 200C.

Toast pinenuts in oven for about 5 minutes until golden. Remove and cool.

Combine 2 tablespoons water and silverbeet in a very large frying pan over medium heat with salt and pepper. Cook, tossing frequently, for 6-8 minutes or until wilted (this may need to be done in 2 batches).

Combine sultanas and vinegar in a small bowl and set aside for 5 minutes, then drain. Tear bread into 2-3cm pieces. Heat 4 tablespoons olive oil in a pan over medium heat and add whole garlic and cook for 1 minute. Remove garlic and add bread pieces and toss until golden and crisp. Season with salt and pepper. Drain on paper towel.

Heat remaining olive oil in a large pan over medium heat and add chopped garlic and anchovies. Stir and add pinenuts, sultanas and silverbeet and stir to heat through. Spoon onto a platter and top with toasted croutons.

Serves 6

Vegetable soup with rice and pesto

1 tbsp butter

1 tbsp olive oil

1 leek, white part only, finely sliced

1 rasher of bacon, chopped

1 clove garlic, finely chopped

1 carrot, diced

1 stick celery, sliced

1 medium-sized potato, cut into dice

1 zucchini, diced

100g baby green beans, halved

2 litres chicken stock

1 x 400g tin chopped tomatoes

1 tbsp tomato paste

100g (¹/₂ cup) long-grain rice

100g silverbeet leaves, shredded

pesto

Heat butter and oil in a large saucepan, add leek and bacon and stir over low heat for 2-3 minutes. Add garlic, carrot, celery, potato, zucchini and beans and stir over medium heat for 3-5 minutes. Stir in chicken stock, tomatoes and their juice and tomato paste. Simmer, covered, over low heat for 30 minutes. Add rice and cook for 10 minutes, then add silverbeet leaves, season to taste and cook a further 2 minutes or until rice is tender. Serve topped with a spoonful of pesto if desired.

Serves 8

Spinach

Spinach is more temperamental than silverbeet and wilts quickly in the heat. It is easily distinguished by its bright, spade-shaped mid-green leaves with pencil-thin stalks and is sold with the pale-pink roots attached.

Baby spinach leaves are sold loose at supermarkets and greengrocers and are delicious raw in salads.

Try cooking spinach in the water left clinging to the leaves after washing, turning it as the leaves on the base of the saucepan wilt. This takes only a few minutes, so remove it while it's still bright-green and refresh under cold water, then drain.

Frozen, chopped spinach is widely available in supermarkets, but is really no substitute for fresh. It contains large amounts of water and needs to be thawed and drained well before using.

Before buying, check that spinach leaves are crisp and fresh, not wilted. Wash them carefully just before using or they may go limp and slimy. To store, place in a plastic bag or container in the crisper of the fridge and use within a couple of days for best results.

Baked eggs with spinach and cherry tomatoes

150g baby spinach leaves

8 free-range eggs

16 cherry tomatoes, halved

salt and cayenne pepper

100g gruyere cheese, grated

grilled chipolata sausages and crisp bacon,
    to serve

Preheat oven to 190C.

Blanch spinach leaves briefly, squeeze out
excess water and coarsely chop. Divide between
4 buttered ovenproof dishes (1-cup capacity).

Crack 2 eggs into each dish and top each with
cherry tomatoes. Season with salt and pepper and
sprinkle with cheese. Bake for about 15 minutes
or until eggs are just cooked and cheese is melted
and golden.

Serve with grilled chipolata sausages and
crisp-fried bacon.

Serves 4

Spinach, walnut and currant salad

200g baby spinach leaves

50g currants

$1/4$ cup red-wine vinegar

100g walnuts, toasted and coarsely chopped

3 red corella pears, sliced

1 tbsp red-wine vinegar

3 tbsp extra virgin olive oil

1 tsp Dijon mustard

salt and cracked black pepper

50g shaved pecorino cheese

Wash and dry spinach leaves and place in a large
bowl. Heat currants with $1/4$ cup of vinegar in a
small pan until boiling, then drain and add to
spinach with walnuts. Add pears to salad.

Whisk 1 tablespoon red-wine vinegar with extra
virgin olive oil, Dijon mustard, salt and pepper to
taste and a pinch of caster sugar, until smooth.
Pour over salad and toss gently.

Scatter with pecorino cheese and serve with
barbecued lamb chops.

Serves 4

Orzo with spinach, semi-dried tomatoes and pinenuts

40g butter

6 brown eschalots, chopped

2 cloves garlic, finely chopped

500g orzo pasta (or risoni)

4 cups hot chicken stock

$^1/_2$ cup dry white wine

150g semi-dried tomatoes, halved

80g baby spinach leaves

2 tbsp flat-leaf parsley, chopped

40g grated parmesan

2 tbsp toasted pinenuts

Melt butter in a large pan over medium heat and add onion and garlic, stirring until onion is soft. Add orzo and toss to coat in butter. Stir in stock and wine, bring to the boil and then simmer, stirring occasionally, until orzo is al dente and stock is almost absorbed. Stir in tomatoes, spinach and parsley.

Serve topped with parmesan and pinenuts.

Serves 4

Ricotta and spinach hotcakes with smoked trout and light sour cream

75g baby spinach

1 green onion

100g plain flour

$^1/_4$ tsp bicarb soda

pinch of salt

2 tsp baking powder

2 eggs, separated

salt and cracked black pepper

1 cup buttermilk

125g ricotta cheese

butter

6 tbsp sour light cream

6 slices smoked trout

4 tbsp chives, snipped

Combine spinach and green onion in a food processor and pulse until chopped. Add plain flour, bicarb soda, pinch of salt and baking powder and process until combined. Add 2 egg yolks, salt and pepper and buttermilk and process until smooth. Add ricotta and process until just combined. Remove to a bowl and fold in 2 stiffly beaten egg whites.

Heat butter in a non-stick pan and drop in 2 tablespoons of mixture and cook over medium heat for about 2 minutes or until golden. Turn and cook until golden and cooked through (about 2 minutes). Keep warm and repeat with remaining mixture, adding more butter as necessary.

To serve, place 2 hotcakes on a warm plate, top with 1 tablespoon light sour cream and 2 slices of smoked trout. Sprinkle with snipped chives.

Serves 6

Sprouts

Sprouts generally come from bean or vegetable seeds and appear as the seeds start to grow. They have been sought-after in China for hundreds of years because of their nutritional value and can be grown easily in a mini-garden on the kitchen window sill.

Fluffy alfalfa, a type of lucerne, is one of the most popular sprouts and grows in four to 10 days. Its texture adds crunch to sandwiches and is often combined with radish sprouts for a spicy flavour burst. Packets labelled beansprouts are usually mung beansprouts, a good source of dietary fibre, sold with or without the green cap of the original bean attached. (Punnets of bean salad include mung beans mixed with red and green lentils and adzuki, Japanese red beans, and are tasty tossed through coleslaw). Creamy yellow soya-beansprouts take about five days to grow, look similar to mung beans, but are larger and require cooking. They are often used in Korean cooking, as the stronger texture teams well with kim chi (pickled cabbage).

Combinations of sprouts such as alfalfa/broccoli are becoming big sellers because of their nutritional benefits. Three-sprout mix comes in small pouches of various sprouts which are handy for scattering on salads and the delicate texture of specialty sprouts such as daikon, beetroot, onion and mustard cress can take dishes to the next level.

Select crisp-looking sprouts that smell fresh. Avoid any that are brown, broken or slimy. There should be no moisture in the base of the container.

Store them in the crisper and use as soon as possible, as they are highly perishable.

Richard Lenoir Market, Paris

Avocado, watercress, mint and orange salad with alfalfa

2 ripe avocado, halved and seeded

2 cups watercress sprigs

1 large orange, peeled and segmented

$^1/_3$ cup torn mint leaves

$^1/_4$ cup extra virgin olive oil

$1^1/_2$ tbsp fresh lime juice

1 tsp Dijon mustard

salt and cracked black pepper

1 cup alfalfa

Scoop flesh from avocado into a large bowl. Add watercress, orange segments and mint leaves.

Whisk olive oil, lime juice, mustard, salt and pepper in a small bowl and pour over salad. Scatter with alfalfa.

Serves 4

Warm salad of prawns, broad beans, brown rice and alfalfa

300g frozen podded broad beans

200g brown rice

2 rashers bacon, finely chopped

1 tbsp olive oil

1 onion, chopped

2 cloves garlic, finely chopped

12 medium-sized green (raw) king prawns, shelled and deveined, tails intact

4 tbsp alfalfa

Dressing

1 anchovy fillet, mashed

180ml extra virgin olive oil

4 tbsp red-wine vinegar

1 tbsp flat-leaf parsley, chopped

2 tsp Dijon mustard

salt and cracked black pepper

For the dressing, combine all the ingredients in a small bowl and whisk until smooth.

Blanch beans in lightly salted, boiling water for 1-2 minutes, drain, refresh under cold water, drain again then peel. Cook rice in plenty of boiling water for about 20 minutes or until tender. Drain.

Cook bacon in a large, non-stick frying pan over medium heat until crisp, then add oil, onion and garlic and cook for 4-5 minutes. Add prawns and cook for about 2 minutes each side or until they just change colour. Combine rice, prawn mixture, beans and dressing in a large bowl. Toss gently and divide between 4 plates. Top with alfalfa.

Serves 5

Lamb and asparagus stir-fry with plum sauce and beansprouts

2 tbsp plain flour

1 tsp Chinese five-spice powder

500g lamb backstraps, thinly sliced

3 tbsp vegetable oil

8 green onions, trimmed, cut into 6cm lengths

200g asparagus, halved

1/2 red capsicum, sliced

1 tbsp soy sacue

1-2 tbsp hot chilli sauce

1/3 cup plum sauce

1 cup beansprouts

boiled rice, to serve

Combine plain flour and Chinese five-spice powder on a plate and dust lamb backstraps. Heat 2 tablespoons vegetable oil in a wok or large pan and stir-fry lamb over high heat for 2-3 minutes or until browned. Remove. Add remaining oil, asparagus and capsicum and stir-fry for 2 minutes. Return lamb to wok and add green onions, soy sauce, hot chilli sauce, plum sauce and 2/3 cup water and stir-fry briefly until heated through. Top with beansprouts and serve with boiled rice.

Serves 4

Chilli-ginger chicken on betel leaves

4 pieces dried cloud-ear fungus

2 tbsp vegetable oil

2 tsp ginger, grated

1 large red chilli, very thinly sliced

1 clove garlic, finely chopped

400g minced chicken

1/2 cup water chestnuts, drained and chopped

2 green onions, thinly sliced

1 tbsp soy sauce

1 tbsp fish sauce

1/2 tsp sesame oil

24 betel leaves, washed and dried

1 1/2 cups mung beansprouts

Cover fungus with hot water and soak for 15 minutes, then drain and cut into very thin strips.

Heat vegetable oil in a wok and add ginger, chilli and garlic and stir-fry over high heat for 2-3 minutes. Add chicken and stir-fry for 2-3 minutes. Add fungus, water chestnuts and green onions and cook for 1 minute. Add soy sauce, fish sauce and sesame oil and stir over high heat, until chicken is cooked.

Place spoonfuls of warm chicken mixture on betel leaves and top with a few mung beansprouts.

Chicken mixture can be made one day ahead and kept covered in the fridge. Reheat before serving.

Makes about 24

Swedes

This bulbous root, with its yellow-beige skin and purple-tipped leaves, is also labelled rutabaga or Swedish turnip. It was first cultivated, as the name suggests, in Sweden.

Swedes can be roasted, boiled, braised or pureed and are usually sweeter and tastier than turnips. They are at their best during the coldest months, and their flavour improves if they are harvested after a frost, when some of the starch converts to sugar.

Select swedes that are firm, small and round, indicating sweet flesh. They should have an earthy aroma. Avoid any with soft spots and don't buy withered or huge Swedes, as they can be woody inside. Keep them in the crisper for up to a week.

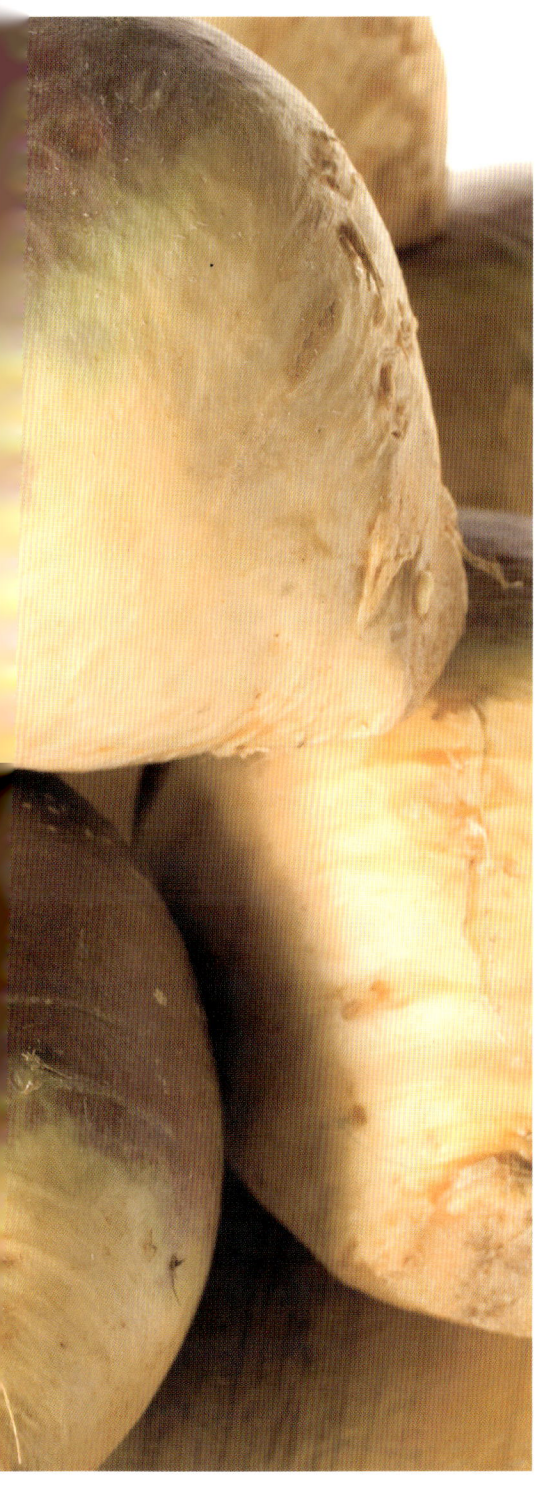

Rustic winter soup with swedes, broad beans and herbs

2 tbsp olive oil

1 carrot, peeled and chopped

2 sticks celery, chopped

1 onion, chopped

2 small swedes, peeled and chopped

150g pancetta, chopped

1 x 400g tin chopped tomatoes

800g broad beans, podded (to produce 400g)

2.5 litres chicken stock

salt and cracked black pepper

100g stellette or other small soup pasta

2 tbsp sage, chopped

2 tbsp flat-leaf parsley, chopped

Combine olive oil in a large saucepan with carrot, celery, onion, swedes and pancetta and cook over medium heat, until lightly coloured. Add tomatoes and cook over low heat for 10 minutes. Add broad beans and chicken stock and bring to the boil. Reduce heat and simmer, covered, stirring occasionally, until vegetables are tender. Remove 1/2 cup of beans and process in the food processor until smooth. Return to saucepan and stir well. Season with salt and pepper.

Just before serving, add soup pasta and simmer for 3-5 minutes or until al dente. Serve in warm soup bowls sprinkled with sage leaves and chopped flat-leaf parsley.

Serves 6

Roasted winter vegetables with bay leaves

1 carrot, peeled and thickly sliced

1 bulb fennel, trimmed and cut into wedges

1 onion, cut into wedges

2 medium-sized desiree potatoes, peeled and cut into chunks

2 small swedes, peeled and cut into chunks

100ml extra virgin olive oil

2 fresh bay leaves

1/2 lemon, finely sliced

salt and cracked black pepper

1 red capsicum, cut into 3cm pieces

Preheat oven to 200C.

Place carrot, fennel, onion, potatoes and swede in a large bowl. Add olive oil, bay leaves, lemon, salt and pepper and combine well. Transfer vegetables to a large, lightly oiled roasting pan and roast at 200C for 15 minutes. Add capsicum, toss to combine, then cook for another 25-30 minutes or until vegetables are golden and tender.

Serve warm roasted vegetables with char-grilled fish fillets or chicken.

Serves 6

Sweetcorn

Sweetcorn originated in Mexico and was one of the plants that sustained the Incas and Aztecs, but there are many varieties grown globally today for various purposes. The juicy kernels are surrounded by tough outer leaves (the husk) with fine yellow hairs (called silk) protruding from the top.

Dent corn, used for making maize flour, is the most widely grown. Some varieties with hard skins, such as flint, are used to make polenta and other types are used for cornflour and making corn tortillas, although much of the cornflour we purchase today is made from wheat. White corn is sweeter than yellow corn, but supplies can be erratic. There is also a blue corn variety, which is ground to make corn chips and tortillas. Baby corn, the immature fruit of sweetcorn, has small pale kernels and is ideal in stir-fries.

When buying, select fresh-looking ears with green husks and glistening silk. The kernels should be full, round and bright-yellow, and if you press a kernel it should produce a spurt of milky juice if fresh. Recently picked cobs should be firm and evenly coloured. Avoid any with dried husks.

Use corn as soon as possible after harvesting, as the sweet flavour deteriorates when the natural sugars start to convert to starch. To store cobs with their husks on, wrap in damp paper towel and refrigerate until ready to use.

Corn and crab soup

6 cobs corn, husks and silk removed

1 tbsp vegetable oil

3 brown eschalots, peeled and chopped

1 clove garlic, finely chopped

3 tsp ginger, grated

4 cups chicken stock

170g tin crabmeat, drained

sea salt and cracked black pepper

2 green onions, finely sliced on the diagonal

½ cup coriander leaves

Cut kernels from cobs and set aside. Heat oil in a large saucepan over medium heat and add eschalots, garlic and ginger and cook for 1-2 minutes, until aromatic. Add corn kernels and cook, stirring frequently over low heat for about 8 minutes. Add stock and simmer for about 5-6 minutes. Remove from heat and blend in a blender or food processor until smooth.

Return soup to saucepan, add crabmeat, salt and pepper and bring to a simmer for 1 minute. Serve topped with green onions and coriander leaves.

Serves 4

Corn and coriander frittatas

These little gems are excellent in lunch boxes or for breakfast with bacon, grilled tomatoes and mushrooms.

2 cobs corn, kernels removed

1 tbsp coriander, chopped

1 tbsp flat-leaf parsley, chopped

60g grated cheddar cheese

sea salt and cracked black pepper

6 eggs

½ cup buttermilk

1-2 tbsp grated parmesan cheese

8 rashers bacon

Preheat oven to 200C.

Combine corn kernels, coriander, parsley and cheddar in a medium-sized bowl. Season with salt and pepper and stir well. Spoon mixture into 8 greased muffin pans (⅓ cup or 80ml capacity).

Combine eggs and buttermilk in a large bowl and whisk until frothy. Pour mixture evenly over corn mixture in muffin pans and sprinkle tops with parmesan. Bake for 15 minutes or until puffed and golden.

Meanwhile, grill bacon rashers until crisp. Serve with the hot frittatas.

Serves 8

Chicken salad with grilled corn and capsicum

3 chicken breast fillets

extra virgin olive oil

3 cobs corn, husks and silk removed

1 small yellow capsicum

1 small red capsicum

1 small green capsicum

1 small red onion, finely chopped

1 small ripe tomato, chopped

$^1/_2$ cup (80g) kalamata olives

$^1/_2$ cup flat-leaf parsley, chopped

$^1/_2$ cup coriander leaves, chopped

Dressing

$^1/_2$ cup extra virgin olive oil

$^1/_4$ cup red-wine vinegar

1 clove garlic, finely chopped

pinch of caster sugar

salt and cracked black pepper

hot garlic bread, to serve

Brush breast fillets with a little extra virgin olive oil and char-grill over high heat for 4-6 minutes each side or until just cooked. Brush corn with a little extra virgin olive oil and char-grill over high heat for about 5-6 minutes, turning frequently, until golden. Cool slightly and cut kernels from cobs. Cut capsicum into 1cm pieces and place in a large bowl. Thinly slice chicken and add to capsicum, add corn, onion, tomato, olives, flat-leaf parsley and coriander leaves. Whisk $^1/_2$ cup extra virgin olive oil, red-wine vinegar, garlic, caster sugar, salt and pepper in a small bowl, pour over chicken and toss gently to combine.

Divide salad among 4 shallow serving plates and accompany with hot garlic bread.

Serves 4

Corn and tomato salsa with grilled baby lamb cutlets

1 large cob corn

1 small red onion, finely chopped

8 cherry tomatoes, chopped

2 tbsp flat-leaf parsley, chopped

1 tbsp oregano, chopped

$^1/_4$ cup extra virgin olive oil

2 tsp balsamic vinegar

pinch of cayenne pepper

salt

12-16 baby lamb cutlets

rocket salad, to serve

Pull down the husk from one large cob of corn, keeping it intact at the base, then remove the silk and replace husk. Chargrill corn, turning frequently for 5-8 minutes or until kernels are cooked. Cool, remove husks then cut the kernels from cob and combine in a bowl with onion, cherry tomatoes, flat-leaf parsley, oregano, extra virgin olive oil, balsamic vinegar and cayenne pepper. Season to taste with sea salt then toss to combine.

Char-grill baby lamb cutlets over medium heat for 2-3 minutes each side or until cooked as desired and serve with corn salsa and a rocket salad.

Serves 4

Sweet potato

These root vegetables have a rich, earthy flavour and are not related to yams or taro as many people think, but are the roots of a trailing vine. They can be boiled, mashed, fried, baked or grated raw into coleslaw, salads and sandwich filings.

There are three main varieties of sweet potato grown in Australia; the slightly drier-fleshed orange type is the most popular and the richest in vitamin C. It is also known by its Maori name kumera (kumara) and pairs beautifully with pork and ham, creating a combination that balances salty and sweet. It is also excellent in puddings.

The brown or beige variety has creamy flesh, which discolours when cut, so drop cut pieces into a bowl of water with a few slices of lemon before cooking. It is perfect for baking.

Purple-red sweet potato has moist, creamy-white flesh, often with a purple fleck through it. It also discolours when cut.

Choose smooth, firm specimens and avoid cracked, bruised or soft examples. The black patches that appear occasionally on the skin are a chilling injury, so keep them out of the fridge. They are best stored in a cool, dark, well-ventilated place and should be eaten as soon as possible.

Sweet potatoes hold their shape much better if roasted with the skin on.

Sweet potato, bacon and orzo soup

2 tbsp extra virgin olive oil

4 rashers bacon, chopped

2 cloves garlic, finely chopped

1 brown onion, chopped

1kg orange sweet potato, peeled
    and coarsely chopped

1.8 litres chicken stock

$^1/_2$ cup (110g) orzo or other small soup pasta

1 cup flat-leaf parsley, torn

2 tbsp oregano leaves, coarsely chopped

toasted sourdough bread, to serve

Heat olive oil in a large saucepan and add bacon. Cook over medium heat for about 5 minutes or until bacon is crisp. Remove using a slotted spoon and drain on absorbent paper.

Add garlic and onion to pan and cook for about 5 minutes or until onion is soft. Add sweet potato, 1 litre of stock and simmer for about 15 minutes or until sweet potato is tender and cooked. Transfer mixture to a food processor or blender and process until smooth. Return mixture to the saucepan and add remaining stock and orzo. Simmer for about 10 minutes or until pasta is cooked.

Ladle soup into warm soup bowls, top with crisp bacon, combine parsley and oregano and scatter over.

Serve with toasted sourdough.

Serves 6

Sweet potato and feta muffins

The following scrumptious savoury muffins are great for breakfast on the run. They freeze very successfully so make a batch on the weekend to enjoy through the week.

200g sweet potato, chopped and cooked

300g (2 cups) self-raising flour

100g (1/2 cup) brown sugar

1/2 tsp ground cardamom

pinch of salt

2 eggs

80g butter, melted

180ml (3/4 cup) milk

125g feta cheese, crumbled

Preheat oven to 200C.

Puree sweet potato in a food processor or mash until smooth.

Sift flour, sugar, cardamom and a pinch of salt into a large bowl. In a medium-sized bowl, stir eggs, butter, milk and sweet potato puree together until blended. Add egg mixture to dry ingredients and stir until just combined. Fold in crumbled feta.

Spoon mixture into 6 standard muffin tins (1/2 cup capacity) and bake for about 25-28 minutes or until muffins are golden and cooked. Cool in pan for 2-3 minutes then transfer to a wire rack to cool.

Makes 6

Sweet potato mash with grilled lamb cutlets

750g sweet potato

1 tbsp butter

pinch of ground cinnamon

4-5 tbsp milk

12 lamb cutlets

2-3 tbsp extra virgin olive oil

2 cups watercress sprigs

1 tbsp vinaigrette dressing

Peel and slice sweet potato and cook in lightly salted, boiling water over medium heat for 10-15 minutes or until tender. Remove and drain. Mash with butter, cinnamon and milk.

Brush lamb cutlets on both sides with olive oil and cook under a hot grill for 3-4 minutes each side or until cooked as desired.

Toss watercress sprigs with vinaigrette dressing and divide between 4 serving plates. Place lamb cutlets on watercress and spoon sweet potato mash to the side.

Serves 4

Roasted sweet potato, artichoke, sugar snap pea and couscous salad

500g sweet potato, peeled and sliced

1 tbsp extra virgin olive oil

1 cup couscous

1 tbsp butter

125g sugar snap peas, trimmed

1 x 100g jar marinated baby artichokes, drained and sliced

1/2 cup torn mint leaves

1/4 cup vinaigrette dressing

1/2 cup plain yoghurt

1 tsp ground cumin

1/4 tsp ground cinnamon

1/2 tsp sugar

Preheat oven to 200C.

Toss sweet potato with olive oil and roast for 20-25 minutes or until tender.

Place couscous in a bowl and add 1 1/4 cups boiling water and butter, stir and cover with plastic wrap then set aside for 5 minutes. Blanch sugar snap peas in lightly salted, boiling water for 1 minute then drain. Place sweet potato, couscous, peas and artichoke hearts in a large bowl and add mint leaves.

Whisk vinaigrette dressing with yoghurt, ground cumin, cinnamon and sugar until smooth and drizzle over salad. Serve with grilled fish fillets.

Serves 4

Tomatoes

Originally from Peru, the name tomato comes from the Mexican *tomatl*. There are hundreds or varieties, which can be divided into a few main groups.

Red and yellow cherry tomatoes are usually sold in punnets or trusses and are ideal for salads, as they contain the highest amounts of sugar. Grape and teardrop tomatoes have a piquant bite and are delicious, low-fat snacks and tom thumbs are slightly larger than cherry varieties with intense, sweet flavour.

Big beefsteak tomatoes are extremely luscious when ripe and have firm, juicy flesh punctuated by pockets of seeds. They are easily distinguished by their ribbed skin and are very tasty in sandwiches and salads.

Round salad tomatoes are the most popular, commonly sold in greengrocers and supermarkets – their flavour improves tremendously if left to ripen on the vine.

There has been a resurgence in heirloom varieties because of their unique flavour. Some of these are green when ripe, but they are not usually as juicy as red varieties. However, they are ideal for making chutney and relishes as are the yellow types, which taste similar. Roma (plum) or egg tomatoes are elongated, with dense flesh and are ideal for cooking and in sauces. They also dry well in the oven sprinkled with a little extra virgin olive oil, salt, pepper and dried herbs.

Select shiny, plump tomatoes with a home-grown aroma for the best flavour. Highly coloured, vine-ripened and truss tomatoes should have the bottle-green calyx intact and feel heavy for their size. Keep them at room temperature, as chilling in the fridge dulls their flavour.

Positano, Italy

Roasted parmesan tomatoes with thyme, parsley and oregano

6 medium-sized vine-ripened tomatoes, halved

100g dried breadcrumbs

50g grated parmesan cheese

1 clove garlic, chopped

salt and cracked black pepper

leaves from 5 sprigs thyme

1 tbsp flat-leaf parsley, chopped

leaves from 2 sprigs oregano

3 tbsp extra virgin olive oil

Preheat oven to 200C.

Gently squeeze juice and seeds from tomatoes in to a bowl. Add breadcrumbs and parmesan and stir well. Add garlic, thyme, parsley, oregano, salt and pepper. Place tomato halves in a lightly greased ovenproof dish, season with salt and drizzle with half the extra virgin olive oil. Divide breadcrumb mixture evenly between tomato halves and drizzle with remaining olive oil. Bake for 15-20 minutes or until tops are golden brown. Serve warm or at room temperature.

Serves 6

Oyster and gazpacho shots with celery salt

(pictured page 319)

750g ripe egg tomatoes

1 red capsicum, coarsely chopped

1 lebanese cucumber, peeled and coarsely chopped

1 small red onion, coarsely chopped

1 clove garlic, chopped

1$^1/_2$ tbsp white-wine vinegar

2 tbsp extra virgin olive oil

$^1/_2$ cup water

cayenne pepper, to taste

salt

$^1/_4$ tsp sugar

$^1/_2$ lemon

celery salt

18-20 Sydney rock oysters, removed from shell

Cut tomatoes in half, then gently squeeze to remove seeds. Place tomatoes, capsicum, cucumber flesh, onion, garlic and vinegar in a food processor until smooth. Transfer to a large bowl, add olive oil and water, season with cayenne, salt and sugar. Stir well. Cover and refrigerate until chilled.

Slide lemon around rim of shot glasses and dip tops of glasses in celery salt.

To serve, place one oyster in each glass and pour gazpacho into glasses.

Gazpacho can be made one day ahead.

Makes 18-20

Oven-roasted tomatoes with anchovies and capers on bruschetta

7 roma tomatoes, halved

3 anchovy fillets

$^1/_2$ cup black olives, pitted

2 cloves garlic, finely chopped

3 tbsp capers, chopped

$^1/_4$ tsp lemon zest

1 tbsp flat-leaf parsley

sea salt and cracked black pepper

1 tbsp lemon juice

6 large slices rustic bread

1 clove garlic

250g fresh goat's curd or cream cheese

1 tbsp red-wine vinegar

3 tbsp extra virgin olive oil

3 cups salad leaves

Preheat oven to 120C.

Place tomatoes on an oven tray and roast for 1 hour.

Soak anchovies in milk for 5 minutes, drain. Place anchovies, olives, garlic, capers, lemon zest and parsley in a food processor and process to a rough paste. Add salt, pepper, lemon juice and tomatoes and pulse a few times.

Toast bread and rub on one side with garlic. Cut bread in 2 slices diagonally. Spread each piece with goat's curd or cream cheese and top with the tomato tapenade.

Whisk red-wine vinegar and oil together in a small bowl. Season to taste.

To serve, place two pieces of bread on each plate, toss the salad leaves with the vinaigrette and pile on top of the bread.

Serves 6

Tuscan bread salad (Panzanella)

4 very thick slices crusty bread, toasted

1 lebanese cucumber, unpeeled, chopped

3 ripe tomatoes, chopped

1 small red onion

$^1/_2$ cup torn basil

2 tbsp red-wine vinegar

120ml extra virgin olive oil

2 cloves garlic, finely chopped

pinch of sugar

salt and cracked black pepper

100g Ligurian olives

Tear bread into 1cm pieces and combine in a bowl with cucumber, tomatoes and red onion. Add basil and stir. Whisk vinegar, olive oil, garlic, sugar, salt and pepper in a small bowl until smooth. Pour the dressing over the salad and toss gently to combine. Top with Ligurian olives.

Serves 4

Seared tuna steaks with chickpea, olive, tomato and herb salad

4 tuna steaks (about 200g each)

2 tbsp extra virgin olive oil

1 x 400g tin rinsed, drained chickpeas

100g kalamata olives

1 punnet (250g) cherry tomatoes, halved

2 tbsp flat-leaf parsley, chopped

2 tbsp mint, torn

2 tbsp basil, torn

Dressing

$1/4$ cup red-wine vinegar

2 cloves garlic, finely chopped

$1/4$ cup extra virgin olive oil

salt and cracked black pepper

pinch of sugar

2 tbsp chives, snipped

Brush tuna steaks on both sides with extra virgin olive oil and sear in a hot non-stick frying pan over high heat for 1-2 minutes each side or until cooked as desired.

Meanwhile, combine chickpeas in a bowl with kalamata olives and cherry tomatoes. Stir well and add flat-leaf parsley, mint and basil.

For the dressing, combine vinegar, garlic and $1/4$ cup extra virgin olive oil in a small bowl. Season with salt, pepper and sugar and whisk until smooth. Pour over chickpea mixture, toss gently and top with chives. Serve tuna steaks topped with salad.

Serves 4

Fattoush

1 slice pita bread, toasted and torn into bite-sized pieces

2 lebanese cucumbers, unpeeled, sliced

2 very ripe tomatoes, coarsely chopped

3 green onions, sliced

$1/2$ green capsicum, chopped

1 cup wild rocket leaves

$1^1/2$ tbsp lemon juice

1 tbsp extra virgin olive oil

1 clove garlic, finely chopped

1 tsp ground sumac

salt and cracked black pepper

barbecued lamb chops, to serve

Combine cucumbers, tomatoes, onions, capsicum and rocket leaves in a large bowl.

Combine lemon juice, extra virgin olive oil, garlic and sumac in a small bowl, season with salt and pepper and whisk until smooth. Add bread to tomato mixture, pour over dressing and toss to combine. Serve with barbecued lamb chops.

Serves 4

Sticky lime lamb kebabs with spiced tomatoes

800g lamb backstraps cut into 3cm pieces

4 tbsp soy sauce

2 tbsp tomato sauce

2 tsp rice vinegar

$1/2$ tsp sesame oil

large pinch of sugar

1 tbsp coriander, chopped

2 limes, cut into quarters

250g cherry tomatoes, halved

1 tsp sweet paprika

1 tsp red-wine vinegar

3 tbsp extra virgin olive oil

salt and cracked black pepper

steamed rice, to serve

Soak 8 bamboo skewers in cold water. Place lamb in a medium-sized bowl and add soy sauce, tomato sauce, rice vinegar, sesame oil, sugar and coriander. Toss to combine, cover and refrigerate for 10 minutes. Thread pieces of lamb onto each skewer and finish with $1/4$ lime threaded lengthwise. Combine cherry tomatoes in a bowl with sweet paprika, red-wine vinegar and 1 tablespoon extra virgin olive oil, season with salt and pepper and toss to combine. Heat a large, heavy-based frying pan over medium-high and add remaining olive oil and cook kebabs, in batches, turning frequently for about 6-8 minutes or until cooked. Alternatively, they can be cooked on the barbecue. Serve the kebabs with the lime wedges squeezed over and accompanied by spiced tomatoes and steamed rice.

Serves 4

Ricotta, chorizo and cherry tomato pizza

1 spicy chorizo sausage (230g), cut into
    5mm thick slices

30cm pizza base

1 tbsp extra virgin olive oil

3 tbsp black olive tapenade

200g ricotta cheese

250g cherry tomatoes, halved

salt and cracked black pepper

3 tbsp toasted pinenuts

$^{1}/_{2}$ cup basil, torn

Preheat oven to 230C and place baking tray
in the oven.

Cook chorizo in a non-stick frying pan over
medium-high heat, turning occasionally, for about
5 minutes or until crisp. Remove and drain on
absorbent paper.

Brush pizza base with extra virgin olive oil. Spread
over tapenade and crumbled ricotta. Scatter
chorizo over ricotta and sprinkle with cherry
tomatoes. Season with salt and pepper and bake
for about 12-15 minutes or until cooked. Remove
and scatter pinenuts and basil over top. Serve hot.

Serves 4 as an appetiser

Watercress

Crisp watercress is the perfect partner to mild-flavoured salad leaves, as it has a tangy, mustardy bite. It is one of the most ancient greens, originating in the eastern Mediterranean, and is rich in calcium, iron and vitamins A and C.

The vivid-green sprigs can be substituted for spinach in many recipes and are an excellent filling for pancakes and omelets. Watercress is a great foil for game, and complements bland flavours such as ricotta and eggs.

Select bright-green, crisp bunches with no yellow leaves and use as soon as possible, as it wilts quickly. The leaves and stems can be used, particularly in soups; the younger leaves are milder and more tender.

To store, trim the stems, stand in a glass of water, cover with a plastic bag and keep in the fridge (or in a plastic bag in the crisper). Wash just before using and dry well.

Quick tomato, asparagus, parmesan and watercress tarts

2 frozen shortcrust pastry sheets, thawed

160g ricotta cheese

25g grated parmesan

1 tbsp oregano, chopped

2 tsp lemon zest

1 tsp thyme leaves

salt and cracked black pepper

4 ripe tomatoes, thickly sliced

4 large asparagus spears, thinly sliced on the diagonal

2 tbsp extra virgin olive oil

2 cups watercress sprigs

parmesan shavings

Preheat oven to 200C.

Cut pastry sheets in half and place on baking paper-lined oven trays. Combine ricotta with grated parmesan, oregano, lemon zest and thyme leaves, salt and pepper. Spread cheese mixture over pastry leaving a 1cm border. Spread tomatoes over cheese mixture and scatter with asparagus. Drizzle each with 2 teaspoons extra virgin olive oil and bake for 18-20 minutes, until pastry is golden and cooked. Scatter each with 1/2 cup watercress sprigs and a few parmesan shavings.

Serves 4

Scallops with watercress, herb and radish salad

36 scallops in shell

1 large green chilli, seeded and finely sliced

1 clove garlic, finely chopped

4 tbsp extra virgin olive oil

18 cherry tomatoes, each sliced into quarters

1 tbsp oregano, chopped

1 tbsp chives, snipped

sprigs from 2 small bunches watercress

9 medium-sized radishes, sliced into matchsticks

Lemon dressing

1 cup vinaigrette dressing

sea salt and cracked black pepper

3 tsp Dijon mustard

1 tbsp lemon juice

For the dressing, combine vinaigrette, salt, pepper, mustard and lemon juice in a small bowl and whisk until smooth.

Preheat oven to 200C.

Trim scallops and place back in the shell. Combine chillies, garlic and olive oil in a bowl and spoon a little on each scallop. Place 2 tomato slices on top of each scallop and place scallops on baking trays. Bake scallops for 5-6 minutes or until just cooked.

Combine oregano, chives, watercress, radishes and half the dressing in a bowl and toss to combine. Remove scallops from oven, place a little of the salad on top of each scallop and drizzle with remaining dressing.

Serves 6

Vietnamese-style salmon with watercress and coriander salad

2 tbsp peanut oil

1 clove garlic, bruised with the back of a knife

1/3 cup brown sugar

2 tbsp fish sauce

2 tsp soy sauce

2 tbsp rice vinegar

4 salmon fillets (about 180-200g)

50g watercress sprigs

1/3 cup mint, coarsely chopped

1/3 cup coriander, coarsely chopped

lime wedges, to serve

Dressing

3 tsp peanut oil

2 tsp rice vinegar

2 tsp lime juice

2 tsp soy sauce

1/2 tsp fish sauce

For the dressing, combine all the ingredients with 2 teaspoons of warm water in a small bowl and stir well.

Heat 1 tablespoon peanut oil in a small saucepan, add garlic and cook for 1 minute. Remove garlic and add sugar, fish sauce, soy sauce, vinegar and 1/2 cup water. Bring to the boil and simmer for 12-15 minutes or until syrupy. Remove from heat and leave to cool.

Brush salmon lightly with remaining peanut oil. Heat a large non-stick frying pan and, when hot, add salmon and cook, skin-side down for 2-3 minutes; then turn and cook for a further 2-3 minutes or until cooked to your liking. When salmon is almost cooked, reduce heat and pour in brown sugar mixture and turn salmon to coat.

Place fish on serving plates with sauce. Combine dressing with watercress, mint and coriander and place on top of salmon. Serve with lime wedges and mash, steamed rice or chips.

Serves 4

Barbecued ocean trout with watercress, cucumber and herb salad

3 lebanese cucumbers, unpeeled

2 tsp salt

1/4 cup light sour cream

3 tbsp extra virgin olive oil

2 tsp lemon juice

1 tbsp oregano, chopped

1 tbsp mint, chopped

2 tbsp chives, snipped

cracked black pepper

3 cups watercress sprigs

4 ocean trout fillets (about 180g each)

lime cheeks, to serve

Halve cucumbers lengthwise and scoop out seeds with a teaspoon. Cut into slices on the diagonal, about 5mm. thick. Toss with salt and place in a colander for 10 minutes. Pat dry with paper towel.

Combine sour cream, 2 tablespoons extra virgin olive oil, lemon juice, oregano, mint leaves, snipped chives and pepper in a large bowl. Add cucumbers and watercress sprigs and toss gently to combine.

Brush trout fillets with remaining olive oil, salt and pepper and cook on a lightly oiled barbecue over medium heat for 3-5 minutes each side or until cooked as desired.

Divide watercress and cucumber salad evenly between 4 plates and top with trout and cheeks of fresh lime. Serve with roasted jacket potatoes.

Serves 4

Witlof

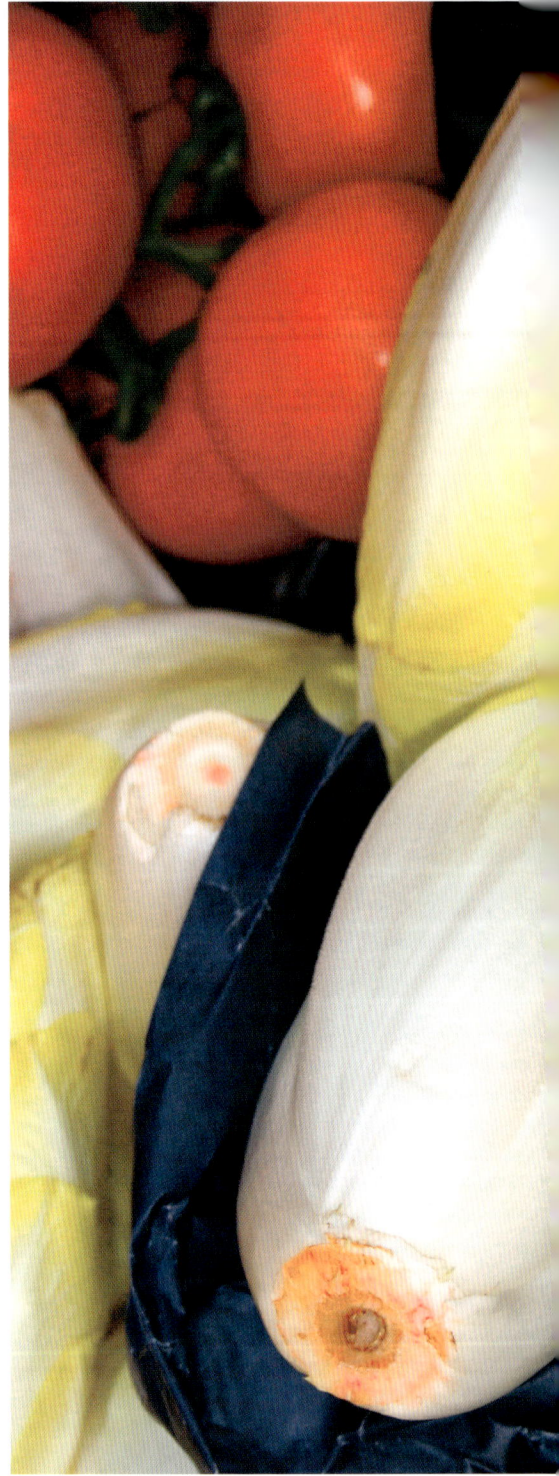

Witlof, a member of the chicory family, is also known as Belgian endive and chicory. The succulent, tightly furled leaves are suitable for many dishes: they add a tart crispness to salads, are meltingly tender in braises and go particularly well with chicken and pork.

Witlof was developed in Belgium in the 1840s by cutting off the foliage and forcing the roots, in darkness, to produce white spears. It is often stored under purple tissue paper at quality greengrocers to protect it from light and prevent it turning bitter.

The two main types available are white with pale-gold or green tips and red. There is little difference in flavour. The red-tipped variety is best eaten raw, as the leaves turn brown when cooked.

Select white spears with compact heads, which will have a more delicate flavour. Do not wash until ready to use. Fresh witlof leaves should not be torn, brown or withered.

Because it deteriorates quickly when exposed to light, it is best stored in a brown paper bag in the crisper. Use as soon as possible.

Richard Lenoir Market, Paris

Calamari, chorizo and witlof salad with chickpeas

800g calamari

2 small chorizo sausages, thinly sliced

1 x 400g tin chickpeas, rinsed and drained

$1/2$ cup flat-leaf parsley, torn

1 lime, segmented

60ml white-wine vinegar

100ml extra virgin olive oil

salt and cracked black pepper

1 clove garlic, finely chopped

1 large green chilli, finely chopped

2 eschalots, finely sliced

4 witlof, trimmed and cut into 3-4cm thick slices

Clean calamari and score inside. Cut into 3-4cm pieces and halve tentacles.

Cook chorizo in a frying pan over high heat for 1-2 minutes each side or until hot and crisp. Remove and drain on paper towel.

Combine chickpeas, parsley and lime in a large bowl, add vinegar and 4 tablespoons olive oil and stir. Season with salt and pepper.

Toss calamari in remaining oil and cook in a large non-stick frying pan over high heat for 1-2 minutes, stirring frequently. Add garlic, chilli and eschalots and cook for 2 minutes then add chorizo and stir for 1 minute.

Remove from heat and add calamari to chickpeas and toss gently.

Scatter sliced witlof over serving plates and top with calamari salad.

Serves 4

Ginger and chilli chicken with water chestnuts in witlof leaves

Separated witlof leaves make perfect little boats in which to hold this spicy filling. The mixture can easily be doubled for a party, cooked ahead and then reheated. Spoon it into the witlof leaves just before serving.

1 tbsp vegetable oil

2 tsp ginger, grated

1 clove garlic, finely chopped

250g minced chicken

2 tsp lemongrass, very finely sliced

$1/4$ cup water chestnuts, chopped

$1/2$ large red chilli, finely chopped

1 tbsp shaoxing wine

$1/2$ tsp caster sugar

1 tbsp soy sauce

3 or 4 large witlof, trimmed and leaves separated

2 green onions, very finely sliced

Heat vegetable oil in a wok, add ginger, garlic and chicken and stir-fry over medium heat for 3-4 minutes or until chicken is half-cooked. Add lemongrass, water chestnuts and red chilli and cook for 2-3 minutes, then add shaoxing wine, caster sugar, oyster sauce, soy sauce and 2 tablespoons water. Simmer for 3-4 minutes.

To serve, place about 2 teaspoons of chicken mixture in witlof leaves and sprinkle with green onions. Serve immediately.

Makes about 16

Zucchini

Zucchini means baby marrow in Italian, and that is just what they are. These members of the squash family are also known as courgettes and, if left on the vine will grow very quickly into a large marrow with thick skin, large seeds and watery flesh.

Some are long and slim while others are bulbous, and they come in dark-green, white (which are actually pale-green) and yellow varieties. Small, dark-green, round types are also available at the markets: they are about 7-8cm in diameter, but supplies can be erratic.

There are two types of zucchini blossoms sold at the markets. The male zucchini flower has a thin stem attached and the female usually has a small zucchini attached to the flower. Cooks often prefer to remove the stamen in the male flower, as it can have a bitter taste, but this is not necessary in female flowers. They can be sauteed, stuffed, baked or chopped and added to risottos, frittatas and soups.

Choose flowers that are firm at the tip, not wilted. The stamen inside the flower should not be brown if fresh. Blossoms that are just starting to open are easier to stuff.

The flowers are extremely perishable and, ideally, should be used on the day of purchase. Store them on damp paper towel, covered, in the fridge for no more than a day or two.

Zucchinis should be firm, shiny and unblemished, with no brown spots. Store them in a plastic bag in the crisper and use within a day or two, as their delicate flavour fades quickly.

Spaghetti primavera

5 tbsp olive oil

1 large red capsicum, cut into strips

1 bunch asparagus, trimmed and cut in half

1 large zucchini, sliced

100g small white mushrooms, sliced

1 medium-sized onion, thinly sliced

5 medium-sized ripe tomatoes, chopped

salt and cracked black pepper

3 tbsp parsley, chopped

2 cloves garlic, finely chopped

400g spaghetti

4 rashers bacon, cooked and chopped

grated parmesan cheese

Heat oil in a large frying pan and add capsicum. Cook over medium heat for 5-6 minutes then add asparagus, zucchini, mushrooms and onion and cook for 4-5 minutes. Add tomatoes, salt and pepper and cook for 8-10 minutes over low heat, stirring frequently. Stir in parsley and garlic.

Cook pasta in plenty of lightly salted, boiling water for 8-10 minutes or until al dente. Drain.

Pour sauce over spaghetti and serve immediately sprinkled with cooked bacon.

Pass grated parmesan cheese.

Serves 4-6

Zucchini, basil and baked ricotta salad

500g firm tiny zucchini

salt and cracked black pepper

2 tsp white-wine vinegar

4 tbsp extra virgin olive oil

1 tsp thyme

$1/3$ cup basil, torn

2 tbsp toasted pinenuts

1 tsp lime zest

150g baked ricotta

Slice zucchinis thinly and place in a bowl. Add salt, pepper, vinegar and olive oil and toss gently. Set aside for 10 minutes then add thyme, basil, pinenuts and lime zest and toss gently.

Crumble ricotta over salad and serve with barbecued steak.

Serves 4

Left: Campo di Fiori, Italy

Summer risotto with zucchini flowers and fresh peas

75g butter

1 onion, peeled and chopped

300g arborio rice

4 tbsp dry white wine

1 litre hot chicken stock

6 small young zucchini, finely sliced

1/2 cup fresh peas

4 small zucchini flowers, torn into strands

40g grated parmesan

1 cup basil leaves, torn

2 tbsp butter

salt

dried chilli flakes, to taste

Melt butter in a large, heavy-based saucepan and cook onion over low heat for 4-5 minutes. Add rice and stir until coated. Add wine and stir until absorbed. Add hot chicken stock, ladle by ladle, stirring until each is absorbed. After about 10 minutes, add zucchini and peas and stir well. When rice is cooked, add zucchini flowers and parmesan. Stir and add basil leaves and butter. Add salt and dried chilli flakes to taste.

Serves 4

Braised chicken, zucchini and capsicum in tomato sauce

2 whole chicken breasts, on the bone
   (or 4 chicken breast fillets)

1 tbsp lemon juice

1 tbsp oregano, chopped

2 cloves garlic, finely chopped

salt and cracked black pepper

1/2 cup (75g) plain flour

1/4 cup extra virgin olive oil

1 large brown onion, sliced

100ml dry white wine

1 tbsp tomato paste

1/2 tsp dried chilli flakes

1 x 400g tin chopped tomatoes

1 small red capsicum, chopped

1 zucchini, sliced 1cm thick

steamed rice, to serve

Preheat oven to 200C.

Cut breasts into quarters and drizzle with lemon juice. Press oregano and garlic all over chicken. Season with salt and pepper. Dust chicken pieces lightly with flour and shake off excess. Heat extra virgin olive oil in a large ovenproof dish and cook chicken over medium to high heat for about 3-4 minutes each side or until browned. Remove from dish.

Add brown onion to dish and cook over medium heat for 3-4 minutes. Return chicken to dish, add white wine, tomato paste, dried chilli flakes, tomatoes and capsicum and cook, covered, in the oven for 15 minutes. Add zucchini and cook a further 10-15 minutes or until chicken is tender. Rest for 5 minutes then serve with steamed rice.

Serves 4

Herbs

Below: Souk, Fez
Right: Souk, Marrakech

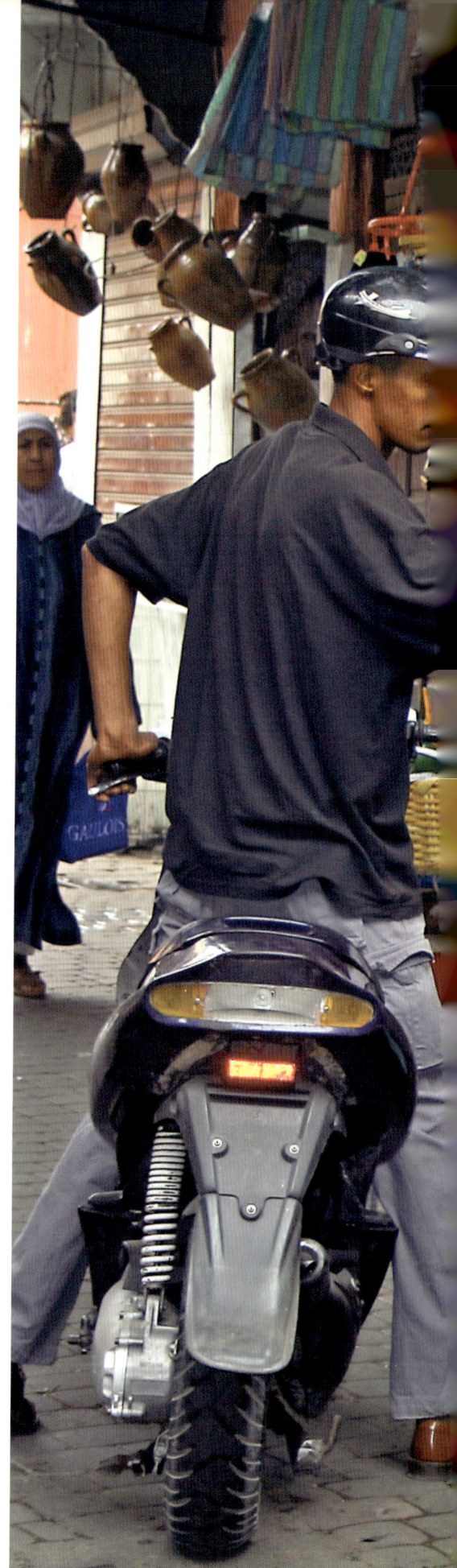

Basil

Aniseed-flavoured basil originated in India and was introduced to Europe in the 16th century. The many varieties include lemon, cinnamon and clove, but sweet basil is the most common variety found in greengrocers and is an outstanding companion to tomatoes. Compact bush basil, with its tiny, mild leaves, is very easy to grow in a pot on the balcony and dark-purple opal basil produces exquisite lavender flowers in autumn.

There are three main varieties used in Thai cooking in particular holy basil, which has slightly hairy, small, green leaves and is often used in fish curries and spicy stir-fries.

The leaves bruise very easily, so don't wash; until you are ready to use them and tear the leaves instead of cutting to avoid them turning black.

Store in the fridge in a glass with a little water and cover with a plastic bag.

Pesto

100g pinenuts

175ml extra-virgin olive oil

1 cup basil, firmly packed

2 cloves garlic

salt and cracked black pepper

100g grated parmesan cheese

Place pinenuts in a small frying pan and dry roast over low heat until golden, tossing frequently to prevent burning.

Place $^1/_2$ cup olive oil and remaining ingredients except cheese in a food processor and blend to a paste. Stir in remaining olive oil and cheese.

Makes about $1^1/_2$ cups

Bay leaves

Sweet bay leaves (*laurus nobilis*) are a vital part of a bouquet garni (with thyme and parsley) and essential in long-simmered braises, stews and soups. The glossy, leathery leaves can be crushed to impart their flavour, but leaving them whole makes for easy retrieval. Dark-green fresh leaves are considerably more bitter then the dried ones, so use them sparingly. Many believe the mellow flavour of the dried leaves is better for cooking, but don't use slightly yellow leaves, as they have probably been exposed to light for too long and are often poor quality.

Store fresh leaves in a plastic bag in the fridge and dried bay leaves in an airtight container.

Corned beef

2kg corned beef

1 tbsp malt vinegar

2 tbsp brown sugar

10-12 black peppercorns

2 bay leaves

Cover beef with cold water and add vinegar, brown sugar, peppercorns and bay leaves. Stir to combine. Bring to a simmer over low heat.

Cover and simmer for $1^1/_2$ hours or until tender. Do not boil.

Remove from heat and cool in stock.

Serves 6-8

Chervil

Chervil has delicate, ferny foliage with a mild anise-and-parsley flavour and is one of the four herbs that make up the traditional *fines herbes* (with chives, tarragon and parsley) popular in French cuisine. The lime-green lacy leaves complement eggs, chicken and fish and team well with creamy potatoes and omelets – or try them sprinkled on sandwich fillings. Add chervil to dishes at the end of cooking to retain the delicate flavour and store it in a plastic bag in the crisper of the fridge.

Char-grilled scotch fillet steaks with quick bearnaise sauce

3 tbsp white-wine vinegar

6 whole black peppercorns

1 sprig tarragon

1 sprig chervil

2 tbsp brandy

1 eschalot, chopped

2 egg yolks, whisked with 1 tbsp water

100g butter, chopped

1 sprig chervil, chopped

4 scotch fillet steaks (about 220g each)

chunky chips, to serve

For the sauce, combine white-wine vinegar, peppercorns, tarragon, chervil, brandy and eschalot in a small saucepan and reduce over high heat by half. Strain, reserving liquid. Place reduced vinegar and egg yolks in a bowl over a saucepan of simmering water and whisk until smooth then beat in 100g chopped butter piece by piece until sauce is thick and smooth. Remove from heat and stir in chopped chervil.

Cook steaks on a lightly oiled char-grill over high heat for 3-4 minutes each side or until cooked as desired. Rest in a warm place for 5 minutes.

Serve steaks topped with bearnaise sauce and hot chunky chips on the side.

Serves 4

Chives

Garlic (or Chinese) chives have flat strappy leaves and starry white flowers with a distinct garlic flavour. They are more robust than onion chives and all parts of the plant are edible raw or cooked. Widely used in Asian dishes, they need to be added towards the end of cooking for best flavour and to retain their fresh green colour.

Onion chives have tubular leaves and don't contain as much sulphur as onions. Their subtle flavour is a perfect match with eggs and smoked salmon, but don't wash them until ready for use or they will deteriorate rapidly. Store both types in a plastic bag in the crisper of the fridge.

Scrambled eggs with chives, smoked salmon and truffle oil

8 eggs

125ml (¹/₂ cup) pouring cream

30g butter

2 tbsp chives, snipped

salt and cracked black pepper

4 slices smoked salmon

truffle oil

thick sourdough toast, to serve

Combine eggs and cream in a large bowl and beat together lightly with a wire whisk. Melt butter in a large, heavy-based pan over low heat and pour in egg mixture. Stir slowly, lifting mixture with a wooden spoon from the bottom to cook evenly. Add chives and season with salt and pepper. When eggs are just set but still creamy, remove from pan and spoon onto 4 serving plates. Top each with a slice of smoked salmon and just a few drops of truffle oil.

Serve with toasted sourdough bread.

Serves 4

Coriander

This is one of the world's oldest known herbs, but it does not store well so use it as soon as possible. All parts of the plant are edible, from the bright-green delicate foliage to the roots, which are an essential ingredient in Thai cooking, and the golden seeds, which contribute spiciness to Indian, Middle Eastern and South-East Asian dishes. Also known as Chinese parsley and cilantro, it is related to carrots and parsley. Add coriander leaves at the last minute to hot dishes, as heat destroys the flavour.

Buy bunches with the root still intact, as this will help to keep the herb fresher longer. Store in a plastic bag in the crisper of the fridge.

Barbecued ocean trout with herb and asparagus salad

4 x 180g ocean trout portions

2 cobs corn, husks removed

olive oil for brushing

sea salt and cracked black pepper

1 bunch asparagus

1 cup basil, torn

1 cup mint leaves, coarsely chopped

$^1/_2$ cup coriander leaves, coarsely chopped

1 long red chilli, seeded and sliced

1 tbsp lime juice

2 tbsp olive oil, extra

lime wedges, to serve

Preheat the barbecue to medium-high.

Brush the ocean trout and corn with oil and season to taste. Cook ocean trout for 3-5 minutes each side (or until cooked as desired) and barbecue corn until tender, turning occasionally. Trim asparagus, cut into 4-5cm pieces and blanch in lightly salted, boiling water for 3-4 minutes. Drain and refresh under cold running water, then drain again. Cut the corn kernels from the cob and place in a medium-sized bowl with the basil, mint, coriander, chilli and asparagus. Drizzle over the lime juice and extra oil, season with salt and pepper and toss to combine.

Place ocean trout on serving plates, top with herb salad and serve with lime wedges.

Serves 4

Dill

Dill's blue-green feathery leaves are a vital ingredient in many dishes, as are the stronger-flavoured seeds so popular in pickles. The leaves look similar to fennel tops, but are smaller and deeper in colour. They wilt quickly after harvesting, so store wrapped in damp paper towel in a plastic bag in the crisper of the fridge.

Dill teams well with potatoes, fish, prawns, salmon, omelets, chicken and eggs. The fresh anise taste diminishes when cooked, so add it to dishes at the last minute.

Pasta salad with bacon, sour cream, chives and dill

400g penne pasta

5 slices rindless bacon, chopped

120ml extra virgin olive oil

4 tbsp sour light cream

60ml red-wine vinegar

$\frac{1}{2}$ bunch chives, snipped

1 tbsp dill, chopped

120g grated parmesan

1 red onion, finely sliced

1 green chilli, finely chopped

salt and cracked black pepper

Cook pasta in plenty of lightly salted, boiling water until al dente. Drain and keep warm. Cook bacon in a non-stick frying pan over medium heat until crisp. Drain on absorbent paper. Combine pasta and bacon in a large dish. Add remaining ingredients and stir well. Add salt and pepper and serve at room temperature with barbecued lamb chops and green salad leaves.

Serves 4-6

Ginger

King prawns with ginger, lemongrass and noodles

400g fresh rice noodles

50ml peanut oil

100g baby corn, halved

12 large green prawns, peeled and deveined,
    tails intact

2 cloves garlic, finely chopped

1 x 2cm piece ginger, peeled and very finely sliced

1 stick lemongrass, white part only,
    finely chopped

2 fresh, small red chillies, finely chopped
    (or to taste)

3 heads baby pak choy, trimmed

100ml chicken stock

50ml oyster sauce

1 tbsp soy sauce

4 green onions, thinly sliced

Cover rice noodles with boiling water, stand for
2 minutes, stir to separate noodles, then drain.

Heat oil in a wok, add corn and stir-fry over
medium heat for 1-2 minutes. Add prawns and
cook a further 2-3 minutes or until prawns just
change colour.

Using a slotted spoon, transfer mixture to a plate.
Add garlic, ginger, lemongrass and chilli to wok
and stir over low heat until aromatic, then add pak
choy and stir until just wilted. Add chicken stock
and sauces, stir to combine, then stir in drained
noodles, prawns and corn and cook until heated
through. Serve topped with sliced green onions.

Serves 4

Ginger forms a perfect marriage with the
flavours of garlic, chilli, lime and coriander and
is therefore used in many Asian recipes. Also
used widely in herbal medicine, the plant is
thought to have originated in South-East Asia,
although gingerbread has been made in Europe
since medieval times. Young ginger has a light
flavour with a lemony freshness; the older it
gets the more pronounced the taste becomes,
sometimes quite hot with a pithy, fibrous texture.
It is marketed in many forms: fresh, dried, pickled,
spiced, ground, candied and preserved.

Always buy ginger that is plump, firm and fresh
looking. Choose pieces with a minimum of
knobbly bits as they will be easier to peel. The
best way to grate the rhizome is to simply rub it
on a ginger grater. Avoid dry, withered specimens
with mouldy ends.

Store in a brown paper bag in the crisper of the
fridge.

Horseradish

Creamy-fleshed horseradish is native to south-eastern Europe. It adds zip to dips, dressings, and sauces and is perfect with roast beef and oily fish. The hard, tough root belongs to the mustard family and needs to be peeled before using. Add it towards the end of cooking for the best flavour.

Wasabi or Japanese horseradish is used with many dishes, in particular as an accompaniment to sashimi, and can be mixed with Japanese soy sauce for dipping.

When fresh rhizomes are out of season, buy jars of horseradish relish or paste, although the flavour won't be as piquant.

Choose fresh horseradish with no soft spots or mould. It should be very firm if fresh and needs to be stored in a plastic bag in the fridge.

Barbecued fillet of beef with horseradish and lime sauce

1 whole scotch fillet, about 2.25kg

Marinade

1 tbsp Dijon mustard

2 tsp thyme leaves

1 tbsp flat-leaf parsley, chopped

1 clove garlic, finely chopped

$^1/_4$ cup extra virgin olive oil

Horseradish sauce

400g sour light cream

3 tbsp fresh lime juice

4 tbsp grated fresh horseradish

$1^1/_2$ tsp salt

1 tsp sugar

1 tbsp flat-leaf parsley, chopped

For the marinade, combine all the ingredients, season to taste and mix well. Place beef in a glass or ceramic dish, spoon marinade over and turn to coat. Cover and refrigerate for 3 hours or overnight. Bring beef to room temperature and barbecue in a covered barbecue, according to the manufacturer's instructions, or roast at 200C for 1 hour for medium-rare (or until cooked as desired). Rest in a warm place for 10 minutes.

For the sauce, combine all the ingredients in a bowl and stir well.

Serve sliced beef with horseradish sauce, boiled baby potatoes tossed in butter and parsley and mixed green salad leaves.

Serves 8

Lemongrass

Known as takrai in Thailand, lemongrass has a citrus flavour similar to lemon zest and is very popular in the tropics, in part because lemons don't thrive in a tropical climate. The tightly furled stalks have razor-like blades that can be used whole to flavour dishes, or the tender inner-white section can be used in curry pastes and sauces, where it needs to be chopped finely so that the pithy fibres do not become tough and chewy.

Also called citronella grass, it was originally used by the Greeks and Romans as a medicine and can now be found year-round in most greengrocers and large supermarkets.

Purchase sticks that are fresh and not dry; they should be firm, pale-green with a white base and not wrinkled. Keep the sticks wrapped in plastic wrap in the fridge.

When using whole stems, bruise them first with the side of a large knife to release maximum fragrance.

Scallop, lemongrass and vermicelli soup

1 litre fish stock

250ml (1 cup) tomato juice

2 sticks lemongrass (white part only), bruised

100g vermicelli

1 ripe tomato, chopped

2 tsp ginger, grated

$^1/_2$ tsp brown sugar

1 clove garlic, finely chopped

20 scallops with roe, trimmed

salt and cracked black pepper

8 Thai basil leaves, torn

2 sprigs coriander leaves, torn

Combine fish stock, tomato juice and lemongrass in a large saucepan, bring to the boil, then simmer for 3 minutes. Remove and discard lemongrass. Add vermicelli, simmer for 2 minutes, then add tomato, grated ginger, brown sugar and garlic and cook for 2 minutes. Add scallops and simmer a further minute or until scallops are almost cooked. Season with salt and pepper and serve sprinkled with basil and coriander leaves.

Serves 4

Mint

Sweet mint tea has been Morocco's favourite beverage for hundreds of years. There are many varieties, all with different aromas and flavours.

Chocolate mint is delicious chopped and tossed through fresh fruit salad while the soft, round, velvety leaves of applemint take berry desserts to the next level. Spearmint is perhaps the most widely used, indispensable in many dishes including mint sauce and salads such as fattoush. Peppermint is often included in sweet-making, but is not used so much in the kitchen because of its strong antiseptic aroma. Vietnamese mint is not a true mint, although the spicy pointed leaves add a piquant accent to Asian salads and soups.

Select mint with bright-green leaves and no yellow patches. Do not wash it until just before using or it turns black. Store in a plastic bag in the crisper of the fridge or in a glass with a little water, covered with a plastic bag in the fridge.

Tomato, mint and chickpea salad

4 ripe tomatoes

2 x 400g tins chickpeas, rinsed and drained

2 cloves garlic, finely chopped

$^2/_3$ cup mint leaves, torn

2 tbsp extra virgin olive oil

1 tbsp red wine vinegar

$^1/_2$ tsp sumac

salt and cracked black pepper

Blanch tomatoes in boiling water for 30 seconds then plunge into ice water. Remove skins and chop coarsely.

Place chopped tomatoes in a large bowl with chickpeas, garlic, mint, olive oil, vinegar and sumac. Season with salt and pepper and toss to combine.

Serve with pan-fried fish.

Serves 6

Oregano

Oregano and marjoram are closely related (both belong to the mint family) and can be substituted in many recipes. Popular in Mediterranean dishes, many chefs believe that using them in their dried form produces a more appealing result. However, use them freshly chopped in salads, scattered over pizza or stirred through an omelet. Oregano's heart-shaped leaves are best stored in a plastic bag in the crisper of the fridge and used as soon as possible.

Char-grilled lamb cutlets with oregano, mustard and olives

2 cloves garlic, finely chopped

2 tsp dried oregano leaves

1 tsp rosemary, chopped

2 tbsp extra virgin olive oil

2 tbsp lemon juice

salt and cracked black pepper

4 double lamb cutlets, trimmed

Dressing

1 tsp Dijon mustard

$2^1/_2$ tbsp red-wine vinegar

100ml extra virgin olive oil

100g feta, crumbled

20 Ligurian olives

1 tbsp fresh oregano leaves

salt and cracked black pepper

100g baby rocket leaves

boiled baby potatoes, to serve

In a bowl, combine garlic, oregano, rosemary, extra virgin olive oil, half the lemon juice, salt and pepper. Add lamb cutlets, toss to coat and rest for 10-15 minutes. Cook cutlets on a barbecue or char-grill for about 6-8 minutes or until cooked as desired.

For the dressing, combine Dijon mustard, red-wine vinegar, remaining lemon juice and extra virgin olive oil in a small saucepan over low heat and stir well. Add feta, olives, fresh oregano leaves, salt and pepper and stir until warm. Serve cutlets on a bed of rocket leaves and pour warm dressing over. Serve potatoes on the side.

Serves 4

Parsley

Parsley is probably the most popuar of all the herbs and comes in two main types. Curly parsley has very bright-green, crinkly leaves and is used widely as a garnish. Flat-leaf parsley, also known as continental or Italian parsley, has darker, serrated flat leaves with a stronger flavour. It teams well with chicken, lentils, zucchini, artichokes and fish and should be washed just before using. If using large amounts for recipes such as tabouli, chop with a knife, as the food processor will bruise the delicate leaves.

Buy bunches with firm stems and fresh-looking leaves and store in a glass with a little water, covered with a plastic bag in the fridge and use within 3-4 days.

Prawn, garlic, chilli and parsley bucatini

350g bucatini or spaghetti
1 tsp extra virgin olive oil

Sauce
2 tbsp extra virgin olive oil
1 large red onion, chopped
4 cloves garlic, finely chopped
2 long red chillies, finely chopped
16 large green (raw) king prawns, shelled and
    deveined, tails intact
1 cup flat-leaf parsley, coarsely chopped
salt and cracked black pepper
extra virgin olive oil, extra

Cook bucatini or spaghetti in plenty of lightly salted boiling water with 1 teaspoon extra virgin olive oil for 8-10 minutes or until al dente. Drain.

For the sauce, meanwhile heat extra virgin olive oil in a large saucepan and cook red onion over low heat for 3-4 minutes or until soft. Add garlic and chillies and stir for 2 minutes. Add prawns and cook for 2-3 minutes on each side or until they just change colour. Remove from heat.

Add drained pasta to prawn mixture. Add parsley and season with salt and pepper and stir.

Serve in four warm pasta bowls and drizzle extra virgin olive oil.

Serves 4

Rosemary

As well as being leathery, aromatic, spiky and drought-tolerant, rosemary is very easy to grow in the garden. The needle-like leaves add a savoury tang to many dishes. It originated in the Mediterranean region, where it is used in Greek, Italian, Spanish and French cooking. The robust stems impart a special fragrance when used as skewers for vegetables, meat or fruit, and a few sprigs stuffed into a leg of lamb before roasting will enhance its flavour.

Buy fresh-looking rosemary that is not dried out, withered or faded and store in a plastic bag in the fridge.

Barbecued lamb chump chops with rosemary, lime and mint

4 large chump lamb chops

1 tsp lime zest

1 tbsp lime juice

2 tsp chopped rosemary leaves

2 tbsp mint, chopped

1 clove garlic, finely chopped

80g feta, crumbled

$^1/_4$ cup extra virgin olive oil

16 baby potatoes, halved

2-3 tbsp butter

$^1/_4$ cup flat-leaf parsley, chopped

Cut a pocket in lamb chops. Combine lime zest, lime juice, rosemary leaves, mint leaves, garlic and feta in a small bowl and stir well. Fill the pockets with the feta mixture and press gently to close. Brush chops on both sides with olive oil and char-grill or barbecue for about 3 minutes each side over medium-high heat or until done to your liking. Remove and rest for 3-4 minutes.

Meanwhile, boil potatoes in lightly salted, boiling water until tender. Drain, toss with butter and parsley.

Serve with lamb chops and green salad leaves.

Serves 4

Sage

This herb makes a beautiful border in the garden, especially in spring when it is smothered in mauve flowers.

The thick, silver-grey leaves are best used fresh, not dried. The younger pale-green leaves of common sage are superior for cooking, as they have a pungent flavour that does not diminish with long, slow braising.

Sage makes an ideal stuffing with onions and breadcrumbs for duck, chicken and pork. Italians use it frequently, fried in butter until crisp then tossed with tortellini or ravioli.

The young leaves of pineapple sage can be chopped and added to fruit salads for a distinct tropical accent.

Store sage in a plastic bag in the crisper of the fridge.

Spaghetti with pan-fried chicken livers, sage and onions

350g spaghetti

1 tsp extra virgin olive oil

Sauce

2 tbsp extra virgin olive oil

2 small red onions, sliced

250g chicken livers, trimmed and chopped

2 tbsp sage, chopped

1 cup light cream

1 egg, lightly beaten

salt and cracked black pepper

3-4 tbsp grated parmesan

Cook spaghetti in lightly salted, boiling water with extra virgin olive oil until al dente. Drain.

For the sauce, meanwhile heat 2 tablespoons olive oil in a large frying pan and cook onions over medium heat for 3-4 minutes. Add chicken livers and cook gently for 2-3 minutes, until they just change colour. Add sage leaves and cream and stir over low heat for 1-2 minutes, until very hot. Remove from heat and add egg, stirring quickly to combine. Season with salt and pepper.

Pour sauce over drained pasta, toss gently and serve sprinkled with parmesan.

Serves 4

Tarragon

French or 'true' tarragon has long slender spear-shaped leaves, a spicy aniseed aroma and a subtle liquorice flavour. Its lesser relative, Russian tarragon, has pale, coarse spikier leaves and very little taste; winter tarragon, with bright-yellow flowers and a warm, aromatic scent, is no match for the French type famous in tartare and bearnaise sauces. Chop the leaves and add at the end of cooking to retain the fresh flavour.

Tarragon is best stored wrapped in damp paper towel then in a plastic bag in the crisper of the fridge.

Rack of lamb with tarragon butter and roasted tomatoes

3 tbsp extra virgin olive oil

2 racks lamb (6 cutlets each), trimmed

3 cloves garlic, finely chopped

12 truss baby tomatoes (in the vine) about 900g

120g soft butter

leaves from 6 sprigs fresh tarragon, chopped

1½ tbsp French grain mustard

1½ tsp white-wine vinegar

salt and cracked black pepper

Preheat oven to 220C.

Heat 1 tablespoon of oil in a frying pan and cook lamb racks over high heat until browned on all sides. Remove and press 2 cloves garlic onto racks and place in a large ovenproof dish. Make a small slit in tomato skins and place around lamb. Pour remaining oil over tomatoes. Roast for about 15 minutes or until lamb and tomatoes are cooked as desired. Rest, lightly covered, for 10 minutes.

For the tarragon butter, meanwhile place butter, remaining garlic, tarragon, mustard, vinegar, salt and pepper in a food processor until smooth.

Slice lamb and serve with a knob of tarragon butter, roast tomatoes and green salad leaves.

Serves 4

Thyme

Pan-fried chicken fillets with thyme, capers and lemon

6 small skinless chicken breast fillets

50ml extra virgin olive oil

10 sprigs fresh thyme

salt and cracked black pepper

1 small lemon, thinly sliced

1 tbsp salted capers, rinsed and drained

100g butter

100ml white wine

300ml chicken stock

3 tbsp flat-leaf parsley

sweet potato mash, to serve

There are many ornamental varieties, but common garden thyme is easily identified by its tiny grey-green leaves and pinkish-white flowers on wiry stalks. It has a warm pungent aroma while lemon thyme has a wonderful citrus fragrance, thick stalks and rounder, dark-green leaves that taste of lemon.

Add sprigs of thyme at the beginning of cooking for best flavour and discard before serving – use lemon thyme in seafood, veal and chicken dishes.

Store thyme in a plastic bag in the crisper of the fridge.

Remove tenderloins from chicken breasts and reserve for another use. Slice chicken in half lengthways and then pound gently between 2 sheets of baking paper, until each slice is 5mm thick. Place in a large dish. Combine oil, thyme, salt and pepper and pour over chicken. Cover with plastic wrap and refrigerate for 1-2 hours.

Combine lemon and capers in a small saucepan and cover with water. Bring to the boil over medium heat then drain. Divide butter between 2 large frying pans and melt over medium heat. Add chicken to pans and cook for 1-2 minutes each side or until just cooked. Remove from pans and rest.

Add white wine and lemon and capers to one of the pans and reduce by half over high heat. Add chicken stock and reduce by half. Stir in parsley, remove from heat and season with salt and pepper.

Serve chicken on warm plates with lemon sauce poured over and sweet potato mash on the side.

Serves 6

Exotics

Left: Rusty's Market, Cairns
Below: Author at Chiang Mai Market, Thailand
Right: Richard Lenoir Market, Paris

Abiu

Abiu resemble brilliant smooth-skinned yellow lemons, but have caramel pulp with rich honey and mango notes. It is native to South America and thrives in warm sub-tropical and tropical climates, where it is considered a delicacy. Its appealing flavour is reminiscent of creme caramel. Slice abiu open and scoop out the succulent translucent white flesh – as with papaya, a few drops of citrus juice enhances the flavour. It can be used to flavour ice-cream.

Black sapote

The black sapote is a chocoholic's dream. Filled with luscious cocoa flavours, but lacking the calories of a chocolate bar, this fruit is closely related to the astringent persimmon and similarly is ripe when very soft. Round in shape with bright-green skin, it can be spotted in specialist fruit and vegetable shops, where it is often tagged chocolate fruit or black persimmon. Black sapote is thought to have originated in Mexico around 4000 BC and is now cultivated in northern Queensland. Try the rich brown pulp with a squeeze of lemon or a splash of white rum for a refreshing instant dessert.

Capers & caperberries

Tiny capers are the unopened flower buds of the caper bush and have been growing wild in the Medierranean for thousands of years. They are referred to as *nonpareilles* in France, the term used for delicate and small. The round, oval-shaped mature fruits are known as caper berries. Those packed in salt are sweeter and more aromatic than those in brine (which are best refrigerated after opening). Rinse capers thoroughly in cold water and pat dry with paper towel before using in salads and mayo.

Dragon fruit

Dragon fruit have fuchsia pink leathery skin (or yellow skin) and brilliant lime-green scales and certainly stand out on the greengrocer's shelves. It is also known as pitaya and strawberry pear. The thin skin encloses sweetly flavoured, white-grey or red pulp (depending on type) with lots of small black seeds. It is delicious chilled and eaten as a snack or can be peeled and cut into wedges and tossed in tropical fruit salads.

Durian

People either love or hate durians, as their smell is very invasive when fully ripe, but the taste is custard-like and hard to resist. This large golden fruit can weigh 1-2kg and has extremely tough skin covered with sharp sturdy spines. The aroma, not the skin colour, is an indication of ripeness. When ripe, the flesh is dense, creamy and extremely sweet. Often called the king of fruits, the durian's rich, glutinous pulp is high in vitamins E and C and makes superb custard and extraordinary ice-cream – the perfect climax to a spicy Asian feast.

Galangal

Galangal is often labelled Thai ginger or Siamese ginger in Asian food stores to distinguish it from the aromatic ginger we use to spice up a marinade or stir-fry. Both are rhizomes from the zingiberaceae family and marry perfectly with garlic, chilli, coriander and lime. Greater galangal (as it is often called) is pinkish-yellow when fresh and has a delicate ginger taste with hints of camphor. It turns to gold and then brownish-red when mature. The striped skin becomes tough as it gets older, but is still ideal for curry pastes. Choose fresh galangal with pink sprouts that are unwrinkled, as it will be easier to peel – scrape off the tough skin then grate or finely slice.

Jujubes

Jujubes look like large acorns and taste like sweet, crunchy pears. Also called red or Chinese dates, this fruit has a very glossy brown skin and small dark seed. They are grown on hardy deciduous trees and have been cultivated in China for over 4000 years. The sweet, pale flesh can be dried or candied and is high in vitamin C. Keep an eye out for fresh jujubes at green grocer and Asian food stores – they only have a short season. Refresh your palate with a handful after a hot, spicy meal.

Mangosteen

Cool, crisp mangosteens are small and round with a thick maroon shell. They are easily identified by four prominent green sepals around the stem. The small white inner segments are delicately sweet, tart and very thirst quenching. One or two of the segments are usually twice the size of the others and these contain soft dark seeds. Mangosteens can be made into jams and sorbets, but the best way to enjoy this fruit is fresh and raw. To open, score the tough thick shell with a sharp knife around the middle of the fruit, leaving the shiny white segments whole.

Micro herbs

These delicate baby leaves come in many varieties and will elevate any salad, pasta, stir-fry or sandwich. They are ideal to enhance dishes where salt and fat have been reduced. Hydroponically grown Italian parsley has a dark-green leaf with a celery flavour and grows up to about 10cm tall. Mild, tangy mizuna has irregularly shaped leaves and is a super garnish on Asian dishes. There are several types of miniature basil available, as well as red and green chard. Lacy, fern-like chervil has a mild aniseed flavour and rocket, sorrel, silverbeet, eschalots, salad burnet, shiso and tatsoi can be found in specialty shops along with several types of cress. Store them in the punnet and snip the sprigs with scissors.

Soursop

Huge pineapple-shaped soursops or prickly custard apples weighing 1-2kg are available at specialist greengrocer and Asian food stores. This elongated fruit has yellow-green skin with short, fleshy hooks on it. The tangy white pulp has toxic seeds that must be removed and the flesh can be very fibrous, requiring straining before being made into tasty sorbets and smoothies. It is ambrosial mixed into fruit salads or made into ice-cream.

Tamarind

Tart tamarind adds an exotic, complex flavour to Asian cooking and is known as asam in Malaysia. It is one of the most popular souring agents because of its high tartaric content, and produces the best flavour when processed as little as possible. The knobbly pods, which grow on tall spreading trees, contain chocolate-brown fibrous pulp and shiny black seeds. The pods turn reddish-brown and become quite brittle when ripe. The pulp develops a dense golden tan colour when it is mature and is then more easily separated from the pod. Sour as vinegar, it is sold in many forms in large supermarkets, but pureed or concentrated are the most convenient to use.

Turmeric

Fresh turmeric should be handled with care because as soon as the rhizome is cut it can stain clothes, hands, chopping boards and knives.

Native to South-East Asia, where it is often called yellow ginger, turmeric has been featured in cooking since 600BC and is also used as a dye to colour fabrics.

A relative of galangal and ginger, it has brown scaly skin and looks similar to thin ginger. The deep-orange, bright-yellow or creamy flesh imparts a warm glow to curries and gives a vibrant-yellow colour to mustards and pickles.

Index